East Asian Screen Industries

East Asian
Screen Industries

Darrell William Davis and Emilie Yueh-yu Yeh

First published in 2008 by the
BRITISH FILM INSTITUTE
21 Stephen Street, London W1T 1LN

The British Film Institute's purpose is to champion moving image culture
in all its richness and diversity across the UK, for the benefit of as wide
an audience as possible, and to create and encourage debate.

Set by D R Bungay Associates, Burghfield, Berkshire
Printed in the UK by The Cromwell Press, Trowbridge, Wiltshire

Cover design: ketchup
Cover illustrations: (front) *Crouching Tiger, Hidden Dragon* (Ang Lee, 2000),
© United China Vision Incorporated/© UCV LLC; (back) *Perhaps Love* (Peter Chan Ho-sun, 2005),
Ruddy/Morgan Productions/Applause Pictures.

British Library Cataloguing-in-Publication Data
A catalogue record for this book is available from the British Library

ISBN 978–1–84457–181–9 (pbk)
ISBN 978–1–84457–180–2 (hbk)

Contents

Acknowledgments

Darrell William Davis thanks UNSW Faculty Research Grants and the university's generous leave policy. Michael Baskett, University of Kansas, offered encouragement and advice. David Bordwell is a constant font of timely information and wisdom. Emilie Yueh-yu Yeh acknowledges funds from Hong Kong Research Grants Council, (Competitive Earmarked Research Grant HKBU2428/05H), Hong Kong Baptist University Faculty Research Grant (FRG/04-05/II-60) and the Chiang Ching-kuo Foundation for International Scholarly Exchange. Both authors are grateful to Michael Curtin and Paul MacDonald, series editors. At the BFI, Andrew Lockett initiated and promoted this work at an early stage. Sarah Watt, Rebecca Barden, and Sophia Contento helped it along to completion. Big thank-yous to Yang Yuanying at Beijing Film Academy, Stephanie Ng Yuet-wah and Lake Wang Hu, in Hong Kong.

Introduction

In the 1990s, East Asian cinema emerged as one of the most influential in the world. Influential because films from Hong Kong, Taiwan, South Korea, Japan and the People's Republic of China (PRC) were consistently rewarded at festivals and markets, and impressed film-makers in the rest of the world who saw Asian film with new regard. Not since the 1960s, when directors like Sergio Leone, Sam Peckinpah and Preston Sturges were borrowing from Akira Kurosawa, had world cinema seen such an influx from East Asia. What is intriguing about this (re)emergence is that it happened while the industry was under threat of obliteration: throughout the 1990s, East Asian screens were besieged by Hollywood exports. In this regard new Asian cinema compares with Italian neo-realism, a movement contending with harsh conditions, but one whose rich creativity inspired film-makers worldwide. East Asian film industries arose from what might easily have been artistic and commercial ashes. Despite dire circumstances, East Asian films and companies have become major players at festivals, markets and on Western screens. This volume describes and assesses current East Asian cinemas from an industrial, aesthetic and critical perspective. It accounts for the choices, costs and negotiations made to revitalise the movies, a lately endangered popular species.

East Asian screen industries have usually been treated within models of national cinema, which take film industries as relatively self-contained enterprises subject to state regulations and specific local, historical conditions. For instance, John Lent's useful primer *The Asian Film Industry* (1990) carves up Asia country-by-country rather than treating the region as an interconnected whole that is susceptible to global political fluctuations and multinational capitalism. As East Asian screen industries have undergone significant restructuring and visible transformation since 1990, there is a need to offer a new volume on the region as a whole. Not only have East Asian industries survived the 'onslaught' of Hollywood, they managed to reconfigure international trade flows. In the 1990s there was a significant migration of films and talent from Asia – especially Hong Kong – to the West, leading to adjustments within the international screen industries. Whether Hong Kong film-makers had lasting impact on Hollywood is debatable, but Hollywood's impact on Asia is not, and specifically the know-how of global movie standards transferred back to East Asia, through experience gained in the West. John Woo is one example, but more recently comedy auteur Stephen Chow took a large step toward global popularity. A major international impact was made by Ang Lee's *Crouching Tiger, Hidden Dragon* (Sony Classics/Columbia-Asia, 2000). This film is explained in Chapter 1 as a benchmark, bringing much-needed revision to the role of blockbusters in East Asia. On the other hand, Chow's work is presented in Chapter 2 as an instance of neo-localisation. These figures, and others, represent East Asian access to models of profitable industrial development and sustainability. The reconfigurations brought by East Asian talent, genre and production prompt the re-thinking of models of national cinema, which in turn depend on the geopolitical boundaries maintained by nation-states. While political boundaries remain intact, there are also structural conditions that challenge greater consolidation of East Asian screen markets. This combination of national sovereignty and regional dynamism provides background for our effort to address recent, ongoing changes in East Asian screen industries.

What have been the structures and policies of East Asian film industries, and how were they regulated? What adaptations and tactics were employed to respond to strenuous challenges in the screen industries here? What accounts for the resilience of film-makers and distributors in unpredictable conditions? New sorts of funding, alliances, technologies, innovations, marketing and transborder talent-sharing are all on the rise. Can these changes be understood as

Zhang Ziyi in *Crouching Tiger, Hidden Dragon*

survival mechanisms in an increasingly interconnected, competitive market-place? Can analysis of national or regional film industries also work dialectically as an account of a global entertainment economy?

East Asia represents an enormous market, an educated, affluent population, turbulent political events and vociferous media contexts. As in the West, large-scale studio-based modes of production have proven unviable. Changes in the region such as the Asian financial crises in the late 1990s, a landslide of dereg-ulation, the 1997 return of Hong Kong to China and China's 1999 accession to the World Trade Organization (WTO) were also key factors in the new forma-tion of East Asian screens. Using case studies, we show how the East Asian screen industry has characteristically negotiated the passing of studio modes to re-emerge as a flexible industrial–cultural force responding to challenges of glo-bal capitalism.

In this book we focus on the structural features of the industry and the strat-egies pursued in Japan, South Korea, Taiwan, Hong Kong and the People's Republic of China. Organisation of this volume is broadly historical and case-specific, outlining overall trends illustrated by clear examples. The basic picture that emerges is one of increasing decentralisation, deregulation and regional co-operation. Flexible production methods and market specialisation has replaced mass-market economies of scale, even as markets expand through trans-border promotion of stars, genres and locations. A key feature of these changes is the interdependence of film industries *within* Asia and prospects for profitable pan-Asian co-operation (Chapter 4). East Asian screens are re-articulated in other ways. As argued in Chapter 5, East Asian film industries and directors are now more visible, thanks to revised frameworks that had remained inside national barriers, such as genres. East Asian producers now go out of their way to sell projects overseas – to each other and to the West – as both finished productions and ongoing business propositions.

However, certain internal conditions are still mandatory. The fundamental elements include (1) basic know-how of the cinematic apparatus, including not only technique, narratives and stars, but the financial tools for launching a plat-form of films or a whole production slate; (2) a coherent policy, strategy, or at least commitment by state authorities to uphold the screen industry as an ongoing business; (3) a sufficient market, that is, a population of moviegoers large enough to form a core audience, like that of Japan and South Korea. Any globally competitive film industry *must* have these elements. An engaged, domestic audience is essential to sustain a popular programme of pictures over many years. As powerhouses of popular film entertainment, Japan and Hong Kong are the best examples of know-how (1), while South Korea's proactive pol-icy initiatives show the benefits of policy (2). As for population (3), the PRC boasts the world's largest, but unless more people devote their leisure time and money to theatrical moviegoing, the market will remain nascent, and in need of further cultivation. Of the fabled one billion consumers of China, only about 150 million actually buy cinema tickets.

All the film industries we examine are thoroughly capitalist, though they vary in degrees of regulation and protectionism. To handle this, we employ a model of flexible production to chart features found across the East Asian film industries. PRC film culture is an exception – a special case – because it still operates within a command economy and propaganda objectives. On the whole, Chinese films are made to satisfy party policies, rather than the ticket-buying public. This situation continues and in fact is the prime reason why state-run film studios faced collapse. Although government subsidies to approved projects and directors continue, independent film-makers persist in practising their craft and getting accepted into festivals, mostly outside China. With the approaching, WTO provisions, independent directors, semi-independents and co-productions are helping steer PRC cinema in a market-oriented direction. The PRC is the most aggressive in its push toward marketisation, perhaps because it is so crucial to manage it, balancing economic momentum with ideological control. Indeed, the PRC is central to key intra-Asian modes of production, as we show in Chapter 4. For now, PRC cinema remains pseudo-socialist and proto-capitalist, requiring special terms of reference. For our purposes 'China' suggests a vast potential market; a prodigious talent pool; and broad cultural traditions underwriting the entire region, more than just a specific film industry.

Several conceptual and methodological points must be outlined, namely questions and debates on media globalisation, media imperialism and Hollywood hegemony. Media imperialism sees globalisation as a diffusion of Western media products, culture and institutions to the rest of the world, assuming a one-way Euro-American projection to non-Western 'peripheries' (Dorfman and Mattlelart, 1975; Schiller, 1976; Wallerstein, 1974–80). This view takes globalisation-as-Americanisation, i.e. cultural homogenisation by Hollywood franchise, to be a powerful model to explain the popularity of American entertainment. But recent studies revised the media imperialism thesis and treat globalisation as a complex process, rather than a one-way, forced imposition of culture and economy (Hannerz, 1996; Robertson, 1995). The relationship between local, indigenous and global media should be seen as a multilayered topography where resistance, assimilation, localisation, de-localisation, and re-localisation constantly interact (Lee, 1979). Not only is there a rise in local innovation and renovation, re-localised to recoup lost markets; we also see more collaboration or co-operation between Western media conglomerates and local players. In many areas, competition is often not with American movies, but with those which share familiar cultural or linguistic traits. In this connection, East Asia provides ample case studies for the 'strange topography' of globalisation (Mosco, 2004).

There are other problems with charges of Hollywood hegemony, or what we call 'Hollywoodism'. Hollywoodism, especially among cultural nationalists and progressive intellectuals, assumes the cloak of dogma. This powerful ideology verges on fascination, but does not really place films within relevant market functions. An ideology invested in commercial dominance, it is exaggerated belief that Hollywood is synonymous with universal popularity, a fatal opiate of enticement, intoxication and mind(less) control.

Hollywood is saddled as the villain in a narrative of media struggle and predatory corporate behaviour. However, a closer look reveals cracks in such typecasting. American blockbusters have a key role in the prospects of East Asian film industries. First, East Asian audiences warmly embraced American imports and this undeniably hampered local production. But, concurrent with Hollywood's impact, a number of Asian rebounds have taken place since the late 1990s. Hollywood pictures reigned, but there came a turning point, and recovery within domestic screen ventures. East Asian responses were initially tentative, encompassing a range of strategies and tactics. One was cultivating local roots to make the kind of movies American pictures could never be, such as comedies, martial arts, period pictures, or vehicles for Asian stars. Alternatively, given the appetite for American-style blockbusters, producers tried to adapt or assimilate Hollywood templates, to co-opt the appeal for high-quality, homemade features. This course had great risks, with high budgets and production values threatening economic ruin if the films flopped. Another way was to partner with Hollywood distributors, who were in a position to share marketing and promotional strategies, a key facet of American movies' appeal. Thus, East Asian film commerce could adopt norms developed for Western imports and, furthermore, reduce the gap between perceptions of East Asian and American pictures. Asian pictures might be *de-localised* in terms of higher quality, especially in marketing, while concurrently *re-localised* in subject matter, stars and genres. Not only pictures themselves, but infrastructure changed too: Japanese customers for distributor Warner Bros.-Japan might enjoy pictures in new theatres built by Warner-Mycal, one of the first corporate partners to construct multiplexes in Japan. Additionally, Japanese crew and technicians might work on big American co-productions, such as *The Last Samurai* (dir. Edward Zwick, 2003), *Memoirs of a Geisha* (dir. Rob Marshall, 2005) or Asian-language pictures bankrolled by Warners or Columbia-Asia (see Chapters 1 and 2). Hollywood's powerful business models may threaten cultural/national traditions, but also hold out promises of export, assimilation and even overthrow, as we shall see in South Korea. A less extreme response was PRC directors' attempts to clone blockbusters with acceptably Chinese characteristics. This can be seen in director Zhang Yimou's martial arts *Hero* (2002), *House of Flying Daggers* (2004), *Curse of the Golden Flower* (2006), Chen Kaige's *The Promise* (2006) and Feng Xiaogang's *The Banquet* (2006). East Asian screen industries turn oft-bitter experience to advantage, incorporating the formulae, logistics and benchmarks of antagonists, reviving and re-establishing markets with expanded margins.

We therefore need to frame the strategies, tactics and experiments taken by East Asian screen industries in the context of global capitalism, within which Hollywood is mistaken for almighty, invincible rival. 'Hollywood owns between 40 per cent and 90 per cent of the movies shown in most parts of the world,' declares Toby Miller at the beginning of *Global Hollywood* (Miller *et al.*, 2001: 3). On the other hand, as organising 'hege-money' it also beckons with fantastic resources to those who play by the new rules of the screen trade-game.

So instead of following the model of the popular *Global Hollywood*, a narrative of homogenising victimisation, we turn to alternative accounts, where heterogenisation is possible. Asia-Pacific as the object of Hollywood strategies is the *subject* of this story. We show the region's difference, resistance and occasional indifference to the dominant global player. Another differentiating factor is the energetic activities of European Union (EU) countries and media companies, as counterweight to the unbridled commercialism of American screen businesses. This triangular structure lends multilateral complexity to East Asian screen industries' ongoing negotiations – with Hollywood, Europe and each other.

Other issues we confront are more practical. There is the problem of timeliness: as a cauldron of simmering ingredients, events in East Asian screens evaporate too quickly to be catalogued in an overview such as this. By the time research is noted and written in a first draft, things might and usually do change completely. Nothing is more frustrating to scholars, and journalists, than a swiftly moving target that threatens confidence in any statement ventured about ongoing situations. We tried to bring our accounts through to the end of 2006. Another problem is verifiable data. While South Korea's Film Commission has been publishing box-office statistics frequently, Taiwan's Government Information Office is less committed, putting out directories and figures in an annual chronicle. Both sets of figures are for major metropolitan markets, with data on suburban districts outside Seoul and Taipei being spotty. As for China, computerised systems of counting tickets have been installed in a few places, but are yet to be widespread and, furthermore, distribution schedules are often disrupted through interruptions by meddling authorities. An accurate picture of the PRC market and its projected box office remains a distant hope.

We place the East Asian screen industry into historical context in order to survey current developments. The old state-sponsored economies of scale are finished, replaced on one hand by flexible modes of independent finance and production; and, on the other, by support from an old antagonist, Hollywood, which may inject its funding and production clout into East Asian screens. This paradox is facilitated by Hollywood's corporate vision: one world market as its own natural habitat, and with a corollary, that Asians are not necessarily prey or competitors, but allies in co-production and branch-office enterprise. This development is described more thoroughly in Chapter 2, where a new localism may be assisted by international agendas. The new localism is endogenous production as a way to propel local talents into global, or at least transborder, currency Asia-wide. In contrast, Chapter 1 takes East Asian benchmarks as alternatives to blockbusters, and also covers the impact of political events and global capitalism on the region. Chapter 3 describes the power of television and video, particularly as it underwrites Japanese and East Asian screen industries. Chapter 4 presents pan-Asian co-production as an emerging business force, attempting to capitalise on East Asia's large population and appetite for large-screen entertainment. Chapter 5 discusses continuities and changes in East Asian genres, arguing that transnational marketing augments genre formulas and aligns specific genres with national cinemas. A flurry of US remakes of East Asian films illustrates this process.

Chapter 6 examines an increasingly central part of the East Asian screen industries – international film festivals, art cinemas and the film authors cultivated in this element. The demand from over 700 film festivals worldwide has encouraged East Asian art film-makers and producers to agglomerate, forming regional exhibition circuits and a proto-industry. With festivals, art cinema has been 'upgraded' in the last decade, formerly an asylum from industrial cinema but now a most favourable global niche for business meetings and marketing. We argue that art cinema is no longer a separated, minority cinema but an integral part of the whole screen industry.

From a distance, the 'Far East' may seem a unique and mysterious region, hard to decipher given linguistic and geographical remoteness from Europe and North America. East Asian screen industries were relatively obscure for various reasons related to the economics of cultural availability. The veil has gradually lifted as global technological flows have intensified contact between cultures, peoples and information. This allowed easier access to examples, statistics and references to a variety of media institutions and practices, making the present volume possible. Knowledge of the region's media was traditionally divided by boundaries of nation, culture and language. This book is a first attempt to identify and describe common trends and traits across individual industries in the area. It is a difficult task as East Asia remains a differentiated, conflicted region and cannot be treated as homogenous. So our objective is to outline the most crucial changes and ongoing developments, not to give a complete overview of East Asian screens. Gaps, omissions and cracks are inevitable in our discussion. We hope future works will continue to supplement and correct our attempts, and flesh out the body of literature on these most vibrant screen industries of the world.

I

East Asian Benchmarks in Policy and Practice

The 1990s were times of deregulation and policies designed to prise open markets. In the global film industry, this process is particularly clear. In the past, East Asian countries imposed quotas and tax barriers to keep out foreign products under assumptions of economic and ideological protection. In 1965, South Korea's military government introduced import limitations and a quota stipulating that exhibitors reserve at least sixty to ninety days per year for Korean films (Lee, 2000: 49). Taiwan limited foreign film exhibition to the circulation of only two prints at a time, until 1994. But East Asia's long-term dependency on the US gave trade negotiators enough leverage to press South Korea, Taiwan and most recently China to open up. Asian protectionist measures were dismantled in the 1990s, bringing deregulation and relaxation toward imports. The shift created a window of opportunity (Curtin, 2003: 254), not only letting Hollywood access an enormous market, but also presenting a make-or-break chance for East Asian companies, based on wholesale restructuring of regional industries. This chapter describes the downfall of East Asian industries in the age of protectionism, followed by an account of specific attempts at redefinition and recovery.

If the downfall of protectionism was a boon for Hollywood, it brought confusion and disarray to the trade in Asian pictures. With strong competitive pressures, industrial mainstays – financing, stars, genres, distribution and marketing – faltered and once-viable national cinemas were in trouble. It would be mistaken to use an across-the-board diagnosis to explain why East Asian cinemas declined in their own territories. The reasons for their struggles vary, depending on specific political, economic and creative conditions in each industry. But we can offer three broad observations that frame an understanding of East Asia's fall as a secure base for national cinemas.

First, there are always trade-offs in economic flows. East Asian national cinemas fell victim to overall high growth in the 1980s and 1990s. Trade negotiators used locally produced movies as a sector to balance huge surpluses with the US, on behalf of industry trade bodies like the Motion Picture Association of America (MPAA). US negotiators demanded that American pictures had an open portal to markets that had been protected by quotas, tariffs and levies imposed on foreign imports. Since 1990, Japan has been Hollywood's largest foreign export market. This is not just because Japanese audiences love American pictures but also due to Japan's maintenance of enormous trade surpluses. These have to be offset and managed for geopolitical as well as macroeconomic stability. Take Taiwan, for similar reasons. Since the late 1980s its economic engine has been driven by its electronics and information technology (IT) industries. To protect these, sectors such as agriculture, financial services and film production – areas in which Taiwan had been self-sufficient – were sacrificed. Trade barriers to these sectors were dismantled and since the 1993 General Agreement on Tariffs and Trade (GATT), Hollywood films enjoyed a steady 70–75 per cent share of the Taiwan market, and in recent years well over 90 per cent (Yeh, 2006: 159). Taiwan's screens were deluged by Hollywood films partly because of the island's success as a net exporter of IT hardware. Annual production averaged over 200 local films in the 1970s and over 100 in the 1980s. Table 1.1 shows the decimation of a once-robust national cinema.

Year	Taiwan film releases	Non-Taiwan film releases (Hollywood, Hong Kong, Asian and European)
1995	18	454
1996	23	230
1997	18	304
1998	15	309
1999	11	306
2000	19	273
2001	10	212
2002	16	250
2003	15	264
2004	23	236
2005	26	288
2006	17	294

Sources:
Data compiled from *Cinema in the Republic of China Yearbook* (1996–2006)
and *TPBO WRETCH* (2006).

Table 1.1 Screen Share in Taiwan (1995–2006)

Second, if Asian high economic growth in the 1980s and 1990s primed the pump for foreign product, there was sluggish, often inept response to imports. As distributors and audiences embraced imports in a newly deregulated environment, local producers were unprepared, having sheltered under longstanding protectionism. Complacent film industries of East Asia were slow to cope with the aggressive entry of foreign marketing. Their structural rigidity made them incapable of handling new challenges, including aging theatres, antiquated publicity campaigns, accelerating piracy, poor production values, overproduction and – thanks to more liberal trade rules – the novelty of extravagant Hollywood block-busters. American businessmen exploited Asian internal weaknesses while at the same time pressing for further access on grounds of deregulation and trade liberalisation.

From the postwar period through the 1980s, domestic Asian industries were sustained by fairly stable separation of locally made and foreign films. Distributors and exhibitors were consistently attached to large studios to ensure regular supplies of genre pictures, serials and occasional specials. Like any goods supplier, distributors for Asian genre pictures brought these to market on screens devoted to Asian films, while American films would play in separate venues. There was little crossover or overlap between distinct markets. Often, vertical integration let the same firms handle production, distribution, exhibition and marketing. As for audiences, a Japanese viewer of *yakuza* crime pictures in the 1960s was unlikely to go to see *Bonnie and Clyde* (Warner Bros., 1967). Chinese audiences for opera films were not in the habit of attending MGM musicals. In the 1990s, these boundaries between audiences for domestic films and those for imports collapsed. Imports by this time lost their foreignness, as mainstream audiences in East Asia acquired a taste for Western movies, multiplexes and marketing practices.

Also, East Asian genre systems have been poorly maintained. This is related to the depletion of established formulae needed to sustain individual industries. Genres specific to East Asian popular cinema such as Japanese yakuza, period pictures (*jidai geki*, samurai films), Hong Kong martial arts and Taiwan's romantic melodramas (*wenyi pian*) were all industrial mainstays, but due to overproduction and competition from TV they lost ground in the 1990s. The difficulty of maintaining popular, local genres prevented the growing of new talent and shortened the lifespan of established stars reliant on genres. (Further discussion of East Asian genres follows in Chapter 5.) Worse, production and exhibition facilities were not sufficiently upgraded to make films with production values and showmanship comparable to imported movies. Furthermore, decades-old advertising schemes were incapable of keeping up with contemporary marketing campaigns characterised by tie-ins, merchandising and clever product placements. Even in mainland China, the state-run film industry was suffering. Production fell from a peak of 166 feature films in 1992 to only seventy-one in 2001. This was a drop of 57 per cent in less than ten years. This was due to poor management and co-ordination across different industry sectors. Deteriorating exhibition facilities and stale content turned the audience away and saw them opt for pirated videos of Hong Kong films over quality domestic production. See Table 1.2 for the fluctuating numbers.

Year	Films Produced
1991	124
1992	166
1993	154
1994	148
1995	146
1996	110
1997	85
1998	82
1999	99
2000	83
2001	71
2002	100
2003	140
2004	212
2005	260
2006	330

Sources:
China Film Yearbook (1991–2005) and *China Film Market* (Jan. 2006).

Table 1.2 China's Annual Feature Film Production (1991–2006)

These industrial and structural problems, given the protected segregation of East Asian screen industries, were heightened when investment was disrupted by the 1997 Asian financial crisis. Capital for film production dried up, unavailable due to losses in the stock and currency markets. This caused a fall in numbers of films produced in Hong Kong, Taiwan and South Korea. The drop in Hong Kong production also hastened the collapse of Chinese-language markets in Taiwan and Southeast Asia that for years had depended on Hong Kong films. Late in 1997, *Titanic* (dir. James Cameron) was launched worldwide, swamping in its wake entire flotillas of once-popular local films. Even the People's Republic of China, the ardent bulwark against 'capitalist spiritual pollution', was drawn into the sinking ship's maelstrom. Former President Jiang Zeming openly praised the film for its promotion of a noble, uplifting spirit. Responding to Jiang's endorsement, all work units ushered people to the decks of *Titanic*, on screens public or private. Since then, China succumbed to this cinematic onslaught, prompting calls to appropriate Hollywood business models and modes of production, with sporadic government backing. China, like the rest of East Asia, was inspired by the Hollywood mode, and by blockbusters such as *Titanic*. Indeed, debates about the concept and uses of blockbusters have arisen, not only in China but around the region. As Chris Berry notes:

In both the People's Republic of China and the Republic of Korea, the rise of blockbuster consciousness is linked to dismantling trade protectionism under intense lobbying from the US and using levers such as 'most favored nation' trading status and access to the World Trade Organization. (Berry, 2003a: 218)

Despite this tremendous pressure, both internal and external, there are striking examples of using the opposition to reclaim lost national markets. These come from three very different practices. In South Korea, the state crafted a cinema boom resulting from capitalist incentives for commercial reinvention of national cinema. The second approach is more laissez-faire. It carefully structures international co-operation between Chinese cosmopolitans and Hollywood majors, exemplified by Ang Lee's *Crouching Tiger, Hidden Dragon*. This pan-Chinese production set a standard and model for East Asian recovery of regional markets and success in the global film business. The third instance comes from Hong Kong, a local trilogy with unexpectedly high production values and regional influence. These three cases can be called 'benchmarks' because they have inspired numerous analyses and imitations. The benchmark idea is not just breaking box-office records, but establishing new patterns for further, long-term activity. Benchmark films may be blockbusters, but not every blockbuster is a benchmark. Executives in numerous East Asian industries take benchmarks as templates, or bearers of future possibility. They are not just economic possibilities but potential synergies, opportunities for new configurations of cultural and financial capital. East Asian benchmarks are outcomes of regional diversity and accommodation within international norms of production and consumption. Benchmarks are not simply Western franchises, ruthlessly homogenising indigenous film craft, but judicious appropriation, blending resistance and assimilation within the global distribution system. Some contemporary industries have successfully capitalised on benchmarks, establishing practical ways of building viable production lines. Three practices – South Korean, pan-Chinese and Hong Kong – provide an understanding of the axis of film policy, Hollywood and transnational capital flows in the survival story of East Asian cinema.

BENCHMARK KOREA
Korean Blockbusters, *Chaebol* and Venture Capital
In 1990 the South Korean film industry faced a sea-change with removal of barriers to direct distribution of foreign products. This meant Korean films were under great pressure, especially from Hollywood imports. Meanwhile, new forms of distribution, production and marketing arose through involvement of *chaebol* (giant conglomerates) and venture capital. *Chaebol* motivation was transparent: their interest in production was to advance the markets for video-

True crime Korean blockbuster *Memories of Murder* (dir. Bong Joon-ho, 2003), starring Song Kang-ho (left)

tape, cable television and home electronics. Companies like Daewoo, Samsung and LG had film production divisions in order to service their primary concerns, video releases within domestic and overseas markets. The conglomerates were horizontally integrated, with the same firm controlling extensive video manufacture, computer software, overseas exports, and leading eventually to joint ventures abroad. For instance, CJ Entertainment was a founding stakeholder in DreamWorks SKG. Technological and corporate diversification drove changes in film financing and distribution by these conglomerates. In the early 1990s, nearly three-quarters of all Korean film distribution was in the hands of *chaebol* (Paquet, n. d. a).

Between 1992 and 1996, Samsung alone produced twenty-two features. Still, at this time the average market share of Korean film was only about 15 to 20 per cent (see Table 1.3). Despite this relatively small share, the *chaebol* investment in the film business brought dramatic changes, including pre-production planning, higher production scale, expanded distribution and marketing. Producers and executives called this 'planned cinema'. Since *chaebol* injected bigger budgets into production, it meant higher risks, which necessitated additional management. Emphasis on stars, well-defined genres and pre-production marketing were important parts of *chaebol* operation. Each project required special treatment, differentiating it from competing films and pushing toward high-concept event films. All possible risks were identified, analysed and minimised.

Each picture was tailored according to market analysis, meticulously doctored scripts and packaging, budget calculations, audience research, and strict time-tables, all relying on a new crop of perfectionist film-makers and technicians. The new business models of corporate co-ordination resulted in the 1999 break-through, *Shiri* (dir. Kang Je-gyu). This Korean blockbuster was the first to overtake the record set by *Titanic*. *Shiri* forecast the contemporary screen industry of South Korea, especially the determination to best Hollywood films on their home court. However, this does not mean mere imitation. The Korean response to American blockbusters is to produce their own versions, while main-land Chinese tend toward refusal (Berry, 2003a: 220). Recognisable to any fan of action film, *Shiri* takes Korean cinema onto a different plane of production and commercial reproduction. Its huge capital gains ensured *Shiri* a place as a benchmark to goad Korean movies toward a renaissance, and an ongoing wheel of creativity and innovation.

Shiri: the Korean Benchmark

The title refers to a fighting fish, signalling the tenacity of South Korean cinema itself. *Shiri* is an explosive genre picture about North Korean agents. It details a top intelligence officer's nightmare. Han Suk-gyu, then Korea's leading star, discovers his girlfriend is really a ruthless spy and killer from the North. Pen-etrating home and heart, she is an undercover sniper sent to assassinate a high

Shiri, explosive political thriller

official. Fatal attraction leads to fatal decision, when Han must choose between the woman he loves and the secret agent he must kill. An unlikely dilemma, but it is culturally and historically resonant, given Korea's stark South–North divide.

The story is visceral, centring on attempts to infiltrate 'free' Korea, and bring Seoul to its knees through massive terrorist strikes. *Shiri* is a political thriller packed with suspense, intrigue, double-crosses and violent action. Yet the film allows sympathy for North Korean characters, emphasising fraternal bonds with their enemies in the South. Emotionally charged, the characters personify the still-intense Cold War conflict and refocus it on matters of heart, including romantic passions and betrayal. The big-budget film has spectacular, gruesome scenes of combat, chases, with fluid camerawork and a powerful climax with a cast of thousands under threat in a sports stadium.

Shiri was a Korean box-office champion, with over 2.5 million admissions in Seoul alone. Long awaited by the industry, it broke the record held by *Sopyonje* (dir. Im Kwon-taek, 1993), a sleeper art-house picture. *Sopyonje* was another *chaebol*-backed melodrama about itinerant musicians caught up in *han*, the term for an irresolvable grudge born of colonial occupation and wartime partition. While *Sopyonje* is culturally specific, *Shiri* addresses any fan of Hollywood thrillers like *Die Hard* (dir. John McTiernan, 1988), *True Lies* (dir. James Cameron, 1994), *Face/Off* (dir. John Woo, 1997) and James Bond. The action formula is patently obvious but the North–South affinities between enemies are unique and powerful. Another record *Shiri* set was its high production budget of US$5 million. With this figure the film was sufficiently attractive to break the Korean box-office record of *Titanic*. Financed by the Samsung group and shot by Kang Je-gyu productions, *Shiri* conforms to the notion of high concept, a recognisable, digestible idea that can be extended and intensified by marketing formulas.

High budget, top stars, loud publicity, soaring returns and broken records – all these reveal *Shiri* as an exemplary planned commodity. The calculation that went into each part, from pre-production, press leaks during shooting and box-office figures, was painstaking. As a strictly commercial object *Shiri* was de-linked from the cushioning effects of government quotas or subsidies. But *chaebol* involvement in film production was already ending. By the time of its release, Samsung was pulling out of distribution, leaving other players to fill the gap. *Shiri* is a benchmark that would spawn other would-be blockbusters. In years following, *Shiri*'s box-office record would be broken by yet another South–North political drama, *Joint Security Area* (dir. Park Chan-wook, 2000), a venture capital project.

Chaebol were not the only investors. Another source of finance was venture capital, which played a key role in film investment after the Asian financial crisis. When the crisis hit South Korea in 1997, *chaebol* soon pulled out of production.

Distribution lines run by *chaebol* also collapsed. Film financing and production was riskier, especially since the sector was a pawn in finance and trade negotiations run by the International Monetary Fund. Venture capitalists like Ilshin Pictures and KDB (Korean Development Bank) stepped in, providing film financing as minority shareholders. This meant less interference in the production process, but tighter accounting. Unlike *chaebol*, whose primary concern was to secure video and cable rights, venture capital wanted high returns in theatrical runs. Films backed by venture capital would follow still more closely the planned cinema model. And unlike *chaebol*, whose production numbers remained modest (due to big investments in infrastructure), venture capital went for quantity, providing opportunities for new directors. By early 2000, the South Korean film industry was very robust, filled with young talent, new ideas and box-office records.

In 2003, gangster epic *Friend* (dir. Kwak Kyung-taek), another venture capital film, would overtake *Joint Security Area* and *Shiri* to set a new box-office record.

Dramatising the DMZ: *Taegukgi* (2004) (left) and *JSA* (2000) (below)

War, action, violence, and espionage formulas have since found new ways to inflate production scale, cost and publicity, resulting in a string of high-profile event films. Two big productions in 2003 and 2004, war epics *Silmido* and *Taegukgi: The Brotherhood of War*, exemplify the tireless reproduction of these patterns.

These films' high performance drew Hollywood's attention. Hollywood's first direct investment came from Columbia Tristar's joint venture with Cinema Service, a new company with a strong commercial bent. *Silmido* (dir. Kang Woo-suk, 2003), an uninhabited island off the west coast of South Korea, was the location of a military coup in 1971. The film details a gruesome historical incident in South Korea's struggle with the North. Based on classified military files, it too concerns the plight of Koreans caught in the South–North divide. It vanquished *The Last Samurai* and *The Lord of the Rings: The Return of the King* at the 2003 box office. Following the release of *Silmido*, *Shiri*'s Kang Je-gyu directed another South–North war epic, *Taegukgi: The Brotherhood of War* (2004), setting another milestone for budget and, until 2006, a box-office record. *Taegukgi* is called South Korea's *Saving Private Ryan* (dir. Steven Spielberg, 1998), with Kang likened to Spielberg.

Shiri is a benchmark, the first in a line of South Korean trends, records and trophies. But its most telling characteristic is the use of historical scars yet to be healed. With North Korea's closed-door policy and the sanction of the US government, the joint security area or demilitarised zone (DMZ) remains the

Jang Dong-gun in *Typhoon* (dir. Kwak Kyung-taek, 2005)

most guarded border in the world. The South–North divide sustains this wound in popular consciousness and in the pipelines of popular culture. Another instalment of these must-see event films was *Typhoon* (dir. Kwak Kyung-taek, 2005) starring Jang Dong-gun as a smouldering North Korean agent. No stranger to the Korean blockbuster, Kwak was the director of 2003's gangster hit *Friend.*

Regulation, Deregulation

The boom of South Korean film since *Shiri* has been called a 'renaissance' or 'New Korean Cinema'. The term echoes the golden era of the late 1950s when Korean cinema excelled in both quantity – annual output of over 200 pictures – and quality, with renowned directors making socially and aesthetically challenging works in the post-Korean War era (Lee, 2000: 46–50). Consider the following statistics and compare them with Hong Kong's decline in Table 1.4. New Korean films are not only embraced at home but also aggressively pushed in the region. Along with K-pop music and K-drama, South Korean film enjoys

Year	Korean Releases	Market Share %	Foreign Releases	Market Share %
1991	86	20.3	176	79.7
1992	68	17.6	201	82.4
1993	51	15.4	215	84.6
1994	52	20.2	238	79.8
1995	62	20.4	307	79.6
1996	55	22.4	320	77.6
1997	60	25.2	271	74.8
1998	43	24.3	244	75.7
1999	42	39.4	233	60.6
2000	62	34.9	277	65.1
2001	52	49.8	228	50.2
2002	82	48.5	192	51.5
2003	65	53.3	175	46.7
2004	74	59.4	194	40.6
2005	83	59	213	41
2006	108	67.4	237	32.6

Sources:
Data compiled from Korean Film Council website. Korean Film Council (2004); *Korean Film News*, 'Statistical Review of Korean Film Industry 2005'; *Statistics*, 'Korean and Foreign Films Produced, Imported and Released by Year', 'Nationwide Box Office Sales by Year' and *Han Cinema* (2007).

Table 1.3 Number of Films Released and Market Share in South Korea (1991–2006)

immense popularity in Japan, Hong Kong and China (see Chapter 3). The commercial reach of South Korean cinema was likened to Hong Kong film of the late 1980s. Seeing the fate of Hong Kong film, the Korean industry fears that its so-called renaissance might become a bubble (Leong, 2002, 2005). Besides industry personnel, the Korean government is concerned with keeping growth manageable. Since 2001, statistics, reports and analysis were made available in English to promote Korean cinema around the world. The government has been flogging the internationalisation of Korean cinema. Without official endorsement and support, South Korean's renaissance-export would take longer to materialise. It has become something of a model, prompting envy and emulation from Japan, Taiwan, Hong Kong and the PRC. Its success is all the more remarkable, given that South Korea used to have the most draconian film laws around. Now, its screen industry is one of the government's star players.

Prior to its growth spurt, South Korea's screen industry was a tug-of-war among various agencies and institutions: strict but capricious government rules, with film exhibitors, foreign importers and distributors forced to act as production houses for quota purposes. The Film Law (1962) is the primary instrument regulating film production, exhibition and distribution. It has gone through more than twenty revisions since its first draft. In a nutshell, the postwar industry is as follows.

The South Korean film industry lacked large-scale production facilities. In lieu of vertically integrated firms or state-run studios, the postwar government adopted a protectionist policy. Instead of directly funding production, government quotas were used to boost investment. The scheme used distribution licences as bait: companies won the rights to a lucrative foreign release only by agreeing to produce a Korean film. Located in a district of Seoul called Chungmuro, most companies were small entrepreneurial affairs, making quick, low-budget films. To ensure exhibition, the government imposed a screen quota system that required all theatres to commit at least 146 days per year to Korean features (Standish, 1994: 74). This protectionist scheme meant the government discouraged film-makers from taking much initiative or risk. In the 1970s, further revision of the Film Law brought heavy-handed rules and censorship to bolster anti-Communist, pro-dictator sentiments. These measures precipitated a downturn for film production and put an end to the 'golden age' of South Korean cinema of the early 1960s.

A dual system (foreign distribution licensing and domestic screen quotas) increased the number of domestic films but eroded their competitiveness and market share. Government licensing ensured that only firms supporting Korean production could distribute a limited number of foreign releases.

The Chungmuro era (1970s–1980s) is a period where imports barely maintained faltering domestic production. The long-term impact of Chungmuro funding was to give local films a reputation for mediocrity ('quota quickies'). This set the stage for the Korean New Wave of the 1980s, a movement toward social consciousness and greater devotion to Korean subjects. The New Wave, however, was more concerned with aesthetics and politics than commercial prospects. Park Kwang-su's *Chilsu and Mansu* (1988), *Black Republic* (1990) and *Berlin Report* (1991), Jang Sun-woo's *Age of Success* (1988) and Chong Chi-yong's *White Badge* (1992) made a reputation for Korean cinema at festivals and generated heated discussions at home. But their immediate impact on commercial cinema was limited.

Despite the unstable conditions, South Korean cinema showed remarkable resilience, re-invigorating itself through new competitive pressures. A carefully planned, well-managed policy was charted by the government and opened roads to financial restructuring. Political changes drove new, aggressive cultural policies in 1998. Kim Tae-chung, the first democratically elected president, and his administration saw culture as an opportunity for enterprise and promoted the film industry, rather than controlling it through restrictions (Paquet, 2005: 44). The government set up targets to increase the national budget for culture and tourism by 100 per cent in the next two years. In 1999, the legislature passed the Culture Industry Promotion Act, establishing official support for culture and entertainment industries. Funds actively promoted Korean cultural production for both domestic consumption and export overseas. The Korean Film Council (KOFIC) is the main unit handling cinema's role in the new Korean culture industry. Charged with raising both quality and quantity of Korean film, KOFIC provides an array of policies, plans, subsidies and financial support for script development, training, marketing and exhibition. These programmes are implemented and constantly updated. The financial incentives are rationalised and carefully distributed. In addition to policy, Korea's screen programmes include infrastructure like the Seoul Studio complex and educational institutions training technical and artistic talent.

Case Study: Korean Film Council

KOFIC is the primary organisation co-ordinating the promotion of Korean films. Established in 1999, KOFIC consists of several institutions: the Korean Motion Picture Promotion Corporation (MPPC, established in 1973); the Korean Academy of Film Arts (est. 1984); the Seoul (Namyangju) Studio complex (est. 1997); and training, outreach and screening centres. The semi-official KOFIC is the highest administrative body in the finance and promotion of South Korean moving images. Funded by the Film Promotion Treasury, it is charged with providing investment, awards and financial aid to projects, individuals and venues that make or show Korean films. For instance, the treasury provides 70 per cent of the costs to theatres undertaking renovation projects. The newly renovated venues are then expected to showcase Korean films. KOFIC's promotions work on two mutually enhancing levels: developing local scripts from the writing stage through to post-production and exhibition; and creating strategies, platforms for regional and international exposure of Korean film. The development process promotes work that can travel to the West, as well as attract Asian cinephiles at regional film festivals.

The domestic side of promotion is characterised by several funds ranging from initiatives on story treatment, scriptwriting skills, animated features, art cinema, documentary, technical advances such as high definition, and promoting co-operation between film and television industries. Through the Art Plus Cinema Network, KOFIC supported theatrical debuts of telefilms by new directors. Funds are raised not only from domestic and government bourses, but also from foreign partners such as large Japanese video and image-processing firms. These partnerships enhance the potential for Korean films to travel. KOFIC has a major commitment to nurture content from the most basic levels. According to KOFIC mission statements, funding low-budget, independent projects gives young film-makers a head start, and helps enhance the creative image of Korean film abroad:

> If KOFIC and its partners are successful in completely financing the production
> cost of the supported films, then it will free filmmakers from the commercial
> pressure to produce works that conform to the marketplace. This will, it is hoped,
> lead to further artistic experiment, ultimately enriching the creativity of Korean
> cinema. (Korean Film Council, 2004)

KOFIC's programmes include lenient repayment terms for advances, and grants for independent, low-budget productions if they are deemed to have limited commercial potential. Funding is generous, up to US$330,000 (400 million Korean won) for art films, with up-front payments rather than matching costs for money scraped together by struggling film-makers. KOFIC does not privilege commercial features but assigns equal value to shorts, unorthodox and non-fiction work. The value in a diverse film culture and an image of a versatile Korean cinema is evident. Short films and independents are of special value for students to learn their craft, hone their talents and rely on KOFIC for completion bonds which are yet to be used in commercial film finance, offered at rates up to 50 per cent less than that of banks.

Developing and Promoting South Korean Cinema

Co-ordinating culture with the commercial film industry, KOFIC and other agencies elicit benefits for both. Multifaceted schemes are provided for developing South Korea's contemporary culture industry. Traditional media such as film and video represent the foundation for the development of new media. Government programmes emphasise digital production and animation. There are attempts to use film education and film culture as a conduit for software development in the IT sectors. Since the late 1990s, the government has formed alliances with *chaebol*s in joint projects on IT products, with research, development and manufacture of digital appliances like LCD (liquid crystal display) screens, mobile phones, PDAs (personal digital assistants), smart appliances and so on. Bringing in 'old' media like film and television assumes that software cannot be neglected, or 'content is king' in Bill Gates's phrase. This prompts a search for design ideas (stories, imagery, characters) that can be grafted onto new platforms like electronic games, streaming video and mobile phones. As one of the most wired countries in the world (over 95 per cent broadband penetration), new forms of funding are available, like investment schemes through online 'netizen' funds that gather contributions for the production of new films (Leong, 2002: 14). There is belief that significant surplus may be extracted from old media like broadcasting and celluloid. Film is not seen as obsolete, a competitor or drag on new media and new technologies. New forms of synergy are envisioned, as in the title of this report: 'The broadcast and film communities: historically divided, now on the same page' (Korean Film Council, 2002).

Successful transfer of people, story ideas and graphic styles is projected and implemented for the mutual benefit of different sectors. The international hit *My Sassy Girl* (dir. Kwak Jae-yong, 2001) began as a novella serialised on the internet, representing a successful crossover. KOFIC's promotion of this film actively facilitates cross-media contact between artistic and commercial work. This proved sustainable with the hit *My Tutor Friend* (dir. Kim Kyeong-hyeong, 2003), a student comedy, breaking out of its internet space into cinemas, bookstores and retail shops. *My Sassy Girl* also travelled, winning audiences in China, Taiwan, Hong Kong, Singapore and Japan. These two titles show the importance of youth, trendspotting and serving the interests (technological, social, cultural) of emerging audiences connected via pan-Asian communication networks. KOFIC and its spokesmen recognise the importance of actively 'growing' audiences in order to sustain a rising number of Korean films, and expanding their appeal. *My Sassy Girl* and its sequel (2004) are both multi-purpose films: assertive chick flick, slapstick, romantic comedy, fantasy, light action and even sci-fi genre film. The film was embraced by viewers in the whole region, and raised Jun Ji-hyun to megastar level.

Record-breaker *Friend*

Under the Korean Culture and Contents Agency, the government encourages all creative industries, including motion pictures, animation, television, popular music and information technology. With South Korea's large population of nearly 50 million people, the agency set about changing the reputation of Korean-made entertainment, in particular weaning people away from televisions into newly improved multiplexes. In addition, the agency worked to give audio-visual exports a boost. The plans included the successful Pusan Film Festival, begun in 1996, opening a showcase for Korean films worldwide (see Chapter 6). The Korean government played an active role, despite regional economic gloom, in providing administrative springboards that support Korean cultural production. This was not window dressing, but building a co-ordinated culture-media industry unprecedented in Asia. With all the subsidies and support, backed by government policy, Korean film production plays an essential role in an integrated culture industry. The effort is paying off, with the immense sup-port from venture capital funds, *chaebol* and even private investors. Here we see a successful alliance between government policy and finance capital to make a sustainable, expanding film industry.

In contrast to this domestic success, there are pan-Asian benchmarks that have been tested by East Asian film-makers such as Ang Lee. Lee's production adopted an international strategy for releasing a Chinese global hit, outside any government support, which unexpectedly turned into a critical and commercial benchmark.

CHINESE-LANGUAGE BENCHMARKS

Crouching Tiger, Hidden Dragon: Transnational Capital, Diaspora Talent

Ang Lee's key film *Crouching Tiger, Hidden Dragon* (2000) rehabilitates the reputation of a whole genre and renders it a beacon of cultural China. The film
redeems or at least makes 'respectable' the pleasure of martial arts films, a genre
with a mixed pedigree. Chinese cinema has long been embedded in the West's
popular imagination, especially action subgenre kung fu, anticipating the work
of Jackie Chan, Yuen Woo-ping, Chow Yun-fat, Jet Li, Michelle Yeoh, Sammo
Hung and others. In contrast, Korean film-makers remain tied to their national
cinema; *Shiri*, and before that *Sopyonje,* set standards for Korean cinema but
their influence stayed largely inside Korea. The Chinese diaspora has long
experience on the edges of the American industry, such as silent star Anna May
Wong, actors Keye Luke and Burt Kwouk, cinematographer James Wong Howe,
Bruce Lee, and directors Wayne Wang and Christine Choy. On the other hand,
Chinese directors from PRC, Hong Kong and Taiwan such as Zhang Yimou,
Chen Kaige, Wong Kar-wai, Hou Hsiao-hsien, Edward Yang and Tsai Ming-liang
are art cinema veterans with critical support in the West. Cosmopolitanism and
access to global film finance and distribution marks the difference between types
of benchmark.

Crouching Tiger, Hidden Dragon was a breakout hit all over the world. Not only
was the film a critical and commercial triumph, it raised the standing of Asian
cinema overall. Lee wanted to revamp a tradition not only aesthetically but
through innovative financing too. *How* the film was made and marketed is more
important even than sensational box office and its many awards (four Academy
Awards, including Best Foreign Film, out of ten nominations, one of which was
Best Picture). It set a very high benchmark, but as time passes its achievement
may well stand as a one-off.

Recent Asian film talents (John Woo, Jackie Chan, Jet Li and so on) made a
mark in the West. Bringing kung fu into Hollywood action film is exciting, but
no matter how big the budget or star, the films have subcultural connotations.
Cross-cultural transposition revalidates on Hollywood terms what are essentially
B-picture conventions. In the 1970s martial arts movies were embraced by viewers worldwide, who found in them an anti-imperialist aesthetic of defiance.
Bruce Lee soon became the most famous star in the world. Ang Lee updates
these past Chinese signifiers, and brings them 'up to code' – technical, dramatic,
cultural and commercial – meeting the standards of the international art film.
Ang Lee strips the aesthetic of defiance and assertive nationalism, but a wistful
longing for cultural China remains.

In contrast to his Hong Kong counterparts, Ang Lee set out to transform Chinese-language cinema by using Hollywood. Rather than exploiting stereotypes

of martial arts, their 'coarseness', as he says, Lee managed to elevate *wuxia pian*, to give martial arts pictures substance; dignity proper to an international form. Because *Crouching Tiger* was distributed in the US through Sony Classics and in Asia through Columbia-Asia, it was assumed to be a Hollywood production. Posters and other promotional materials displayed prominent logos of Columbia Pictures and other Hollywood trademarks. But where capital was concerned, *Crouching Tiger* was actually a diaspora Chinese film (Klein, 2004: 18). The project was initiated, financed and bonded through individual efforts outside Hollywood, and outside America. This project was packaged in several countries, by Hsu Li-kung of Zoom Hunt (Taiwan); Bill Kong, of Edko films (Hong Kong); and by Lee and James Schamus, through New York-based Good Machine. These figures combined their faith in the major markets of Taiwan, Hong Kong/China and North America. The trio was able to get a completion bond through a negative pickup of three buyers: Sony Pictures Classics, Columbia Pictures-Asia, and Warner Bros., France. Negative pickup is a sale completed after the film is finished, as opposed to pre-production finance. Most negative pickups are films produced without knowledge of major distributors, but Ang Lee's track record helped secure distribution commitments before *Crouching Tiger* wrapped. This was after all the director who made the single most profitable film of 1993, *The Wedding Banquet*. These large markets were pre-sold, and this allowed production to commence (Zhang and Lee, 2002: 381–2). This shows the domination of international distribution by Hollywood companies. Yet Hollywood still allows outside products into its system, even as a foreign language, Asian picture. It was *marketed*, however, as a Hollywood picture, and this profited it immensely.

If the financing was innovative, independent and international, the film is also a benchmark in visual design. Hong Kong action choreographer Yuen Woo-ping was hired to stage action sequences. Yuen had pioneered wirework techniques, and further popularised them through his work on *The Matrix* (dir. Andy and Larry Wachowski, 1999). But in *Crouching Tiger*, Lee wanted a different kind of visual effect, more ethereal and dance-like. Yuen was then asked to devise a new type of martial arts action that would seem to float. This stylistic revision affords an expansion of the audience, opening a visual appeal in a genre traditionally linked with masculine violence and pain. In this Lee aestheticises physical combat, the key element of the genre. He also brought a wide array of talent, from Hong Kong, Taiwan and mainland China, an Oscar-winning score by composer Tan Dun, stunning location work in China's far west, and production values that belie the film's budget of US$15 million. At the Oscars Tan said, '*Crouching Tiger* is for a new era. It's not just for China. All the cultural boundaries have been crossed. I am honored to have been part of that' (Hayes, 2001: 1).

Because the film is not dubbed, with actors speaking Mandarin with English subtitles, this lends classic quality and substance, traits usually associated with European art films, rather than badly dubbed kung fu B pictures. With a cautious marketing campaign the film opened slowly in successive cities across the US at the end of 2000. It broke all records for a subtitled film, taking US$128 million in the US alone, with US$85 million in international box office. In the US another $112 million was earned in video rentals and sales (Klein, 2004: 18).

Successfully crossing over from art house to multiplex, *Crouching Tiger* spent thirteen of its fourteen weeks of release in the top ten. This reverses the usual blockbuster pattern, opening wide in the hope of quickly amortising costs in the large US market, then going on to capitalise on international territories, where local films cannot compete. *Crouching Tiger* was a blockbuster indeed but a peculiar one, requiring adjustments in the very concept of blockbuster movies and the art of entertainment.

China Replies: *Hero* and its Offshoots

Zhang Yimou's *Hero* (2002) is regularly measured by the aesthetic, critical and economic patterns set by *Crouching Tiger*. Zhang acknowledges the benchmark status of Lee's film and said that raising funds for his martial epic was easy as a result. *Hero* was the first officially sanctioned martial arts film in the PRC since the People's Revolution in 1949. The film has similar ingredients to Ang Lee's package: a pan-Chinese cast and crew with Jet Li, Maggie Cheung, Tony Leung and Zhang Ziyi; glossy production values, and a big budget. *Hero* also boasts a high-profile international crew including cinematographer Chris Doyle, world-class Japanese costume designer Emi Wada, and Ching Siu-tung, the renowned Hong Kong action director. Crucially, *Hero* had the same finance package: executive produced by Bill Kong of Edko in Hong Kong, together with government support on the mainland. It also looked to captivate the West, with an aggressive American distributor, Miramax. Although *Hero*'s US release was delayed by two years, it grossed a total of US$53m, becoming the PRC's most profitable export ever.

Crouching Tiger's failure in China was due to scant government support, since by the time it opened in theatres most Chinese had already seen bootleg copies on DVD or unauthorised television broadcasts. Seeing this, Chinese authorities took steps to ensure box-office success for their own martial arts epic, *Hero*. They clamped down on video pirates, initiated a strict computerised accounting system for urban theatres, and prevented in-house duping. This strict protection continued with Zhang's *House of Flying Daggers*. When it opened in Hong Kong in the summer of 2004, two officers with badges made an announcement, explaining to the house why they would be standing in front and monitoring the audience for the entire show. They hoped that this would not interfere with patrons' enjoyment. Furthermore, no other Chinese films were released during *Flying Daggers'* first run in China. This film and *Hero* both enjoyed a near-monopoly exposure authorised by SARFT, the State Administration of Film, Radio and Television. This paid off spectacularly, with a US$29m domestic box office for *Hero* and a US$18.5m take for *House of Flying Daggers*. With these results, the Chinese benchmark pattern was established.

Other films that followed the *Tiger*'s trail include *The Touch*, directed by Peter Pau, Lee's cinematographer on *Crouching Tiger*, Jackie Chan's failed *The Medallion* (2003, backed by Miramax), and Stephen Chow's *Kung Fu Hustle* (2004) (Frater, 2003b: 29). Finally, there was Tsui Hark's 2005 summer hit *Seven Swords*. In South Korea, a martial arts picture *Bichunmoo* (2000) was among the first to try to match *Crouching Tiger* (Leong, 2002: 76).

Differences between *Hero* and other films that followed *Crouching Tiger* reveal much about conditions within the PRC industry and those of a transnational, diaspora co-production. First, *Hero*'s source material is from Chinese history, not martial arts fiction; this is important because martial arts stories remain ideologically suspect in the PRC. With a true story from the historical record, its martial arts genre could be doctored and approved. The same story was covered before by Chen Kaige, in the Kurosawa-like *The Emperor and the Assassin* (backed by Sony Classics, 1999). Second, there are narrative convolutions, a story told from different perspectives that viewers are invited to compare. *Hero*'s narrative structure is more complex and puzzling than *Crouching Tiger*. Though just as beautiful as Peter Pau's Oscar-calibre cinematography, the film's colour scheme, shot by Chris Doyle, lends symbolic weight to the director's vision, signalling stark divisions between characters' points of view and their respective attitudes toward authority. Third, there was high-level government support. Though riding on *Crouching Tiger*'s success, *Hero* was an official Chinese product, not 'imitation Hollywood' drawing on decadent vernacular fiction. If *Crouching Tiger* is primarily romance, an elegiac fantasy of lost China, *Hero* teaches powerful history lessons, apropos of its authorised, official backing. *Hero* offers a corrective to the diaspora diffusions of Chinese culture, as depicted by the wistful *jianghu* world of *Crouching Tiger*. (*Jianghu* refers to the drifting movements, and morals, of itinerant mercenaries in martial arts fiction.) *Hero* sought to establish a new, orthodox benchmark, competing not only in critical and commercial success but also in cultural terms. Chinese blockbuster films would henceforth be infused with sublime motifs of Oedipal rebellion and its inevitable failure: *The Promise*, *The Banquest*, and *Curse of the Golden Flower* are only the beginning of this cycle begun by *Hero*.

Setting a benchmark therefore means not just popularity, but influence: establishing a new template, genre or franchise.

Infernal Affairs: Hong Kong benchmark

Another significant benchmark comes from Hong Kong. *Infernal Affairs* (dir. Andrew Lau and Alan Mak, 2002) shuttles in between, synthesising local genre elements with international styles and norms. Like *Crouching Tiger*, it contemporises a genre from Hong Kong's long line of police–triad stories. But it also reaches outward toward the PRC, especially in its subsequent instalments, and was remade in the US by Warner Bros. as *The Departed* (2006) with Martin Scorsese directing. In scope and ambition *Infernal Affairs* is at once local, regional and international.

Infernal Affairs' industrial significance must be seen in the context of steep falls in films produced since the 1997 handover. Moreover, subsequent catastrophes in Hong Kong – financial crisis, the SARS (severe acute respiratory syndrome) outbreak – further undermined confidence. Although Stephen Chow's kung fu comedy *Shaolin Soccer* (2001) inspired optimism, the credit was attributed to Chow's own popularity and charisma. The industry remained cautious of a rebound until *Infernal Affairs* and its sequels attracted an unexpected number of admissions in late 2002.

The success of *Infernal Affairs* should be recounted when an exodus of talent to the West accompanied Hong Kong's 1997 return to China. Once the most vigorous regional production centre, Hong Kong lost momentum with two major blows. First, output dropped after years of soaring quantity, giving way to Hollywood and other Asian films in the late 1990s. From 1996 to 2006, the total number of releases dropped from 100 to fifty-one, a decline of nearly half. And in the period between 2000 and 2006, the drop is steeper yet, at over 60 per cent. Zoom in further to 2001 and 2002, just one year, the decline is close to 30 per cent. Furthermore, market share of Hong Kong films in 2002 was recorded at its lowest percentage of 38 per cent, an 11 per cent drop from 1997, and falling 4 per cent from the previous year (see Table 1.5). This was alarming to a skittish industry used to high growth and big returns in the early 1990s. In late 2002, local production and distribution company Media Asia released its first event film *Infernal Affairs* after a major restructuring (see Chapter 4).

Released in late 2002, *Infernal Affairs* was a hit for Media Asia in the Christmas–New Year season, climbing through the Chinese New Year in February. It topped the box office at US$7.1 million (HK$55 million), doubling that of *Hero*, released at the same time. Within a few months, it spawned two solid follow-ups. Like most Chinese holiday films it boasts a stable of Hong Kong's biggest stars – Tony Leung, Andy Lau, Anthony Wong, Eric Tsang, Kelly Chen,

Year	Number of Releases
1996	100
1997	82
1998	84
1999	148
2000	146
2001	121
2002	87
2003	76
2004	64
2005	55
2006	51

Sources:
Data compiled from *City Entertainment* (1996–2006); *hkfilmart.com* website ('Weekly Box Office').

Table 1.4 Hong Kong Film Annual Releases (1996–2006)

Sammi Cheng – but there the familiarity ends. Its cool minimalism in perform-ance, production design and cinematography signals a different thriller than most happy holiday movies or swaggering gangster melodramas. In Hong Kong cinema, cops going under cover are nothing new, like the John Woo-inspired policiers of the 1990s or Alex Cheung's deeply ironic *Man on the Brink* (1981), a pioneering film in the Hong Kong New Wave. But *Infernal Affairs* is surpris-ingly restrained, even repressed. Police and gangsters no longer represent a Manichean opposition, but a *ying-yang* equilibrium, a kind of moral détente. Loyalties of the heroes and indeed of heroism itself become thoroughly con-fused: Leung takes the familiar position of police mole infiltrating the mob, while Lau works against him, impersonating a model cop, and reporting to an avuncular triad godfather (Eric Tsang Chi-wai). With leading cinematographer Chris Doyle as 'visual consultant', the film has a controlled blue-slate colour scheme far removed from the lush symbolist palette of Doyle's work on *Hero*.

The film is reminiscent of such stylish films as Michael Mann's *Heat* (1995) and *Collateral* (2004) rather than the violent hoodlum cycle of the *Young and Dangerous* comic book series. Andrew Lau and Alan Mak co-directed seven *Young and Dangerous* instalments between 1996 and 2000. Lau also then directed two of the biggest hits of the late 1990s, *The Stormriders* (1998) and its nationalist sequel, *A Man Called Hero* (1999). These two hit films, like the *Young and Dangerous* series, were also taken from a comic series, Ma Wing-shing's *Fung Wan*. Unlike the gritty streets of the *Young and Dangerous*, these effects-laden fantasies were calling cards to videogame and comics buffs, as if courting Chi-nese fans of *The Terminator* (dir. James Cameron, 1984). According to Tony Rayns, Lau's work, especially his *To Live and Die in Tsimshatsui* (1994), a remake of *Man on the Brink*, represents the worst excesses of Hong Kong film in the 1990s: 'glossy, hyperbolically violent, slackly plotted and deeply insincere' (Rayns, 2004: 26).

Infernal Affairs is none of these. But in all three *Infernal Affairs* films the film-makers and Media Asia shrewdly catered to local tastes, updating tried-and-true formulae. Their work exemplifies Hong Kong's on-the-fly culture of excess but the *Infernal Affairs* films show new restraint and discipline. In subject matter and stars *Infernal Affairs* represents continuity, but in style and mode of production it is a great change from traditional methods. What makes the *Infernal Affairs* films impressive is that they do not appear like conventional Hong Kong pictures at all. Instead, their careful scripting and planning, matched by a high level of craftsmanship, avoids local parochialism. The story flows seamlessly and with believable characters; this alone makes *Internal Affairs* stand out, while the high production values are striking.

Who better than former perpetrators of excess to purvey an aesthetic of discipline? Lau says, 'We have been in the business of making Hong Kong movies for quite a long time and we wanted our film to be different from previous Hong Kong movies. If we don't change, we'll die' (Rayns, 2004: 29). But what is being changed into is a wardrobe already comfortable to the majority of Hong Kong viewers: the structural reliability, and control, of Hollywood. It is only relative to expectations of Hong Kong films and especially policiers that *Infernal Affairs* offers significant novelty. Like audiences elsewhere, Hong Kong viewers are

Eric Tsang in *Infernal Affairs*

Year		Hong Kong	Foreign Films			
			Japan	Hollywood	Europe	Others
1997	No. of films (Total)	29%	71%			
			5%	49%	5%	12%
	Box Office (Total)	49%	51%			
			1%	46%	3%	1%
	No. of films (Foreign)	/	8%	68%	17%	7%
	Box Office (Foreign)	/	2%	91%	5%	2%
1998	No. of films (Total)	29%	71%			
			6%	44%	16%	5%
	Box Office (Total)	39%	61%			
			1%	59%	1%	0%
	No. of films (Foreign)	/	8%	63%	22%	7%
	Box Office (Foreign)	/	2%	96%	2%	0%
1999	No. of films (Total)	45%	55%			
			8%	30%	11%	6%
	Box Office (Total)	41%	59%			
			4%	50%	3%	2%
	No. of films (Foreign)	/	15%	55%	20%	10%
	Box Office (Foreign)	/	6%	86%	3%	5%
2000	No of films (Total)	41%	59%			
			7%	34%	10%	8%
	Box Office (Total)	40%	60%			
			3%	49%	3%	5%
	No. of films (Foreign)	/	11%	58%	17%	14%
	Box Office (Foreign)	/	5%	83%	4%	8%
2001	No of films (Total)	38%	62%			
			7%	38%	7%	10%
	Box Office (Total)	42%	58%			
			5%	48%	2%	3%
	No. of films (Foreign)	/	12%	61%	11%	16%
	Box Office (Foreign)	/	9%	83%	3%	5%
2002	No. of films (Total)	30%	70%			
			8%	36%	12%	14%
	Box Office (Total)	38%	62%			
			3%	48%	3%	8%
	No. of films (Foreign)	/	11%	52%	18%	19%
	Box Office (Foreign)	/	5%	78%	4%	13%
2003	No. of films (Total)	31%	69%			

Year	Category					
			6%	40%	8%	15%
	Box Office (Total)	48%		52%		
			2%	45%	2%	3%
	No. of films (Foreign)	/	8%	58%	12%	22%
	Box Office (Foreign)	/	3%	86%	4%	7%
2004	No. of films (Total)	26%		74%		
			4%	45%	11%	14%
	Box Office (Total)	43%		57%		
			3%	46%	1%	7%
	No. of films (Foreign)	/	5%	61%	15%	19%
	Box Office (Foreign)	/	5%	81%	2%	12%
2005	No. of films (Total)	21%		79%		
			9%	40%	14%	16%
	Box Office (Total)	32%		68%		
			6%	55%	3%	4%
	No. of films (Foreign)	/	11%	50%	19%	20%
	Box Office (Foreign)	/	9%	80%	5%	6%
2006	No. of films (Total)	21%		79%		
			12%	39%	9%	19%
	Box Office (Total)	27%		73%		
			8%	56%	1%	7%
	No. of films (Foreign)	/	15%	50%	11%	24%
	Box Office (Foreign)	/	11%	77%	2%	10%

Sources:
Data compiled from *City Entertainment* (1996–2006) and *hkfilmart.com* website ('Weekly Box Office').

Table 1.5 Numerical Proportion and Box-Office Share, Hong Kong (1997–2006)

unwilling to split apart the norms and expectations of domestic and Hollywood films. The directors are quite open in their appropriation of *The Godfather* (dir. Francis Ford Coppola, 1972) in Part Two of their trilogy. This too is standard procedure; Hong Kong film-makers have endlessly pilfered Hollywood in the 1980s and 1990s, only this time, the comparison is apt. Though *Infernal Affairs II* is no masterpiece, it goes beyond simple homage. Francis Ng stands out as Hau, a quiet mob boss with a charismatic villainy. Ng's usual persona is a character actor specialising in psychotic killers. The sequel has an operatic lushness very different from the metallic sheen of the first film. Co-produced by Singapore's MediaCorp-Raintree, the film's October release grossed an impressive US$3.2 million (HK$25 million).

As for the third instalment, the producers explicitly courted the mainland. Missing is the mirror-image theme of moral confusion. China's popular television actor Chen Daoming (*Hero*) is cast as a gangster from across the border, possibly in league with a corrupt Hong Kong inspector. Chen's presence signals the need to include a mainlander in the ensemble. The story resolves in the triumph of law and order, and Chen is revealed to be an undercover public security bureau officer. Reversing old Cold War stereotypes, this infiltration by 'red' Chinese authorities is benevolent, operating incognito within a corrupt capitalist demimonde, whose detectives need correction. This is the way party cadres see Hong Kong society, a flock to be coaxed back to the national fold. The film ends with friendly fraternal bickering; officer Chen upbraids his Hong Kong counterparts for their poor Mandarin. Part Three takes the premise of the first two films and transposes it into terms that please mainland authorities and audiences. Beijing-born Leon Lai, a big star in both Hong Kong and the mainland, plays a cold double agent. The changes were noted by Hong Kong critics, as well as a slackening narrative structure and production values. Despite efforts to assimilate a Hong Kong formula to PRC requirements, the translation stalls. The result is diluted, with producers aiming at external marketing over internal quality, but the gamble paid off. The film earned US$4.5 million (RMB 36 million) on the mainland and topped the Hong Kong annual box-office chart with US$3.87 million (HK$ 30 million). The film's combined box office of US$8.37 million surpassed the US$7.1 million taken by the initial instalment in Hong Kong.

Like *Hero*, *Infernal Affairs III* received pirate repellent. To pre-empt copying, authorised DVDs of the film were on sale in mainland shops just three days after the film's theatrical release. Going for only 8 RMB ($1.00) the disks cost the same as fakes, and carry 'For Sale in Mainland Only' warnings with a Mandarin language track and no subtitles. Through timeliness and price, distributors pre-empted the illegal trade in dupes, eliminating the incentives offered by unauthorised dealers.

Infernal Affairs' moral ambiguity

As a trilogy, Media Asia's *Infernal Affairs* represents a benchmark project. At a time of great anxiety in the industry, it backed an expensive three-part ensemble film that recalls Western models. In the second and third parts, it made casting and thematic changes to hasten the film's travel into China. This was a radical move, since the first *Infernal Affairs* was banned outright on the mainland. In China, Part Two received a quiet release, while the final instalment was the country's third-highest grossing film of the year. It would seem that Media Asia was committed to a China route for its products, even if it meant diluting the property. The dilution is not just thematic, but a calculated trade-off: though *Infernal Affairs III* retreated from records set by Part One in Hong Kong, its overall take was higher, as a fanfare release in China, in addition to Hong Kong and other Asian territories.

The *Infernal Affairs* trilogy is both a local and regional benchmark, serving the old markets of Taiwan and Southeast Asia as well as making inroads into China. The first swept the Taiwan Golden Horse awards, Chinese-language film's most prestigious event. Despite its appeal to American buyers, the series is unlikely to restore lasting faith in Hong Kong's screen industry, let alone recover the 1990s boom. Instead, its northward turn acknowledges the mainland as the main road to continuing production and profits. Pragmatic Hong Kong producers are sure to serve whoever keeps the cameras rolling; and shrewd Chinese bureaucrats know how to provide incentives through selected market access points. Though the first two films evoke apprehensions that Hong Kong society has toward its new master, ultimate success comes only from central authorities' approval. Winning over the Hong Kong audience and selling options to Hollywood represent a remarkable success but, ultimately, the final arbiter post-97 is acceptance by China's gatekeepers. While this may be seen as Chinese efforts to embrace a market economy, the main object is still a green light from mainland censors. A benchmark in the PRC requires both economic *and* ideological reliability; yes, a spectacularly large market beckons in China but it is closely guarded, mined with stipulations and rules that change without warning. On this note, forecasts differ between the screen policies of South Korea and the PRC. The former, while continuing, expects a sunny ending while China's outlook remains overcast, with possible storms.

CONCLUSION

We have outlined three distinct benchmarks in East Asia, noting sources of film capital, production packaging, projected markets and the roles played by policy, whether state-driven or deriving from other structural conditions. Benchmarks, we argue, are not identical to blockbusters, or even a successful series. The term describes a milestone or interchange at which film industries alter course. A benchmark is a film, company policy or state strategy that not only pays off but is a standard by which to gauge subsequent efforts. Benchmarks respond to the challenges and opportunities of East Asian mediascapes and are object lessons in competitive, groundbreaking cinema. These lessons entail new kinds of storytelling (their blockbuster function) but also the ability to seize occasions presented by post-protectionist Asian markets. These benchmarks have industrial, geographical and legislative aspects.

South Korea's twenty-first-century film boom is largely domestic, achieving objectives through a combination of financial incentives, flexible policies and marketing Korean film as a national priority. Its economic and cultural success, including box office, commercial appeal and specifically Korean themes, is the envy of neighbouring countries. South Korea's screen industry is not without pitfalls, but East Asian counterparts scramble to learn from its experience and policies, seeking out those that can be transplanted. In this regard the Korean benchmark proves potentially exportable, overflowing its place of origin. *Crouching Tiger, Hidden Dragon* is just one film, but behind it stands an array of stakeholders that orchestrated an East Asian tour de force. Its importance is marked by outstanding box office, of course, but also a careful alignment of pan-Chinese and global markets. There are lessons here that beckon not only in successful packaging, production and marketing but in the film's problems as well. *Crouching Tiger* failed to reap much benefit from its most likely target, mainland China. This was the very market targeted by Media Asia in its handling of the *Infernal Affairs* trilogy, a commodity that remade its texture and ideology to conform to China's conditions. Using censorship as creative enabler, Media Asia showed how a banned film could be recouped in a way that not only satisfied censors but also widened a regional market accessible to further exports and co-productions. As we shall show in subsequent chapters, Media Asia's experience with *Infernal Affairs* showed that the way forward was the road to China. Other producers in Hong Kong, and nearly every media enterprise in Asia-Pacific, have embarked on that journey.

2

The New Localism:
Alternatives to Blockbuster Benchmarks

Since 2000, two trends emerged in the screen industries of East Asia. One is a greater resilience, adopting Hollywood modes of production such as market research and script development, completion bonds and meticulous post-production, with digitally enhanced attractions. This represents an impulse toward direct competition with the world's dominant commercial cinema. Sometimes fuelled by nationalism, and often supported by Asian governments, this trend has been described at length in Chapter 1. But not every sector follows Hollywood's line. Beyond would-be blockbusters there are vigorous attempts to resuscitate narrative styles specific to the national, regional and local. This other approach is the second important trend in contemporary East Asian screen practices. It is a new breed of local production employing resources specific to given markets, combined with key elements of global entertainment production, that are in turn characteristic of the first trend.

We call this second trend the new localism. The new localism is not limited to independents but also includes transnational companies, as well as Hollywood majors Columbia-Asia and Warner Bros., which have production offices in East Asia. In late 2004, Warner Bros. set up the first production partnership on the Chinese mainland, Warner China Film HG Corp. The new partnership aimed to produce, market and distribute Chinese-language co-productions, including feature films, made-for-TV movies and animation. The company also began similar branch production ventures in Spain and Italy. The establishment of these production branch offices, as opposed to just sales, clearly shows the difference between blockbuster benchmarks and the new localism: Hollywood majors now see local audiences as a sufficient condition for Asia-based production, not just millions of additional viewers of global American pictures. So, just as some East Asian pictures duplicate the action-adventure templates of global Hollywood, Hollywood firms have themselves commenced finance and production aimed directly at national and regional markets within Asia. In this sense new localism is not local at all; it is international, yet decentralised and Asia-specific. Smaller, independent firms such as Arc Light (Taiwan), Applause Pictures (Hong Kong) and Office Kitano (Tokyo) also employ flexible financing and market research to package and produce quasi-art films catering to both festival and commercial tastes.

The new localism revives interest in servicing local and regional audiences by area, and targeting specialised markets by genre or demographic. Rather than outdoing Hollywood, the new localism tightens its prior rapport with East Asian tastes. It is logical that both Asian media firms and Hollywood multinationals take this line, as the former enjoys a head start in entertaining East Asians, while the latter seeks greater market share in the most populous area of the globe. Since the 1990s Hollywood films have tapped East Asian audiences as a mighty revenue stream, with an enormous population base and high disposable incomes. In the previous chapter we described the means by which projects in South Korea, China, and Hong Kong pursued innovations in policy, genre and style to compete with Hollywood blockbusters head to head. A string of blockbusters served notice that enough talent and know-how could be assembled to score huge returns, refuting any notions of East Asian mediocrity. *Crouching Tiger, Hidden Dragon* may be the best case of Asian financing and production capably appropriating state-of-the-art methods. Given his experience, Ang Lee used international models and world-class production, conceiving, implementing and exhibiting a high-quality product with minimal outlay. The US$15 million film was a breakout global hit (US$213 million in theatrical release alone), but the question is whether Asian markets have been fully primed, serviced and recouped. Have audiences renewed their trust in locally made films? Industry people in Chinese-language cinema were dubious because *Crouching Tiger* appeared to re-confirm Hollywood's power. The film was seen as an embrace of the Hollywood model as much as signs of East Asian ingenuity. But there is another example, this time from Hong Kong, a box-office record-breaker firmly wedded to Chinese industrial practice and narrative conventions.

LOCAL HERO: STEPHEN CHOW AND *SHAOLIN SOCCER* (2001)

Shaolin Soccer is an exemplar in its differentiation from American pictures, returning to more distinctive subjects, styles and genres, specific to local popular taste. Usually the return is accompanied by a reduction in scale and ambition, but not always. Occasionally a film will surprise its makers, achieving big business such as Stephen Chow Sing-chi's kung fu sports comedy *Shaolin Soccer*, which was later bought by Miramax for North American release. *Shaolin Soccer* broke all records in Hong Kong, at US$8 million (HK$60.7 million), remaining – until Chow's next effort – the highest grossing locally made picture. No wonder Miramax paid attention.

Stephen Chow's *Shaolin Soccer* (2001)

Chow plays Sing, ex-Shaolin disciple, who uses his kung fu to earn meagre tips. His dream is to make martial arts a part of daily life in what has become materialistic China. Ex-soccer ace Fung (Ng Man-tat) discovers Sing. Because he threw a game, Fung was earlier crippled by his teammate/rival Hung (Patrick Tse) and Hung is now a big wheel in the soccer business and owner of Team Evil. Sing and Fung form the Shaolin Team to challenge Hung, assembling other wandering Shaolin disciples. In the final game, the Shaolin team triumphs by willpower, showing that team spirit and iron-fisted determination bring victory.

Chow, like most Hong Kong stars, began his career in television, hosting children's programmes. In the 1990s he was one of the most bankable stars in the industry, next to Chow Yun-fat and Jet Li. Stephen Chow soon gained a following among PRC college students with his *Chinese Odyssey* (dir. Jeff Lau, 1995) in which Chow plays Monkey King, legendary hero in the Chinese classic *Journey to the West*. But this is a different hero: a hilarious deity who must give up his human dispositions to achieve divinity. Chow uses his trademark 'mo lei tau' (nonsense) humour in his modern rendition of a character staple from television series and popular films.

Shaolin Soccer took Chow over two years to make, then an unheard-of time in Hong Kong production. It boasts expensive special effects from John Chu's Centro Digital Media, a local post-production lab known for its vision during the worst of Hong Kong's financial crisis. The film synthesises kung fu (Shaolin refers to Shaolin Temple, China's martial arts mecca) and soccer. The sports theme tied in with the World Cup held in the summer of 2002, in Japan and South Korea. The film boasts local and mainland actors speaking colloquial slang peppered with bons mots, sight gags and songs. Vicky Zhao Wei's performance stands out as a dumpling-maker with spectacular kung fu skills. She not only charms Sing with her flying hands but also represents a romantic attachment between Hong Kong popular culture and mainland serenity. Zhao Wei, a mainland actress, was red-hot in the region with her appearance in the *My Fair Princess* television series (1998–9) a Taiwan-China co-production. In *Shaolin Soccer* there are many fond references to classic Hong Kong movies, such as John Woo's *A Better Tomorrow* (1986) and the Bruce Lee films.

All these show *Shaolin Soccer*'s timeliness and awareness of local concerns; this cultural locality – story, action, characterisation, and topicality – is framed within a regional, contemporary context. Shot as a co-production on the mainland, the story takes place in a generic Chinese city embracing both Hong Kong and Shanghai. The underdog motif, together with Chow's persona as hapless wisecracker, struck a chord with local audiences. Hong Kong pictures formerly employed put-downs of Chinese migrants, but *Shaolin Soccer* is more generous. This is due to a reversal of fortunes. High unemployment and plummeting property prices afflicted Hong Kong after 2000; Hong Kong identity seemed downtrodden; and the film industry was sinking, with a low output of movies. Overall revenue was drying up, as well as a declining number of theatrical releases (see Table 1.4). Despite a respectable market share for Hong Kong films, the total revenue for theatrical receipts dropped over 50 per cent between US$200 million (HK$1.5 billion) in 1993 to US$58 million (HK$450 million) in 2001 (Mok, 2002).

Chow's film was embraced by audiences, critics and industry leaders. *Shaolin* signified a commercial rebound where wounded parties could be consoled and satisfied. Audiences felt well entertained; Hong Kong's top local paper *Apple Daily* celebrated the recovery of 'Hong Kong can-do spirit' and the industry regained some faith in local talent, techniques and storytelling. This collective rejoicing in the underdog's triumph peaked with the awarding of six prizes to *Shaolin Soccer* at the Hong Kong Film Awards in 2002, including best director and picture. In *Shaolin Soccer*'s reception, we see an urge to reassure a vulnerable local identity. Unlike the hybrid, global *Crouching Tiger*, *Shaolin* seems a familiar, comforting picture, at least to audiences in Hong Kong. The picture is locally owned and made, produced by Chow's Star East and Universe, an independent local video distributor. Without the need of outside assistance, it took local cinema to a new level of finesse.

A double commitment was apparent: loyalty to the local and an endeavour to make quality pictures; this makes *Shaolin Soccer* stand out in recent Hong Kong film history (Lau and Chan, 2001). The movie has a characteristically Hong Kong take on Chinese patriotism, signalling a departure from Chow's earlier 'films [that] have often been retreads of Western genres' (Elley, 2001). Chow's retreads and parodies are comedic craft, and derive from his work with producer Wong Jing. The Wong–Chow partnerships are typical of 1980s Hong Kong style: derivative, brash and vulgar. But now, Chow prided himself in specifically Chinese forms of virtuosity, invoking not only Shaolin kung fu but also a homegrown story, with unified attractions and special effects. *Shaolin Soccer* moves the game forward, changing the Hong Kong reputation from shoddy colonial escapism to more affirmative Chinese values. Production values, emotional value and ideological value – all were solidly in place. When Miramax announced purchase of the film's US rights for US$10 million, Chow and Hong Kong were elated. To make it palatable to Americans, Miramax recut and dubbed, and failed to give the film a proper marketing campaign. It was butchered, but Miramax tried, however clumsily, to leverage an emerging market for Asian popular – not only art house – film in the West. With his next project, *Kung Fu Hustle* (2004), Chow took a big step toward a global audience but, because of this local success, he now had Hollywood finance and marketing (see Chapter 5).

The significance of *Shaolin Soccer* surpasses box office to suggest a rehabilitation of elements specific to East Asian screens. This contrasts with tactics used to assimilate and contest Hollywood, as discussed in Chapter 1. Ultimately *Crouching Tiger*'s success may not be reproducible, though not for lack of effort. The more urgent question for local industries is not how to duplicate *Crouching Tiger*, but how to entice audiences back to the cinema on a regular basis. This priority resonates when we recall failed attempts to simply copy the packaging of *Crouching Tiger*, as in Michelle Yeoh and partner Thomas Chung's *The Touch*, *Silver Hawk* (dir. Jingle Ma, 2004) and Jackie Chan's ill-fated *The Medallion* (co-produced with Miramax).

Witnessing the risks of cloning blockbusters, local film-makers in the region sought safer projects, affirming a new localism – with new styles, talent and subject matter rooted in the local but having strong stories and regional appeal. The essence of new localism: use local languages, settings, references, genres or characters to expand audiences. Unlike benchmarking, direct competition with giant blockbusters is avoided. The new localism is not limited to a single country, language or popular form. It embraces regional co-productions: pan-Chinese, pan-Asian cinema and even co-productions with Europe and Hollywood. An example is the work of Hong Kong directors Johnnie To and Wai Ka-fai, who received funds from both Hollywood and Singapore to adapt a popular Taiwanese comic, Jimmy Liao's *Turn Left, Turn Right* (2003, see below). The new localism cultivates new genres, drawing on prior cultural traditions and folk arts; tapping specific communities like students, ethnic minorities, gay/lesbian, and repackaging extra-cinematic ingredients into engaging movie entertainment.

New localism is not a strategy specific to Hong Kong but a trend at work in almost every East Asian territory. It employs source material grounded in local genres, stars, styles and cross-media alliance. These are endogenous to East Asian popular culture, updated and raised to higher quality levels. In the rest of our discussion, we cover key companies and talents in the East Asian screen trade. Focus is on textual innovation, corporate negotiation and marketing practices. By extending new localism to a wider industry account, it is evident that East Asian film-makers are not simply reacting to the agendas of Hollywood, either adopting or rejecting. Hollywood hegemony is no doubt the most powerful norm, but it remains under scrutiny by more sophisticated, enhanced forms of localisation practice. It is partly Hollywood hegemony that set these enhancements in motion. Hong Kong film-makers Johnnie To Kei-fung and partner Wai Ka-fai, the complete star Andy Lau, successful PRC director Feng Xiaogang and Taiwan producer-director Chen Kuo-fu all skilfully combine transnational capital with local production, distribution and marketing.

RECYCLING LOCAL FORMS:
JOHNNIE TO KEI-FUNG AND WAI KA-FAI

Johnnie To and Wai Ka-fai were the most prolific film-makers in the post-1997 decline. The decline was attributable less to political changes than to internal problems of overproduction, depleted genres and creative paralysis. John Woo, Tsui Hark, Ringo Lam and Stanley Tong were defecting to Hollywood and better prospects. To and Wai's Milkyway Image production company, formed in 1996, was little affected by the negative environment. Coming from a stint in television, To, Wai and their backers recycled local genres and production methods, injecting needed vitality into the industry. From 1996 to 2004, To and Wai directed and produced over thirty films. Between them, working together and separately, they averaged three to four films per year since 2000. Such high productivity recalls the 'glory days' of the 1980s when big stars like Chow Yun-fat or Maggie Cheung would average ten pictures every year. Now three to four pictures a year is considered prolific. Noteworthy about To and Wai is their box-office power, as well as rising critical acclaim. Since 2000, To and Wai dominated the summer and winter hit seasons until 2003, when *Infernal Affairs* broke their hold. Every year, To and Wai were nominated for awards in Hong Kong and Taipei. Before the advent of Media Asia's *Infernal Affairs* trilogy, To and Wai were the most successful film-makers in Hong Kong, both critically and commercially.

Johnnie To and Wai Ka-fai come from the old guard, veterans of the Shaws entertainment empire. In the 1970s and the early 1980s, To was a director for TVB, Hong Kong's dominant network established by the major studio Shaw

Johnnie To Kei-fung on set

Brothers in the 1960s. In 1986, he left television and directed for Cinema City, a production house owned and operated by film-makers, and backed by local distributors. Cinema City was known for its calculating, efficient and effective production strategy. In years following, To established himself as an experienced director-producer, capable of working across different types of movies, like most successful film-makers in the industry. Among the genres in which he worked, male melodramas were notable. His 1989 *All About Ah-long* (as director) and 1990 *A Moment of Romance* (as producer) were the best-known classics of the 1980s, along with John Woo's *A Better Tomorrow*. *Ah-long*, with Chow Yun-fat and Sylvia Chang, remade the lachrymose Jon Voight–Faye Dunaway *The Champ* (1979, itself a remake of King Vidor's 1931 classic). Chow is Ah-long, an aging motorcycle racer who struggles between career and single fatherhood. His young son, Porky, provides an irresistible source of pity. The film reworks themes of maternal sacrifice, centring on masculine father–son pathos. But there is more to this conventional soapy story – the racing subplot allows for spectacular action sequences, balancing the cloying sentimentality. The combination of high-speed competitive sports and melodrama successfully pushed Chow's acting career forward after his gangster triumph, *A Better Tomorrow*. This mix-and-match continued in To's next hit, *A Moment of Romance*. Starring a young Andy Lau,

Year	Title	*Box Office (in HK$ million)	Local Box-Office Ranking
1997	*Lifeline* (dir. Johnnie To and Yau Tat-chi)	20.8	6
1998	*A Hero Never Dies* (dir. Johnnie To)	6.8	18
1999	*Where a Good Man Goes* (dir. Johnnie To)	3.8	23
	Running Out of Time (dir. Johnnie To)	14.66	8
	The Mission (dir. Johnnie To)	4.6	17
2000	*Needing You* (dir. Johnnie To and Wai Ka-fai)	35.21	1
	Help!!! (dir. Johnnie To and Wai Ka-fai)	14.22	10
2001	*Love On a Diet* (dir. Johnnie To and Wai Ka-fai)	40.44	2
	Running Out of Time 2 (dir. Johnnie To and Law Wing-cheong)	5.94	19
	Wu Yen (dir. Johnnie To and Wai Ka-fai)	27.24	4
	Fulltime Killer (dir. Johnnie To and Wai Ka-fai)	25.68	5
2002	*My Left Eye Sees Ghosts* (dir. Johnnie To and Wai Ka-fai)	20.71	4
	Fat Choi Spirit (dir. Johnnie To and Wai Ka-fai)	19.22	5
2003	*Love For All Seasons* (dir. Johnnie To and Wai Ka-fai)	24.73	6
	PTU (dir. Johnnie To)	2.98	31
	Turn Left, Turn Right (dir. Johnnie To and Wai Ka-fai)	13.91	13
	Running On Karma (dir. Johnnie To and Wai Ka-fai)	26.34	3
2004	*Breaking News* (dir. Johnnie To)	7.84	21
	Yesterday Once More (dir. Johnnie To)	15.48	6
	Throw Down (dir. Johnnie To)	8.23	20
2005	*Election* (dir. Johnnie To)	15.89	5
2006	*Election II* (dir. Johnnie To)	13.54	6
	Exiled (dir. Johnnie To)	5.47	18

*HK$7.75 = US$1

Sources:
Data compiled from *City Entertainment* ('Annual Box Office Supplements', 1996–2006); Chen (2000); Hong Kong Film Archive Website; Hong Kong Trade Development Council ('Weekly Box Office') and Milkyway Image Website.

Table 2.1 Milkyway Image: Filmography and Box Office (1997–2006)

A Moment has triad confrontations, motorcycle chases and a love story. The film, with To as producer, generated two more sequels in 1992 and 1996.

Wai Ka-fai, Johnnie To's partner in Milkyway, was a colleague from TVB. Wai was a senior scriptwriter, responsible for writing assembly-line drama, but he managed to produce two critically acclaimed series in the early 1990s: *The Great Times of Man* and *Looking Back in Anger*. Wai worked mostly as the principal writer for Milkyway Image, though he often switch-hit, co-directing with To on at least one picture a year. (See Table 2.1.)

Johnnie To's extensive experience in the business pre-Milkyway meant he had excellent connections in the distribution establishment, besides being a skilful commercial director. With Wai's television writing skills – timely, expedient and proficient – Milkyway operated with adequate funds, smoothly, efficiently and flexibly.

Milkyway's significance is its strategy of working with major stars and allying with big companies such as China Star, Media Asia and Warner Bros. This permits Milkyway to work with ample financial and distribution resources, regardless of the products delivered to investors. Milkyway therefore flexibly alternates between comedy star vehicles and smaller, edgier crime pictures. Together, this continues to satisfy pickier local audiences and to fulfil the filmmakers' ambition to remain leaders in Hong Kong cinema.

'Flexibility in everything!' To said in an interview, responding to a question about his facility with genres, from farce to romantic comedy to thrillers. 'If necessary everything can change, all at once. And in the next day's shooting maybe everything will change again. … Hollywood can't do this. But we can: *we* can change things whenever we want' (Kraicer, 2001). While To refers to daily adjustments of performance, script and rushes, his appetite for variety could just as well describe his genres, budget and production values, including action-adventure, martial arts, costume films and such supernatural concept pictures as *My Left Eye Sees Ghosts* (2002) and *Running on Karma* (2003).

To and Wai clearly reveal the new localism of Hong Kong cinema. For Milkyway to distinguish itself from – not assimilate or comply with – Hollywood, it pursues conscious product differentiation to forge alternatives to the global hegemony. Continuing with old, abandoned working patterns demonstrates clinging to local forms. This entails risks: of reprising depleted models, of falling into false nostalgia, of failing to excite a new generation of moviegoers. It also risks arousing critical doubts whether these movies might actually contribute to the industry's decline by running outmoded machines into the ground:

> From a strictly business point of view, giving a stylish new spin to shopworn genre material lays no foundations for the reconstruction of a film industry in trouble.

This kind of success is inherently short-lived; it defers collapse rather than rescinding it. Ironically, [Johnnie To] has been pursuing exactly this policy for more than ten years already: To (sometimes with his creative partner Wai Ka-fai, sometimes without) directs and produces heavily burnished updates of old genre formulas, including his share of police-triad thrillers. Despite stolid support from Hong Kong critics and a couple of international festivals, his work hasn't ushered in a return to the glory days of the 1980s. (Rayns, 2004: 29)

Rayns's scepticism reflects disappointment that Milkyway's films are not very innovative and perhaps too commercial. This view places Milkyway in the canons of art and independent cinema, within the discourse of international film festivals. Compared with previous artistic work from Hong Kong, including the Hong Kong New Wave, films by Wong Kar-wai and Fruit Chan, Milkyway fails to pass muster with critics using the standards of art cinema. But this 'failure' also shows a disinclination to recognise the creative energy brought to the industry by Milkyway Image. Because of this critical misapprehension, and other marketplace risks, we can place To and Wai in the East Asian new localism.

A clear decision not to go 'global' (to Hollywood) or 'international' (to Western art houses) places Milkyway firmly at home, reworking old material in new ways. Milkyway contracts with local outfits for financing, distribution and marketing. It organises production around Hong Kong stars, genre formulas, local settings and content. To make this assembly line work, To and Wai happily recycle from a hodgepodge of familiar materials, including manga (Japanese comics), samurai films, Kitano Takeshi, Japanese television drama, pop songs, John Woo, Meg Ryan, Westerns, and their own previous work.

The choice to stay local and to make films for Hong Kong audiences does not entail isolation or parochialism. Since *The Mission* (dir. Johnnie To, 1999), Milkyway's artistry has been internationally recognised. Given the wider brief of contemporary festivals, it was time for Milkyway to cross over to festival circuits. Ever since Italy's Udine Far East Film Festival did a retrospective on him in 2003, Johnnie To gained a reputation as a Hong Kong auteur. Auteurism in East Asia signifies transnational investment and sometimes a shift in market and audiences. But so far, Milkyway's productions have remained unaffected in financing and distribution. But in terms of content, the company is moving toward political critique, just when most local films have become politically cautious, eager to be integrated with a larger China constituency.

Between 2005 and 2006, Johnnie To completed two crime pictures on Hong Kong triad history, *Election* and *Election II*. *Election* entered competition at Venice in 2005, under director Marco Muller, known for his support for Asian cinemas. *Election II* was the closing film for the Hong Kong International Film

Wai Ka-fai, screenwriter-director

Johnnie To's triad parable, *Election*

Festival. Both films detail power struggles within crime families and the tactics used by contenders for the position of godfather. Unlike Hong Kong itself, these triads undertake open democratic campaigns complete with charismatic candidates, bribery, torture and other dirty tricks. *Election* ends with the victory of the most unassuming, but totally depraved, player (Simon Yam). *Election II* concludes with a high-ranking Chinese security officer welcoming the godfather-elect to the lucrative trade in the Pearl River Delta. Local audiences applauded at the end of *Election II* for its wry twist on China's suffocating embrace. Both films performed well in the local box office. *Election* received US$2 million (HK$15.89 million) and ranked fifth for the year while *Election II* took US$1.75 million (HK$13.54 million) in the low, pre-summer season (see Table 2.1). The first passed Chinese censors with significant revisions. First, like *Infernal Affairs* a major triad member is revealed to be an undercover cop; second, To shot a new ending with the undercover police charging from the bushes to arrest the boss and see justice prevail. Perhaps due to complaints on the internet from both mainland and local audiences, Milkyway did not provide a China-ready version for *Election II*.

To's triad trilogy answers Media Asia's *Infernal Affairs* trilogy in contrarian mockery. *Infernal Affairs III* was supported by the mainland, but *Election* and *Election II* seem made to annoy Chinese authority. *Infernal Affairs II* romanticises the formation of a powerful triad godfather but *Election* depicts the routine savagery behind democratic manoeuvring. *Infernal Affairs III* is about the close partnership between Hong Kong and the Chinese police in maintaining social stability but *Election II* ends with a shocking revelation of China's parental control.

As To's international reputation rose, Wai Ka-fai found a separate career. After *Running on Karma* (2003), To and Wai ended their partnership. In 2005, Milkyway was acquired by a property speculator, Alex Law, who granted To complete artistic control over production. Johnnie To remains the creative centre of the company, continuing his collaboration with Hong Kong's major distributors, China Star and Media Asia. It seems Johnnie To's commitments will sustain his updating of local film standards.

Hits from Milkyway Image

Needing You (2000, China Star/Milkyway/One Hundred Years) was a hit and launched Cantopop diva Sammi Cheng as a movie star. It is a romantic comedy à la Meg Ryan, to whom Cheng is often compared. This film reworked 'trendy drama' with local sensibilities and references. It features a couple with personality disorders who eventually unite after a series of challenges. A bashful office girl (Cheng) meets a self-made investment broker (Lau), a smart-alec executive who takes other people too casually. The pairing capitalises on Andy Lau's star power and Sammi Cheng's popularity with young women. Lau had by now achieved unprecedented stardom in all Chinese-speaking territories. In Hong Kong cinema's decline, the much-needed success of *Needing You*, as well as its breezy tone, allowed To and Wai to continue their reworking of local themes and packages.

Turn Left, Turn Right (2003, Warner Bros.) is a pan-Chinese production with a combination of regional talent, crew and location. Set in Taipei, it stars a top pan-Asian idol, Takeshi Kaneshiro, and Gigi Leung, another Cantopop and movie star. Kaneshiro is a classical violinist and Gigi is supposed to be a translator of Polish poetry. The film is patently fairy-tale. This fantasy was adapted from an illustrated storybook by Taiwan's Jimmy Liao, popular throughout Chinese communities in the region. The film has the flavour of Japanese television drama, manga (comics), romantic melodrama and topical references. Mention is made of the September 2002 earthquake in central Taiwan that killed thousands of people. *Turn Left, Turn Right* is premised on an attempted reunion of two classmates who keep missing each other, though they live in adjacent flats.

Bankrolled by Warner Bros., this film was directed exclusively at young East Asian audiences, not only to Chinese-speaking territories but also Japan and Korea. A film initiated through distribution channels, it is a package directed solely to the region, and not back to the US. The writing and production values are not up to To and Wai's usual standards, as the style is not polished enough for J-dorama (Japanese television drama), even though the concept and original property place it in that framework. There's an otherworldly quality to the story in keeping with the original work by Liao, and J-dorama, but alien to the grittier work of To and Wai.

Running on Karma (Milkyway/One Hundred Years, 2003) is a strange, uneven concept picture capitalising on Andy Lau, especially at first where it treads close to exploitation. A martial arts fantasy, *Running* is about a monk (Lau) who tries to apostasise, initially working as a muscular stripper. Because he can see people's karma – their future and their past – a police investigation ensues. To catch a murderer, the film takes a strange turn into the metaphysical. Lau's co-star Cecilia Cheung cannot escape her karma, and dies a gruesome death. What begins as wild comedy ends as dark parable of redemption and retribution.

A STAR IS WORN:
ANDY LAU AND THE 'FOUR GREAT HEAVENLY KINGS'

In the centre of Johnnie To and Wai Ka-fai's successful collaboration is the star Andy Lau Tak-wah, whose huge fan base supports Milkyway lines of credit. Andy Lau (b. 1960) is the Tom Cruise of Hong Kong and China screen trade. Not only is Lau the number one box-office leading man, he also assumes leadership in the industry. Also, Lau may be more visible than Cruise. From 1981 to 2007, Lau starred in 130 movies. And, he can sing! Between 1985 and 2007 Lau released 138 albums. In 2000 he was credited with a Guinness Book of Records citation for selling the most Cantopop records. To many his acting remained superfluous, a sideline to Lau's real popularity as a singer.

Though none are as prolific as Lau, every Asian star must be able to perform musically, especially on annual talent and variety shows for broadcast. Many screen actors started out in music and/or television, under long-term contracts that exploited every appearance. More recently stars have come to the screen from talent agencies, trained to be all-round celebrities, not just actors. In Hong Kong this has been standard practice since the 1970s, and in Japan, the 'idol' system has been operating since the 1960s, based on agreements between talent agencies and television. Japan's top idol group SMAP ('Sports Music Assemble People') is owned and operated by the agency Johnnie's Jimusho, or Johnnie and Associates (est. 1963), proprietor Kitagawa Johnnie. It has dominated the most lucrative pop culture ventures (variety, commercials, drama, recording and radio) for decades. 'Multimedia talent' comes out of Kitagawa's push to reverse the decline of the Japanese star system in the 1990s. All-round celebrities enable Asian firms to lease their talents to commercial ad agencies, live concert promoters and recording companies.

Andy Lau Tak-wah with Maggie Q, *Magic Kitchen* (2004)

Stars in feature films are just one of many platforms to generate revenue, publicity and career advancement.

Andy Lau's success is not based on some mystical star quality but on his indefatigable appetite for continuous work. This is a punishing grind, as Lau is a workaholic, exercising up to six hours per day in addition to squeezing deals, sales meetings and publicity campaigns into daily regimens to further his career. His longevity in the entertainment industry will bring him legendary status in the future. For now, though, acclaim in the West has eluded him.

Like many top Hong Kong show-business talents, Lau comes from working-class stock. Raised in the semi-rural New Territories, he began as a hair stylist before entering TVB, former studio mogul Run Run Shaws' television network. As Lau worked his way up from television drama in the early 1980s to supporting roles in features, from his first appearance in the critically acclaimed *Boat People* (dir. Ann Hui, 1981) to Chow Yun-fat's sidekick in the first two of Wong Jing's five-part *God of Gamblers* series (1989–96), he maintained a reputation for reliability and charm. He was finally cast as a romantic lead in *A Moment of Romance* (dir. Benny Chan, 1990) though by this time he had many years of experience.

Andy Lau's career shot skyward when he was raised into the 'Four Great Heavenly Kings' pantheon of Hong Kong entertainment. This was a Cantopop publicity gimmick invented by TVB to push four in-house male idols to heart-throb rank in the recording industry: Jacky Cheung, Leon Lai, Aaron Kwok and Andy Lau. Throughout the 1990s, Andy Lau consolidated his star billing by entering the top echelon, singing both Cantonese and Mandarin hits. He would win scores of awards as the most popular male vocal artist from 1994 to 1996, on Billboard, Channel V and MTV charts.

In the late 1990s with the film industry in a slump, Lau began collaboration with Johnnie To and Wai Ka-fai and was subsequently taken seriously for versatile roles in *Running Out of Time* (1999), *Needing You* and *Fulltime Killer* (2001). Lau was well and truly a 'Heavenly King', only the phrase was now defunct, nostalgically reflecting Lau's regenerated stardom. Lau draws the female audience right through from age eight to eighty. The more successful he is, the higher the stakes in potential changes made in his screen persona.

Andy Lau tirelessly endorses everything from toilet fixtures to public service announcements reminding clerks to 'smile when you serve'. Lau has a huge following across the whole region, from the PRC to Taiwan, Singapore, Malaysia, South Korea and Japan (Fung, 2003). One thing that endears him so widely is his down-to-earth persona. Among his versatile activities spanning film, television, ad campaigns, commercials, recording, live concerts and producing, the only thing he hasn't ventured is the theatrical stage.

Still, Andy Lau avoids taking the same roles, since typecasting would fail to satisfy fans. He has starred in martial arts, historical epic, nostalgia, detective, period pictures, action, comedy, police thrillers, fantasy, and art films, including Wong Kar-wai's first picture *As Tears Go By* (1988). Consider his presence in such wildly different pictures as *Running on Karma*, *Love on a Diet* (2001), as opposed to the charismatic assassin in *Fulltime Killer* (on which he also served as producer) and the Thai kickboxing champ in *A Fighter's Blues* (dir. Daniel Lee, 2000). Not to be overlooked are appearances in PRC cinema, like Zhang Yimou's *House of Flying Daggers* and Feng Xiaogang's *A World Without Thieves* (2004). In 2004 alone, five Lau films released: *Magic Kitchen*, *Jianghu*, *Yesterday Once More* as well as the two PRC films directed by Zhang and Feng.

Andy Lau is vigorous in his involvement with local production and promotion. The One Hundred Years of Film Company was the result of a 1999 merger between Andy Lau Tak-wah's Teamwork (est. 1991) and Hong Kong's major distributor China Star. Lau worked as producer on *Jianghu*, *Infernal Affairs*, *Fulltime Killer* and Fruit Chan's independent debut, *Made in Hong Kong* (1997), its sequel *The Longest Summer* (Chan again, 1998), *McDull II: Prince De la Bun* (dir. Toe Yuen, 2004, and also the voice of McBing, the porcine hero's father). Lau's Focus First Cuts series of high-definition video features serves as a training ground for young directors from all around Asia. In 2006, Focus First Cuts launched a pan-Asian series of films: *The Shoe Fairy* (dir. Robin Lee, Taiwan, 2006), *I'll Call U* (dir. Lam Tze-chung, Hong Kong, 2006), *Love Story* (dir. Kelvin Tong, Singapore, 2006), *Crazy Stone* (dir. Ning Hao, China, 2006), *Rain Dogs* (dir. Ho Yuhang, Malaysia, 2006) and *My Mother is a Belly Dancer* (dir. Lee Kung-lok, Hong Kong, 2006). *Crazy Stone* topped China's box-office chart for domestic film in the summer of 2006 (Yu, 2006).

For another Hong Kong-based production company Applause Pictures (see Chapter 4), Lau appeared in the first *Golden Chicken* (dir. Samson Chiu, 2002), but not the second, except for a cameo as the Chief Executive of Hong Kong in the year 2046. Lau's popularity takes political advantage, as well as his fitness and good looks that border on immortality. Unlike Jackie Chan, the kung fu action star, Lau boasts an impressive versatility and commercial adaptability. Andy Lau can (and does) sell *everything,* including the Hong Kong film industry itself. But his various roles behind the camera and in business meetings are just as protean and productive, making him a cultural ambassador for China itself: the only major star who does not appear in any foreign films, a stardom seemingly rooted in East Asia.

If Andy Lau Tak-wah is Hong Kong's leading man, adored for his musical talent, work ethic and versatility, he has been overlooked in the West. Other talents have worked in America and Europe – Chow Yun-fat, Jet Li, Gong Li, Zhang

Ziyi, Maggie Cheung and Tony Leung Chiu-wai, among others. Another twist is that the first Hong Kong film remade in the US was *Infernal Affairs* – starring Andy Lau Tak-wah. Its story, style or genre American buyers found noteworthy, and paid to capitalise on a new source of entertainment value. It was rumoured that Lau sought a cameo in Martin Scorsese's Boston remake, *The Departed*, but it was not to be. If Lau remains unknown in the West, he is a wildly celebrated talent and industry spokesman all over Asia.

In late 2006, Andy Lau's achievements were recognised by the Pusan International Film Festival, the region's leading festival. Lau was awarded 'Asian Film-maker of the Year' for his promotion of young, independent Asian films and his devotion as an Asian actor for over two decades.

POST-SOCIALIST COMEDY: FENG XIAOGANG AND THE BEIJING FORBIDDEN CITY FILM COMPANY

As elsewhere in East Asia, there is rising synergy in China between cinema and television, as PRC media diversifies. Compared to earlier eras of central planning, China's media today is remarkably free. Product differentiation is

Feng Xiaogang, market-oriented director

promoted through cross-marketing of broadcast and theatrical films, online promotion, and greater awareness of regional audiences. With some Hollywood imports allowed, the People's Republic of China still maintains its official position and regularly produces mainstream policy films, the so-called *zhu xuanlü*, 'main melody' films. These pictures are directed at the Chinese masses, often with free admission and compulsory attendance. *The Opium War* (dir. Xie Jin, 1997), a policy film commemorating Hong Kong's return, boasted a box-office record of US$6.25 million (RMB 50 million). But in 2001, since joining the WTO, China's state-monopoly system was restructured toward market-driven production. State-run studios have been corporatised, if not privatised, as with the Shanghai Film Group (est. 2001), a conglomerate that owns Shanghai Film Studio, Shanghai Animation Studio, Shanghai Dubbing Film Studio, Shanghai Science and Educational as well as Shanghai Film Studio Laboratory, formerly independent entities under the Shanghai municipal government. The current Chinese conglomerates of distribution, production and exhibition were reconstructed from the ashes of old state-owned enterprises.

Feng Xiaogang typifies this market-driven revamp. He began as a set painter for the People's Liberation Army Theatre Troupe. His career blossomed with China's marketisation drive. In the early 1990s Feng went into television as a writer, and enjoyed some comic hits. His fame was secured with *Beijingers in New York* (1992), a multimillion-dollar melodrama shot on location in the US, starring China's leading man, Jiang Wen (*Hibiscus Town* [dir. Xie Jin, 1986], *Red Sorghum* [dir. Zhang Yimou, 1987], *Devils on the Doorstep* [dir. Jiang Wen, 2000], etc.). It concerns a poor musician who arrives in the city with his wife, who achieves success, but at the cost of a happy home. Since then, Feng Xiaogang has become a director of satirical comedies about social changes in contemporary Chinese life.

In 1997, Feng and partner Wang Shuo formed a consulting firm called Sweet Dream. Wang, teleplay writer of *Beijingers in New York* and *Stories of the Editing Room*, was popular for 'hooligan literature', a new type of fiction about unemployed Beijing hustlers in the early 1990s. Feng's third feature *Part A, Part B* (1998) was Sweet Dream's calling card to Beijing Forbidden City Film Company, a state-funded entity founded in 1997 as a flexible financing, production and marketing venture. Forbidden City is an interesting case in the film industry of the late 1990s. With a new annual ten-picture limit on foreign imports, the so-called 'Big Ten' initiated in 1994, the Chinese government started a 'boutique film' policy, inviting qualifying projects to compete with Big Ten blockbusters. This involved astute marketing plans and cultivation of subjects closer to the daily life of Chinese audiences. In addition, film-makers were encouraged to adopt both Hollywood and Hong Kong

Year	Title	*Box Office (in RMB million)	Box-Office Ranking
1998	*Part A, Part B*	10	3
1999	*Be There or Be Square*	Over 30	1
2000	*Sorry Baby*	30	2
2000	*A Sigh*	Around 30	3
2001	*Big Shot's Funeral*	40	1
2003	*Cell Phone*	53	1
2004	*A World Without Thieves*	103	3
2006	*The Banquet*	130	2

*RMB 8 = US$1

Sources:
Data compiled from *Film Art* (1999, no. 3; 2000, no. 3; 2001, no. 3; 2002, no. 3), Ying and Wang (2005a, 2005b) and Yeung (2007).

Table 2.2 Box Office of Feng Xiaogang's Films (1998–2006)

models to save Chinese film from box-office oblivion. One of Forbidden City's targets was the so-called *hesui pian*, 'Celebration Pictures', a term used for Jackie Chan's lunar New Year extravaganzas. Since 1995, Jackie Chan dominated this slot every year in Hong Kong, Taiwan and the mainland. This was the market objective of *Part A, Part B*, released in time for the lunar New Year of 1998. With strong government backing the film was a hit, taking US$4.13 million (RMB 33 million), only a few hundred thousand behind the season's policy film, and a biopic on China's former premier *Zhou Enlai* (see Table 2.2). Feng's subsequent films would take the same road to popular success. With Forbidden City behind him, Feng triumphed with wry urban comedies *Part A, Part B*, *Be There or Be Square* (1999), *Sorry Baby* (2000), *Big Shot's Funeral* (2001) and *Cell Phone* (2003). Later, Feng would get backing from Hong Kong's Media Asia for *A World Without Thieves*. In all these films Feng explores China's new rich: a rising bourgeoisie of entrepreneurs and entertainers, aspirational opportunists in show business and the arts. Together, Feng and Forbidden City created a new production trend in China, with many film-makers later tapping into this *hesui pian* concept. Zhang Yimou's failed *Happy Times* (2001) and his sensational success *Hero* were also *hesui pian*. Feng Xiaogang opened a door, henceforth hailed as the first genuinely commercial director in contemporary China.

According to Feng, two ingredients are central to his films: a down-to-earth, populist perspective (*renmin xing*, 'the people's feelings') and a fantastic, legendary quality. The first is about depicting desires and imagination of the masses. The second expands and fulfils the people's imagined wishes, a 'sweet dream', as Feng named his start-up company. This appeal to the popular was once consigned to Hong Kong films. It also created a cushion for domestic films' competition with Hollywood, and can be seen as China's variation on the new localism. These ingredients seem peculiarly Chinese; they are neither Hong Kong nor Hollywood, but represent a new PRC, a Populist Regime of Consumers, entranced by images and stories desired by ordinary Chinese. In this regard, China's leading director Zhang Yimou is an evil twin of Feng Xiaogang. Both make popular films but by very different routes: one via highest state of the art, the other granting multitudes their wishes, a new state of vernacular Chinese entertainment. With *The Banquet* (2006), though, Feng clearly wishes to ascend into the prestige sector of official production and international awards.

The new localism of Feng's films is evident in their titles. The Chinese title of *Part A, Part B – jiafang yifang* – refers to the legal term for contracts related to investments, property, rentals, marriage and divorce. *Meiwan meiliao* (*Sorry Baby*) is colloquial Chinese for 'endless, inconclusive'. This is a tale of a cab driver and a kidnapping gone awry. A rich fool is outwitted by the driver, in cahoots with the rich man's mistress. *Cell Phone*'s Chinese title *Shou ji* (hand device) is likened to hand grenades (*shou lei*), a time bomb that exposes the web of deceit and extramarital affairs of affluent Chinese. *Big Shot's Funeral* is simply called *Da wan'er* (big shot) in Chinese, in argot specific to urbanites of the capital. The common trait of these titles is their specificity, making them immediately recognisable to city dwellers of Beijing and its surrounds. *Be There or Be Square*, a film about Beijingers in Los Angeles, shows Feng's satirical inversion of socialist slogans into survival skills for overseas Chinese. Liu is a drifting Beijinger in Los Angeles, looking for fun, money and a carefree, American-style life. One of his schemes is to tutor the LA police in Chinese to help their patrols in suburbs with large diaspora populations. Liu wryly makes fun of the cops by training them to say, 'serving the people' (*wei renmin fuwu*, a Communist motto) as a standard Chinese greeting. This is amusing because the film initially depicts the Los Angeles Police Department (LAPD) as menacing and racist, not servants of the people. Feng thus affords Chinese immigrants some control by extracting surplus value from passé political expressions. An English-language critic presents the case on Feng Xiaogang:

> As mainstream entertainment goes, *Cell Phone* is a slick and enjoyable film for a home audience. It sits nicely in the context of a domestic [PRC] cinema, which has only just been allowed to deal more honestly with infidelity and other minor social problems. But future distributors should take care when listening to all the sociological bluster that has surrounded the film, as there's really little more than a single, albeit fun, idea at its center. (Havis, 2004: 64)

But there is an additional, industrial aspect to Feng's success. A semi-official film-maker with access to the coveted Chinese holiday audience, Feng lards his stories with soft lessons for contemporary consumers: crime doesn't pay; infidelity will out; honesty is the best policy; respect authority. Prominent films made by Feng must toe the line set by the Chinese censors. Dealing with an exploding consumer society and its attendant problems is an ideological requirement for Feng's pictures to have official endorsement. Mild critiques of individualism, selfishness, lust and other 'spiritual pollution' must be there, and Feng's material is amenable to such didacticism. But what we see in sets, costumes and production values is hog wallowing in luxurious indulgence. Feng's movies are loaded with product placements, opulent settings and glossy production values.

A World Without Thieves (no thieves under heaven, *tianxia wu zei*) rephrases another Chinese proverb, *tianxia wu di* (invincible under heaven). This too hints at an ideal socialist world, now infested with post-socialist wolves and foxes. The first part of *A World Without Thieves* looks like a parody of a TV commercial. A stolen BMW is the setting, in which a gorgeous couple roars through the gate on the road to Tibet. As they speed away, a liveried guard salutes smartly. The hero (Andy Lau) stops the car, reverses and scolds the guard, demanding to know why people with fancy cars might not also be thieves. 'Do your job' (serve the people), he commands. 'Don't make silly assumptions based on possessions.' Here, spectators have their consumer cake and eat it too. The lesson is clearly spelled out but images of glamour, comfort and success dominate, letting spectators gorge on product-placed fantasies of the good life. Such scenes are typical in Feng's movies: one line of meaning for vigilant censors, another for the aspirational viewer dreaming visions of luxury. Within the same sequence Feng caters to both sides of modern China, the socialist and the consumerist. Interestingly, this scene of the hero scolding the nonplussed guard is missing from the Hong Kong version of the film. The remainder of the film is a road movie about a train journey to and from Tibet where thieves prey on migrant workers with loads of cash.

A World Without Thieves was the first co-production between Hong Kong-based Media Asia, Forbidden City and Huayi Brothers, an advertising agency-cum-marketing firm, with distribution by the state-run China Film Corporation. This backing explains the film's larding with product placement for Nokia, China Mobile and internet portal Taobao, in addition to BMW. The film's ambition goes beyond the China–Hong Kong nexus. It has input from Taiwan, including Taiwan's Rene Liu as Andy Lau's female counterpart and crediting Taiwan director-producer Chen Kuo-fu as executive producer, possibly the creative force behind the train sequences, clearly inspired by Hitchcock thrillers and espionage stories.

Feng is notable for creation of a third space in Chinese cinema. Film in the PRC has been stuck in a dichotomy, a state organ of socialist propaganda on one side, and on the other an art cinema with international prestige exemplified by the Fifth Generation films. While these two poles yielded the most interesting Chinese cinema in the past, each bears risks of different sorts. State propaganda brings little profit and thus makes no sense at all in a market-driven economy. It also hampers the liberal, peaceful image that China is keen to project to the world. Art cinema, on the other hand, has been completely transformed into globally appealing genre pictures at the hands of once-critical artists like Zhang Yimou and Chen Kaige. Feng's pictures stand between and mediate these extremes. They are concerned with mobility among the middle classes, worried about reputation, consumption, ethics and culture. Full of Westernised temptations, Feng's films reverse the exoticising of Chinese historical experience, whether revolutionary or dynastic. These popular films are warmly embraced by local audiences, and have little currency outside the mainland. This is confirmed by Hong Kong distributors' difficulty in marketing these films to their audiences, due to the colloquial topicality of Feng's stories.

Feng Xiaogang presents himself as a kind of ordinary worker, in touch with the average Chinese. He communicates in down-to-earth, even raunchy images. With a journalist one night at dinner, he tells a parable about China's films.

Horror sleeper *Double Vision* (Chen Kuo-fu, 2002)

He likens Chinese art films to seafood, while his pictures are more like the lowly chilli. 'Look at this prawn,' he says, 'delicious, luscious, easy to eat.' He takes the prawn and places it over the tiny red chilli next to it. The chilli disappears. 'Now,' he asks, 'when you get up in the morning, which do you remember in the toilet, prawn or chilli?' (Beech, 2001).

DOUBLE VISION (2002): GLOCAL PRODUCT FROM TAIWAN

Like the PRC, Taiwan has been known for its art cinema, not its popular films. But for decades, the Taiwan film industry was a mass-production line of hundreds of genre pictures every year. As a popular cinema produced by a cottage industry for quick returns, money poured into production that kept cash flow rapid, maintaining a viable distribution system. This pipeline for local pictures flowed freely from the late 1950s for about thirty years, relying on a large regional appetite, especially in Southeast Asia. During this period Taiwan was under martial law (1947–89), which suspended freedom of speech, public assembly and the media. Beginning in the early 1980s, Taiwan film markets at home and abroad began to dry up. Audiences rejected domestic films in favour of Hong Kong imports, especially comedies and action pictures. To revive local production the government embarked on a policy to cultivate young directors in hope of attracting a new generation of viewers back to cinemas. Thus arrived the Taiwan New Cinema of early Hou Hsiao-hsien, Edward Yang, Wan Ren, Wu Nien-chen and several others. Instead, the New Cinema emerged as an acclaimed movement in international festivals and resisted turning its artistry toward commercial ends (Yeh and Davis, 2005: 55–89). The New Cinema's international reputation, though totally dismissed by local distributors and exhibitors, was a major inspiration to young film-makers. In the 1990s they would choose personal expression (albeit internationally favoured) over domestic commercial entertainment. Hence Taiwan popular cinema was abandoned, allowing imports to fill the empty screens.

Since the late 1980s, with media deregulation, Hollywood majors have been making exorbitant returns in Taiwan. Usually their distribution takes up less than 30 per cent of all films shown in Taiwan, but their revenue share continuously remains above 70 per cent (*Cinema in the ROC 2002 Yearbook*, 2002: 38). Presently, while there is plenty of investment in foreign distribution, there is little money for local production.

Co-financing *Crouching Tiger*, Columbia Pictures-Asia and others initiated a synthetic 'glocal' line for local consumption. This strategy taps local taste and production know-how, with finance, distribution and marketing extended on US lines. Long accustomed to making art films, it was hard for Taiwan film-makers to defer to Hollywood. Having forgotten recipes for popular cinema, they see little demand as it is unlikely that they could outdo Steven Spielberg, Ron Howard or Peter Jackson. But Taiwan directors also fear overspecialisation, which is evident in audiences' automatic rejection of Taiwan-made product. Some directors aspire to make popular film but dare not, especially since fundraising is nearly impossible for a locally made genre picture. It is very risky compared to the well-trodden art film path, with their high international profile and track record; these have no difficulty attracting money from government or international sources. Hou Hsiao-hsien's Shochiku-produced *Café Lumière* (2003), for which Hou does not even have Taiwan distribution rights, needed special permission for a Taipei screening in late October 2004. For all intents and purposes *Café Lumière* is a Japanese film. With *Double Vision* it was Hollywood backing that sought to partner with Taiwan talent to engage the Chinese-language market.

For *Double Vision*, the glocal strategy paid off. It was a trial that hit the mark, especially in marketing and distribution: US$2.6 million (NT$80 million) in box office (*Cinema in the ROC 2002 Yearbook*, 2002: 39). The film was directed by Chen Kuo-fu, a longtime veteran of the Taiwan New Cinema, and written by Su Chao-bin, a popular thriller writer. Chen seems an unlikely reviver of Taiwan popular film. Chen never worked the commercial mainstream, unlike Hou Hsiao-hsien, but he always wanted to make interesting thrillers, à la Hitchcock. As a cinephile critic, Chen was highly familiar with Hollywood and European classics. His earlier films *Treasure Island* (1993) and *The Personals* (1998) are stylish fusions of genre elements and personal flourishes.

Double Vision was financed and produced by Sony Pictures-Columbia-Asia in order to gain inroads into Taiwan's lucrative box office. Since 1994 Taiwan has always been among the top global earners for Hollywood pictures. As with *Crouching Tiger*, Sony Pictures-Columbia-Asia wanted production as well as distribution benefits, as well as those of distribution. It shrewdly combined local Taiwanese and Hollywood ingredients: the pitch for *Double Vision* was simply 'Taoist Se7en', after the 1995 David Fincher thriller. It contains a Taiwan–America cultural theme, with American character actor David Morse appearing in Taipei as an FBI (Federal Bureau of Investigation) agent probing a series of bizarre murders. The Morse character is like the film itself: a Taiwan story unfolding through a Hollywood narrative formula. It covers contemporary Taiwanese social problems like the spiritual rot belying high-tech materialism, with much suffering by the whistle-blowing hero. Hong Kong actor Tony Leung Ka-fai stars as a police detective in charge of international affairs. He is about to lose his family and job because of his intolerance of police corruption, and that in turn leads to a cousin's suicide. Consequently, Leung's character is wracked with guilt and depression. The American notices, and proceeds to first annoy – as only

Yanks can – then provoke, befriend and strongly support his Taiwan counterpart. So in addition to other affiliations, the film is also a familiar inter-cultural buddy film.

The title *Double Vision* epitomises a parallel between the narrative and the making of the film. A 'double vision' sees things in twos: a spiritual and economic outlook; reason (FBI forensics) and superstition (Taoist intuition); local production (location, story) and Hollywood management (Columbia-Asia's production schedule, accounting methods, supervision). Funds from Hollywood also allowed Nan Fan (Southern), the production company headed by Chen Kuo-fu, to design a marketing campaign that turned the enigmatic narrative of the film into an online puzzle to rouse pre-release curiosity (Liang, 2002). Chen and company saw that in order to lure audiences back to locally made films, one vision is insufficient. You must have another eye on marketing to inform, entice and promote. Chen's marketing scheme, capitalising on his Hollywood connection, paid off. It was the key to the success of *Double Vision*, whose US$1.22 million (NT$ 39 million) in the capital Taipei alone surpassed Universal's thriller *Red Dragon*'s (2002) US$840,000 (NT$27 million) and prompted Columbia's CEO to fly from Los Angeles to congratulate Chen. Chen Kuo-fu turned water into wine, miraculously transforming a B-grade noir-thriller into a local blockbuster (Liang, 2002).

The key to *Double Vision*'s victory, similar to that of *Crouching Tiger*, is its combination of local know-how, setting and Hollywood backing, not only through financial support but its administrative resources channelled through Taiwan expertise. Ironically, Hollywood collaboration appears to be the only way to revive local commercial cinema, and to change perceptions of Taiwan film. *Double Vision* proved that Taiwan can and will make popular films even if it requires a former critic and art film director. Taiwan film-makers now rely on Hollywood, the main beneficiary of the vanishing domestic popular cinema, to claw back a share of the local market. This is a peculiar feature of screen industry globalisation. In 2002 *Double Vision* scored high in the foreign movie chart, alongside *The Lord of the Rings: The Two Towers* and the second *Harry Potter* film.

Double Vision could well be a one-off, like *Crouching Tiger*, whose producers seem to have opted out of franchise possibility. Columbia-Asia also backed Taiwan-born actress/director/producer Sylvia Chang's 2004 romantic comedy *20: 30: 40*, a woman's film about love, career and aging, with Chen Kuo-fu as executive producer. The film competed at the Berlin International Film Festival. But its box-office take in Taiwan and Hong Kong was modest. Most local producers believe that projects like *Double Vision* and *Crouching Tiger* are migrating birds for which Taiwan is temporary refuge. Only films with Taiwan

characteristics can attract the attention of local, popular audiences for entertainment. But local features are insufficient; they must offer higher production
values and narrative ingenuity, as well as shiny marketing and packaging. In the
post-*Crouching Tiger* renewal, a fresh but still nascent force is 're-growing' the
market for Taiwan pictures. Clearly producers are reaching out to audiences who
wish to be entertained by storytellers who dwell among them, not just by blockbusters from afar.

CONCLUSION

The new localism is a resurgence of East Asian subjects, conventions and confidence. It is a faith that local audiences still like to be entertained by films in
their own language and cultural idiom, cultivating local roots to make the kind
of movies American pictures cannot be, such as martial arts, period pictures, or
comedy vehicles for Asian stars. Multinational companies recognise this too and
want to get in on the new localism. They sometimes partner with local production talent to help revive the market. Our main examples are balanced between
local heroes in Hong Kong – Stephen Chow, Milkyway Image and Andy Lau –
that pursued product differentiation as alternatives to Hollywood's global
hegemony. Milkyway persisted with old, almost-abandoned patterns that rework
local forms like triad stories. Versatile, hardworking Andy Lau promotes Hong
Kong film every possible way, as star, salesman and executive producer of First
Cuts, a programme of digital features by young directors. Stephen Chow, after
rejuvenating the Hong Kong industry in 2001, joined Columbia Pictures-Asia
for his next project and changed direction, to the chagrin of many Chinese fans.

Similarly Feng Xiaogang's post-socialist comedies of the 1990s have turned
to bigger budgets and spectacle, led by investment from multinational firms with
wide ambitions. The dual impulse to consumerism and didacticism embedded
in Feng's earlier work in television and film comedies still resonates in his latest
spectacular epic. Finally, we see Hollywood involved again in the new localism
of Taiwan: Chen Kuo-fu's shrewd blending of local themes, transcultural genre
and clever marketing. A Los Angeles executive flies to Taipei to congratulate
Chen, a Taiwan film-maker, for outselling nearly every Hollywood blockbuster
that year. This odd configuration of interests and agendas typifies new localism
in a global film industry.

3

The Power of Small Screens

For fifteen years, *America's Funniest Home Videos* was licensed from Tokyo Broadcasting System, modelled on a variety show called *Fun TV with Kato-chan and Ken-chan* (TBS Global Site, 2005). Since *America's Funniest Home Videos* is franchised worldwide, this makes TBS's *Fun TV* the mother of all contemporary reality shows. If this seems odd, it is because Japan is in an atypical position. Japan's postwar recovery, its large domestic market, its often hermetic media and its attachment to American movies incline it more toward global media than to East Asian screen industries. Japan's huge production, consumption and intricate distribution networks make it the area heavyweight, the biggest screen player – yet set apart from regional trends. East Asia moves rapidly towards regional integration and corporate tie-ups in media finance, distribution and marketing, though Japan's involvement seems cautious, even aloof (Shackleton, 2006c). However, Japanese media influence around the region remains strong. For decades, Japanese television provided irresistible formats and source materials to networks in neighbouring areas. By 1963, television penetration in Japan stood at 65 per cent (Lent, 1990: 37). From drama series to comedy and animation, news to documentaries, stations in Taiwan, Hong Kong and South Korea employed proven Japanese models to fill their broadcasting hours. Before, Japan's influence was diluted not only by national barriers, but also with formats being remade with local characteristics, like Japanese cartoons and *America's Funniest Home Videos* much later. But from the 1990s, Japanese programmes themselves were available via satellite, cable and video dupes. Audiences from Taiwan to Thailand, Singapore to Seoul could enjoy Japanese programmes at low cost, despite official disapproval and import restrictions. Sometimes Asian consumers took advantage of new, unauthorised technologies. Proliferation of VCDs (video CDs) and DVDs cut obstacles imposed by local censors and by release windows, especially in Southeast Asia and China. If Japanese cinema was Asia's leading cinema in the postwar era, then in the twenty-first century Japanese television made important regional inroads directly into East Asia.

Before approaching Japanese television, we can outline the shape of the industry in Japan. Japanese companies are *keiretsu* (interlocking) structures, with firms tightly conglomerated through cognate businesses, and through shared board members across different, affiliated companies. The screen industry is a gigantic enterprise with complex links between film, video, television, telecommunication, animation, publishing, advertising and game design. An example is the reconstitution of Japan's publishing giant, the Kadokawa Group.

Restructured in 2003 as Kadokawa Holdings, Inc., this media conglomerate soon jumped into the first tier of the Tokyo Stock Exchange in late 2004. Publishing, movie/visual and digital content are the three main business areas for Kadokawa Holdings. Each business is supported by many subdivisions that handle a variety of activities, from production, distribution, licensing and merchandising, to collaboration with foreign partners. Kadokawa Group began in 1945 as Kadokawa Book Store, specialising in publishing literature, art, historical and language books. Despite severe shortages, publishers and media companies rushed to supply a huge postwar market starved for entertainment.

Kadokawa Book Store recently became known as a major player in the film industry through its successful marketing of horror films in the 1990s, known as J-horror. Drawing on its publication of horror fiction, Kadokawa initiated a slate of J-horror film production by collaborating with major distributors and injected a strong dose of stimulant into the still-sleepy film industry. The regional and international impact of J-horror will be covered in more detail in Chapter 5. In 2002 Kadokawa took over Daiei studio (est. 1943) for its library of 1600 films, production facilities and distribution channels. Its roots in publishing allow Kadokawa to make tie-ins with literary, cinematic, musical and advertising material. In 1976 it pioneered the multimarket blockbuster strategy (*taisaku-shugi*), exploiting production of *The Inugami Family* (dir. Ichikawa Kon) adapted from its popular detective novel by Yokomizo Seishi (Lent, 1990: 39). Kadokawa Group now calls itself a 'Mega Content Provider' and a 'comprehensive media enterprise in the publishing and movie/visual business.' (Kadokawa Holdings, Inc., 2005). Kadokawa also aims to capitalise on a perceived softness in the domestic market for imports: 'Hollywood films are in decline. They have less and less to say to Japanese audiences today. We think we can do better,' said Kuroi Kazuo, president at Kadokawa Pictures (Schilling, 2004d: 20). With Kadokawa's resurgence, Japan's big three studios (Toho, Shochiku, Toei) are now a big four.

Kadokawa is integrated along many lines: by area (Hokkaido, Hong Kong, China, Taiwan, US), demographic (Kids Net) and media format (publishing, toys, games, cinema). In this sprawling network, each module depends on the others, forming a unique, interlocking mediascape (see Figure 3.1). Without much segregation or autonomy in Japanese media structure, each branch is expected to support the whole. Thus, these media giants are vertically and horizontally integrated corporations with direct control of their production, distribution and sales.

In Japan media structure appears totalised, inclined toward monsters like Kadokawa: integrated, rationalised combines producing talent, facilities and content management across all access points. But in the centre is television, the major engine and stockholder. As in other rich countries with large populations, Japanese television is central in terms of size, organisation, creativity, productivity and dominance in Japanese popular culture. Even 'Mega Content Provider' Kadokawa accommodates the clout of Japanese television, as do other film producers in Japan and East Asia. Twenty-first-century Japanese television is a key

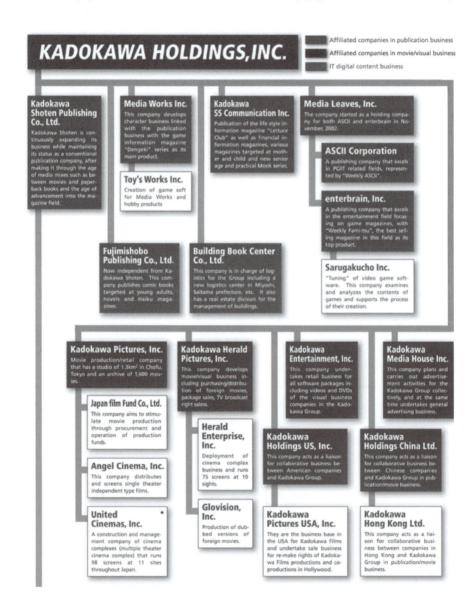

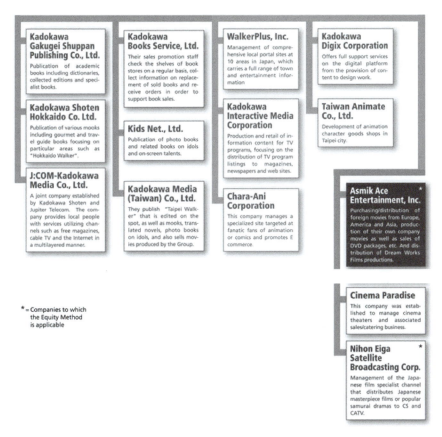

Source: Kadokawa Holdings, Inc. website, 2005.

Figure 3.1 Corporate Structure of the Kadokawa Group

factor in the resurgence of theatrical films, genre variations and changing styles. Because Japanese television is consumed across the whole region, most East Asian screen industries, even China's, are shaped by developments in Japan.

Japanese television rests on a dual system established in the early 1950s. There is public and private, state and commercial broadcasting. There are two founding images, one British, the other American. Public broadcasting is a giant network, the NHK (Nihon Hoso Kyokai or Japan Broadcasting Corporation, est. 1925), with income from mandatory fees every set owner pays. In 1999, NHK's income was US$5 billion (¥645 billion) (Watanabe, 2003: 646). Modelled on the BBC, it began television broadcasting in 1953. The commercial broadcasters are TBS (Tokyo Broadcasting System), Fuji TV, TV Asahi, NTV (Nihon TV) and TV Tokyo, the five major networks, plus more than 200 stations, affiliates and companies broadcasting either television or radio, or both.

This takes after American commercial television, except that all five broadcasters are embedded within newspaper empires, forming cross-media cartels. This has serious implications for investigation, reporting and programming of public affairs. Checks and balances between broadcast, print and online information are weak; tightly consolidated media means less competition, and information circulates between fewer channels. Journalism has been characterised as a 'Media Atrocity', with charges that the Japanese public has been 'betrayed' (Gamble and Watanabe, 2004). Although there were longstanding rules about cross-media ownership, they were amended in 1989 and 2001 in moves to deregulate and stimulate markets (Sinclair and Turner, 2004: 103–4). A consequence is that Japanese television networks are very powerful. In 2004 Fuji TV brought net sales of US$4.41 billion (¥476.7 billion; Fujisankei Communications Group, Corporate Data, 2005). TBS earned revenue of US$2.79 billion (¥301.7 billion; TBS Global Site, 2005). In economic, creative and cultural terms, the Japanese small screen is commanding.

This chapter considers television's impact in three areas of East Asian screen trade: commercial and independent cinema, 'trendy drama' and animation.

Market disproportion between television and cinema provides broadcasters tremendous leverage and drives new initiatives in production, including independents and other screen industries outside Japan. With little government intervention, Japan is approaching a renaissance in screen entertainment that rivals that of South Korea; domestic television is the main reason for this resurgence of production, marketing and audiences:

> 2006 has seen Japan's powerful TV network oligopoly fully utilize its media clout to produce and market feature films offering spectacle on a scale equal to Hollywood and stories that appeal to local audiences. An elusive demographic until now, young people have also been flocking to cinemas to see local fare in higher numbers than ever before. (Gray, 2006b)

We also focus on the specific contributions of television to formats and styles connected with cinema, again, moving out toward East Asian industrial variations. Finally, we discuss the importance of Japanese animation for film industries in East Asia and international audiences, pausing on the blockbuster films of Studio Ghibli.

TELEVISION AND COMMERCIAL CINEMA

In Japan, it would be a mistake to overestimate the market for Japanese cinema, relative to other domestic entertainment. Like the rest of East Asia, domestic films suffered a decline since the golden age of the 1950s and 1960s (see Table

3.1). The standard explanation for this is the rise of television, though this is too simple. Though 1997 saw some recovery with a 41 per cent market share of the box office, Japanese films' performance still lagged behind that of imported movies. The year 2002 even recorded an all-time low of 27.1 per cent market share. With the economy finally emerging from decades of recession, domestic film rebounded in 2004 by growing 4.5 per cent. In 2004, Japanese films earned US$76 million (¥79 billion), a healthy 37.5 per cent share of a total box office worth over US$2 billion (¥210 billion). That year also saw 310 domestic releases. Subsequently, in 2005 Japanese films achieved the highest market share since 1997, of 41.3 per cent (US$71 million, ¥81.8 billion).[1] This despite a 6 per cent fall in total box office from 2004 (*ScreenDaily.com*, 2006). Domestic film in 2006 outperformed imports for the first time since 1985, taking over half the market (Gray, 2006b). Japanese film may follow South Korea in achieving dominance on its home field, twenty years after its loss to foreign imports in 1986. This prospect has had great impact on regional screen industries already.

By European standards, these numbers are strong. For 2000, France's domestic market share was 28.5 per cent; Great Britain, 19.5 per cent; and Germany, 12.5 per cent (Kim, 2004b: 270). Statistics project a rosy picture for Japanese cinema, but film is dwarfed by the so-called Big Four: television, newspapers, magazines and radio. Together, Big Four media brought in almost US$36.1 billion (¥3,971 billion) in 2000. The smallest of the four is radio, and grossed ¥207

Year	Japanese film	Market share %	Box-Office gross (in Yen billion)
1960	547	78.3	31.1
1970	423	59.	18.5
1980	320	55	34.9
1990	239	41.4	29.4
1997	278	41.5	32.57
1998	249	30.2	26.4
1999	270	31.9	26.42
2000	282	31.8	54.3
2001	281	39	78.14
2002	293	27.1	53.5
2003	287	33	67.1
2004	310	37.5	79
2005	356	41.3	81.78
2006	417	53	107.7

Sources:
Data compiled from Motion Picture Producers Association of Japan, Inc. (Eiren) website.

Table 3.1 Selected Statistics for Japanese Films (1960–2006)

billion, 3.4 per cent of total media revenue (Watanabe, 2003). Japanese movies earned just ¥54.33 billion and total film exhibition gross was ¥171 billion, including imports, in 2000. Of course, film revenues have been rising quickly since then.

These numbers pale against annual revenues for television, at over US$18.9 billion (¥2,079 billion), more than half the Big Four total. Small wonder that film gets short shrift by media brokers and policy wonks. Proximity to TV is the key definition of success. As a journalist writes, 'Now, more than ever, TV is a center pillar in the Japanese movie industry, both financially and human-resources-wise' (Kaifu, 2006). If a Japanese film remakes television series, or otherwise links to TV, then this is the popular golden calf, more than star power, genre or even box office itself. Television is the great multiplier: fertile seed for moving images and narratives to sprout, grow and migrate to allied markets like internet, games, mobile phones and the cinema.

The live-action films, *Bayside Shakedown* and *Bayside Shakedown 2* (dir. Katsuyuki Motohiro, 1998, 2003) were sourced from television, bringing windfalls of US$80 million and US$158 million, respectively. *Bayside Shakedown 2* set a new box-office record for a non-animated film. *Negotiator* (dir. Motohiro Katsuyuki, 2005), a second sequel, grossed US$36.2 million; its follow-up *Suspect* (dir. Kimizuka Ryoichi, 2005) took US$33.5 million. These are extraordinary figures for domestic films. But these features all grew out of a much bigger tele-

Bayside Shakedown producer Kameyama Chihiro, of Toho

vision series, *Odoru Daisosasen* (1997–8) from Fuji TV. Fuji TV belongs to the Fujisankei Communications Group, a media conglomerate comprising nearly 100 companies and owner of the most powerful network of television, radio, newspapers, publishing, music and video. The group also owns Pony Canyon, a major video and music distributor in Japan. By 2005, the network made more than 150 films and six of them were among the top highest grossing live-action films (Fujisankei Communications Group, 2005). In 2004, Fuji TV co-distributed the *The Lord of the Rings: The Fellowship of the Ring* (dir. Peter Jackson, 2001), *Lost in Translation* (dir. Sofia Coppola, 2003) and in 2005 *Kung Fu Hustle*. In 2006, Pony Canyon became a subsidiary of the network, consolidating Fuji's hold on the film industry. The company says its success comes from 'abundant and superior production staff, exceptional casting capability, and the usage of the television media to promote and broadcast a feature film. [Thus] Television has contributed greatly to Fuji Television's success in motion pictures' (Fujisankei Communications Group, 2005).

Unlike US spin-offs, Japanese theatrical features do not camp up their TV sources, nor rely on in-depth knowledge of the series. For *Bayside Shakedown*, absorbing, humorous and suspenseful detective stories were delivered by director Motohiro Katsuyuki, based on carefully wrought scripts. The producer, Toho's Kameyama Chihiro, said the *Bayside Shakedown 2* plot was based on Pixar-Disney's *Toy Story* (dir. John Lasseter, 1995), with a clean, three-act structure derived from *Star Wars* (Schilling, 2004c). Because of its television provenance and commitment to modest, human-interest entertainment over widescreen spectacle, *Bayside Shakedown* signals the enduring influence of television. Television underwriting of the Japanese screen industry is a key factor in the resurgence of domestic films, with Japanese films taking half the market in 2006.

TELEVISION AND INDEPENDENT CINEMA
Kitano Takeshi and T-Mark

The famous Japanese film director Kitano 'Beat' Takeshi is also an example of how television power leads to big-screen success. In Japan's mega-media, Kitano has roots in live comedy (*manzai*), traditional burlesque, and television. His TBS reality show, *Takeshi's Castle*, was exported overseas and in the US remade as *Most Extreme Elimination Challenge*. In 1985 Kitano appeared in *Iesu no Hakobune* (The Ark of Jesus, TBS) in which he played Sengoku Iesu, a cult leader who wanders the country with his mostly female apostles. Kitano also starred in the NHK television novel series *Takeshi kun, Hai!* about his colourful childhood years (Sata and Hirahara, 1991: 198). Kitano's early career thus straddled both commercial and public broadcasting sectors.

With a meteoric rise as comic raconteur, Kitano tried acting in Oshima Nagisa's war film, *Merry Christmas, Mr Lawrence* (1983), cast as a savage prison camp officer. Japanese viewers were baffled, seeing something odd about Kitano, a standup comic, in an intense melodrama about passions ablaze between military officers – like watching Jackie Chan play a sadistic drill sergeant. In 1989, Kitano began directing, again against type, with ultra-violent yakuza (gangster) fare, often with homosexual subtexts. *Violent Cop* (1989), *Boiling Point* (1990), *Sonatine* (1993) and *Kids' Return* (1996) are a mixed bag, combining yakuza, sports and police procedurals with erratic art cinema techniques. In between these, Kitano tried slapstick, *Getting Any?* (1994), a near-silent surf film, *A Scene at the Sea* (1991), and a road movie about a boy and a softhearted yakuza, *Kikujiro* (1999). He appeared as an actor in a number of Western pictures, including *Erotic Liaisons* (1992), *Gonin* (1995), American independent *Johnny Mnemonic* (dir. Robert Longo, 1995), and Japan-France co-production *Tokyo Eyes* (dir. Jean-Pierre Limosin, 1998). Okinawa-set *Sonatine* impressed many international critics and *Kids Return* was a modest hit in Japan, evidence of local audience acceptance of Kitano as a film-maker. 1997 saw *Hana-Bi* (*Fireworks*) win the Golden Lion prize at the Venice Film Festival, and in 2003 Kitano received the Silver Lion for best director in his martial arts remake, *Zatoichi*. By the time Kitano appeared in another Oshima film, *Gohatto* (*Taboo*, 1999), he was already a bona fide international enterprise.

Auteur, celebrity and regional sponsor Kitano Takeshi

Kitano's importance in Japan is not only because of his international reputation, and almost daily appearances on television and in magazines, but also due to Office Kitano, his multimedia firm that manages a variety of film–television–publication–distribution–PR–advertisement–internet–sponsorsh ip activities. Office Kitano subsidiary T-Mark pursues film acquisition and funds emerging Asian film-makers such as Chinese director Jia Zhangke (see Chapter 6), and Iranian directors Samira Makhmalbaf and Abolfazl Jalili.

The major figure in T-Mark is Ichiyama Shozo, a seasoned producer specialising in Asian co-productions with a track record covering Hou Hsiao-hsien's *Good Men, Good Women* (1995), *Goodbye South, Goodbye* (1996) and *Flowers of Shanghai* (1999) for Shochiku. T-Mark employs Ichiyama to contact Asian talent around the region, funding or underwriting it, in order to ensure rights and access to other future projects at ground level. Office Kitano does not have the same leverage as mega-media combines Kadokawa, Toho, Shochiku or Avex (a multimedia agency rising from pop music). Rather than competing head-to-head with giants, T-Mark operates on a smaller scale, distributing/sublicensing low-budget films and building relationships with Chinese and Asian distributors. The objective is to gradually build trust and confidence in handling partner films in the large Japanese market, leading to production deals with budding directors, all by shepherding smaller deals and project management, without promise of immediate financial gain. In this way Office Kitano avoids big risks, knowing that partnerships with Jia and Hu Tong films will pay off at festivals, and that bigger rewards will be won than by simply sublicensing other companies' films. Through T-Mark, it invests in people and syndicates with a potential to become another Kitano, Wong Kar-wai or Hou Hsiao-hsien.[2] Here, Office Kitano operates like other regional players such as Fortissimo (Chapter 4), methodically building relationships and transnational links between sales, distribution, production, presentation and promotion: a picture of informal vertical/horizontal integration in motion.

Sento Takenori and Satellite TV

Television also spurred prolific independent producer Sento Takenori. Sento, a young producer passionate about art cinema and genre pictures alike, inspired a cohort of edgy, brilliant film-makers in the 1990s. These in turn transformed the reputation of Japanese films, mainly through recognition at foreign festivals. Sento helped initiate a shift in packaging films for cable, developing material for pay channel Wowow on JSB, Japan Satellite Broadcasting. Known for strict control of budgets, organisational acumen and impeccable taste, Sento takes credit for a large number of foreign festival prizes. Already in the 1990s Sento said, 'The Japanese film industry is lagging behind that of Europe and the US. I would like to introduce Western production methods into that industry as soon as possible. That is one of the missions I hope to accomplish ...' (Schilling, 1999: 32). Sento's activities included J-Movie Wars, a low-budget series begun in 1992 to make shorts and art-house films. The series helped the careers of Nakata Hideo, the director of *The Ring* (1997) and documentary/art-house director Kawase Naomi. Kawase won the 1997 *Caméra d'Or* prize at Cannes with her film *Suzaku* (1997).

Suncent Cinema Works was a broader slate of pictures organised by Sento in late 1998. This aimed at a wider market of cable subscribers to Wowow. The Suncent series collapsed in late 2001, and several strong films were left hanging without distribution (Mes and Sharp, 2005: 221). Sento's Project J-Cine-X proposed theatrical pictures for a world market, 'a major project that will assemble directors who have gained strong reputations at foreign film festivals and make films with them aimed at the overseas market' (Schilling, 1999: 32). The directors – Kawase, Kore-eda Hirokazu, Shinozaki Makoto, Riju Go and Aoyama Shinji – all work under Sento's package-unit system, a method of spreading resources and risk in order to boost production. More recently, the Wowow channel has moved into theatrical and DVD distribution of films initially broadcast to subscribers. It wants to be Japan's answer to HBO, says Kimizuka Shoko, its development manager (Schilling, 2005a: 4).

GENRES FROM TELEVISION

Another legacy of small screens was the 'J-dorama' boom of the 1990s. Also called 'trendy drama', these primetime serials present romance, fashion and career conundrums. Trendy drama television series centre on beautiful dwellings, people, and their glamorous problems, enduring unrequited love, illness and psychological trauma. They are pitched at young female audiences, and have high production values, strong stories and catchy scores.

Fuji and TBS are the major networks responsible for the popularity of J-dorama. Fuji TV produced hits like *Tokyo Love Story* (1991), *Long Vacation* (1996), *Love Generation* (1997) and *God, Please Give Me More Time* (1998) while TBS had *Junen ai* ('Pure love', 1992), *Concerto* (1998), *Witches' Requirement* (1999) and *Beautiful Life* (2000). These were so influential in the 1990s that they spawned a second wave of J-dorama, a spate of TV series and theatrical features with the dorama aesthetic, like *Fried Dragon Fish* (dir. Iwai Shunji, 1993), *Love Letter* (Iwai, 1995), *April Story* (Iwai, 1998) and *Twixt Calm and Passion* (dir. Nakae Isamu, 2002). With a background in advertising and music video, Iwai Shunji is a key link in the J-dorama–cinema chain: 'Iwai effectively brought in a new visual aesthetic sense adopted from the pop promo world, filling his work with musical interludes set to contemporary music and a host of visual tricks culled from the video mixing desk' (Mes and Sharp, 2005: 289).

Still more interesting was the evolution of several pan-Asian spin-offs. These television and film by-products came from regional saturation of Japanese dorama by box sets of VCD and DVDs, initially pirated, but eventually syndicated on cable and terrestrial broadcast (Yeh and Davis, 2002). In the post-97 Asian mediascape, J-dorama held point position for Hong Kong, Taiwan, Singapore and South Korean audiences. Given this, a large number of Chinese language and Korean series were made, along with many theatrical features capitalising on the boom. Television examples include: *Meteor Garden* (CTV, Taiwan, 2001) and *As Sure as Fate*, *A Place of One's Own*, *Till When Do We Part*, *A Master of Business* (all TVB, Hong Kong 1998–9). Feature films indebted to J-dorama include *Christmas in August* (dir. Hur Jin-ho, 1998, South Korea), *Love Generation Hong Kong* (dir. Wong Jing, 1998), *Tempting Heart* (dir. Silvia Chang, 1999, Hong Kong), *Lavender* (dir. Jingle Ma, 2000, Hong Kong) and *Blue Gate Crossing* (dir. Yee Chih-yen, 2002, Taiwan). Chapter 2 described the formation of China Star and Andy Lau's One Hundred Years of Film. Its first effort was a J-dorama spin-off, *Okinawa Rendezvous* (dir. Gordon Chan, 1999), starring the late Leslie Cheung (Hong Kong's pop idol through the 1980s and the early 1990s), Faye Wong (diva of pan-Chinese markets) and Tony Leung Ka-fai (Hong Kong's all-round actor, known for his role in the Marguerite Duras autobiography, *The Lover*, dir. Jean-Jacques Annaud, 1992). Despite the star appeal and the allure of location, this holiday romance failed. The lukewarm response showed that simply copying Japanese television drama wouldn't work. It also indicated a hard fact: aging stars such as Cheung and Leung were miscast in a romance aimed at teenage to twenty-something viewers.

Taiwan art film director Hou Hsiao-hsien was not immune to J-dorama, as in his tribute film to Ozu Yasujiro, *Café Lumière* (2003, Shochiku). This romantic melodrama about a Japanese girl who falls pregnant by her Taiwanese boyfriend is a charming, understated employment of dorama conventions. J-dorama is also a readymade formula in pan-Asian cinema (see Chapter 4). *About Love* (2005), a pan-Asian urban romance, has intricate storylines linking Tokyo, Taipei and Shanghai. The omnibus film was a co-production between Japan (Toho, Movie-eye Entertainment) and China (Tianjin Film Studio), with segments directed by Shimoyama Ten (Japan), Yee Chih-yen (Taiwan), Zhang Yibai (China) and distributed around Asia by Hong Kong-based Celestial Pictures. In this recombinant variety, we see East Asian projection of J-dorama into features, fashions and regional stardom. Most importantly J-dorama represents an identifiable format and sustainable entertainment package popular all over East Asia.

J-dorama and its cousins peaked in the late 1990s and early 2000s, and were soon eclipsed by Korean melodrama in regional popularity. As a longstanding genre for the whole region, Japanese romantic melodramas remain strong in regional markets. The year 2004 saw a huge comeback with *Crying out Love in the Center of the World* (dir. Yukisada Isao), the year's second-highest grossing film at US$82.5 million; it was produced by TBS, Tokyo Broadcasting System, which also made the popular television series of the same name. Just behind *Crying out Love* was another latter-day dorama, *Be with You* (2004) at US$46.6 million. In 2005, *shojo manga* (girl comics) adaptation *Nana* (dir. Otani Kentaro, 2005) grossed US$34.8 million, one of the strongest performers that year. Despite keen competition from Korea, Japan remains enthralled by its own romantic melodramas.

In the wake of J-drama, 2000 saw a strong Korean wind blowing into Japan, Hong Kong, Taiwan and the PRC. South Korean TV drama, hip-hop, films, stars and festivals flooded the media. Korean drama replaced J-drama in many East Asian television schedules, prompting Taiwan's broadcasting authority to regulate the hours devoted to it. A Korean family melodrama, *Whatever Love Is*, was sold and broadcast to CCTV, China's official channel, and enjoyed ratings that were the third highest in China's history (Kim, 2004b: 311). Media pundits in China pronounced the Korean trend *hanliu* ('cool wave') in the late 90s and early 2000s.

The Korean appeal is based on packaging innocent heart-throbs who became household names through television exposure. Bae Yong-jun in *Winter Sonata* (2002, Korean Broadcasting System) became a huge star in Japan and went on to appear in a romantic feature, *April Snow*, (dir. Hur Jin-ho, 2005). *April Snow* set a record in its opening week in Japan, and its Japanese box office of US$22 million became the second highest grossing Korean film in Japanese history. Japanese housewives conferred the royal-sounding 'Yong sama' (Yong highness) on the star. Song Hye-kyo, Song Seung-hun and Won Bin reached transnational stardom through their work in *Endless Love* (KBS, 2000), another Korean drama that became a regional hit.

On the big screen, Won Bin evolved into an A-list star as the lead in *Taegukgi* (South Korea's *Saving Private Ryan*), a top-grossing Korean film in 2004. Kim Hee-sun from *Sad Love Story* (MBC, 2005) also starred in *Bichunmoo* (2000), one of the first films to challenge Ang Lee's *Crouching Tiger*. Kim also co-starred with Jackie Chan in *The Myth* (dir. Stanley Tong, 2005). Known as 'the most beautiful woman in Asia', Kim's casting is a ploy to boost her popularity among Chinese audiences (Leong, 2002: 235). In the West, Kim Yoon-jin was seen in the primetime American series *Lost*, but unlike the rest she is US- and UK-trained, and considerably older, having starred in Kang Je-gyu's ground-breaking *Shiri* (1999, see Chapter 1). Jun Ji-hyun, star of *My Sassy Girl*, became a ubiquitous advertising face in China, Korea and Japan in 2004–5. All these new faces – the emerging mega-media icons of East Asia – eclipsed J-dorama idols such as Tokiwa Takako and Kimura Takuya via television exposure and advertising. These transnational idols were first presented in romantic melodramas and made the crossover to pop music, commercials and movies. They are indicative of forms of new localism with regional traction in East Asia, and not confined within the borders of single national screen industries.

The epicentre of Korean *hanliu* is not fluffy romantic drama, but something closer to home. The costume series *Dae Jang Geum* (*Great Jang Geum*, aka *Jewel in the Palace*, 2003), from South Korean broadcast network MBC, is about a royal physician, Dr Jang. Her tenacious feminine wisdom mesmerised Chinese-speaking audiences around the world. The usual markets of China, Taiwan, Hong Kong and Malaysia tuned in but also communities in the San Francisco Bay Area, Australia and New York – all were captivated by The Great Doctor. Unlike previous J-dorama or *hanliu*, which appealed to females, *Dae Jang Geum* recorded a high proportion of men in its audience, and captured every major demographic. This allowed the lead, Lee Young-ae, to make a grand comeback. Lee was in earlier hits such as *JSA* and *One Fine Spring Day* (2001), but was considered too old for the latest industry boom. So she moved to television, and her performance as the fastidious Confucian physician achieved stardom rivalling all the young idols. She was recycled again by director Park Chan-wook, against type, for his Venice film festival premiere, *Sympathy for Lady Vengeance* (2005).

When the *hanliu* first arose, flame wars erupted online between devotees of trendy Japanese and Korean dorama; the former derided *hanliu* as second-rate, derivative. Producers in Korea fended off accusations of borrowing and even plagiarism, with one MBC executive saying, 'I am grieved at the watchman's view of our culture, which keeps questioning whether a quality product is actually a copy from foreign culture' (Lee, 2004: 263). Since then (1992), South Korean pop culture has flourished. The key point is that J-dorama, a television format aimed first at Japanese females, stimulated new projects not only in Japanese cinema but also media and fashions throughout the region. Eventually dorama, and cousin K-drama, became a regular feature in East Asia's mediascape, a romantic vortex at once local, transnational and regional.

ANIME: TV OUTPUT TO INTERNATIONAL SCREENS

Above, we argued for the mobility of Japanese and Korean television, with popular formats and genres bounced between media platforms in several East Asian territories. At first their migration was consumer driven, but soon producer-distributors saw chances to capitalise. Another powerful Japanese export to global screens is anime, which also sprung from television dating back to the 1950s.

Anime, Japanese animated film and video, is a key media industry with a solid local identity and a distinct reputation abroad. Anime is firmly rooted in the

Japanese market and embedded in the television industry. Since the 1960s, television series abounded with animals, sports, fantasy, robots and family comedies, all animated, with crossover from multi-volume manga (comic books). Famous ones are *Astro Boy*; *Kimba the White Lion*; *Lupin III*; *Black Jack*; *City Hunter*; *Doraemon*; *Dragon Ball Z*; *Neon Genesis Evangelion*; *Mobile Suit Gundam*; *Miss Sazae*; *Ah! My Goddess*; *Gigantor*; *Pokemon*; *Sailor Moon*; *Star Blazers*; *Urusei Yatsura*: *Beautiful Dreamer*, *Yu-Gi-Oh*, these being are a few that were successfully exported. Like J-dorama in East Asia, these animated series were embraced in the West, then fan-circulated by viewers who elucidated, annotated and often subtitled the material for a select few. Animation in the West is still associated with children's programmes, though this is changing, with the Cartoon Network claiming two-thirds of its audience are adults and teens. *The Simpsons* is approaching its twentieth birthday. Still, 'Japan-anime' excites in its huge variation, freely crossing age, social and gender divides, appealing not just to children, but also to teenagers, adults, housewives, salarymen, students, academics and *otaku* fan boys and girls. In Japan there is commercial targeting of what were once *otaku* subcultures, creating a giant market called *moe* (literally 'blooming'), with thousands of customers craving characters of comic, screen and electronic graphics. The Kadokawa Group subsidiary has the Chara-Ani Corporation (character animation), which pursues 'specialized targeting of fanatic fans of anime or cartoons [through] e-commerce' (see Figure 3.1). There is also a middle category between television and features called OVA (original video animation), work produced for video alone, and not accountable to standards and practices of networks or theatrical distribution. This large, direct-to-video platform allows production of a wider range of subject matter, technical training and pathways to new opportunities.

In 2003, anime made up 60 per cent of all broadcast animation worldwide and is projected to be worth over ¥10 trillion (Ridout, 2006). Anime, then, is not only lucrative; it is essential to the identity of Japanese popular culture. Film critic Donald Richie, no fan of anime, describes it as an unstoppable force, a juggernaut:

> The enormous popularity of both manga and anime is such that they have come to dominate all visual markets and in terms of box-office figures, to represent Japanese filmmaking to its audience ... manga accounts for a third of all books sold in Japan and anime accounts for half of all Japanese-movie tickets sold. (Richie, 2001: 252)

Consider television series *Doraemon*, a cheeky robo-cat hero from the 1970s. Like most successful manga, *Doraemon* was first broadcast domestically in 1978 as an animated series. *Doraemon* was widely exported in the 1980s, primarily to Asia, but also to Italy, Spain, Russia, Brazil, Latin America and the Middle East (Ching, 2000: 250). *Doraemon* and other animated serials were dubbed and sold to dozens of countries, exemplifying again Japanese television's adaptability. Despite official prohibition on Japanese material, South Korean broadcasters were free to show anime as early as the 1960s, though 'Korean audiences were unable to find any clue that the program was produced in Japan' (Lee Dong-Hoo, 2004: 260). In Korea and worldwide, this was true of a whole generation of children growing up with Japanese-made, locally adapted animation. In the mid-1980s, multifunctional *Doraemon* came to big screens to amuse small children on their summer holidays, and has become a seasonal treat in most East Asian cinemas. Such early global warnings heralded the wide embrace of Japanese theatrical anime in the 1990s with Otomo Katsuhiro's dystopic *Akira* (1988), whose ardour shows no sign of cooling. Anime itself is not only a significant market sector; live-action films use it through citation and spin-offs. These include Japanese films like the experimental cyberpunk *Tetsuo* (1989, dir. Tsukamoto Shinya). With no subtitles, *Tetsuo* electrified the Fantastic Film Festival in Rome and opened the way for contemporary Japanese cinema revival in the West (Mes and Sharp, 2005: 147). In America, *Kill Bill Vol. 1* (dir. Quentin Tarantino, 2003) trumpets outré Asian taste by placing an anime segment within the live action story. This kinetic, violent insert was contracted to Production I.G. The company released many notable anime features: *Patlabor I* and *II* (1989, 1993), *Ghost in the Shell* (1995) and its sequel *Innocence* (2004). *Animatrix* (2003) was another 'Japanimated' offshoot of the *Matrix* franchise, an imaginative echo of the Wachowski brothers' trilogy. Theatrical films *Neon Genesis Evangelion* (1995), *Patlabor* (with versions made for television, OVA and theatrical release), *Pokemon* (1997, plus sequels), *Doraemon* (1985, plus annual sequels) and other kids' fare are all spin-offs from TV, and capitalise on characters and situations whose familiarity goes back years. Nonetheless, they found great success outside Japan, either through mass merchandising or youth subcultures whose collective fantasies were highly stimulated. Dave Kehr notes that 'Japanese film has probably never been as popular internationally as it is now', and much of that is due to animation from TV serials (Kehr, 2002).

Miyazaki Hayao and Studio Ghibli

At the other end of the market, we find the animated family blockbusters of Studio Ghibli. Japanese film had a good year in 1997, with a high market share of 41.5 per cent. This hefty slice was due to *Princess Mononoke*, a Studio Ghibli film directed by Miyazaki Hayao. That year in Japan, only *Titanic* did better, and *Mononoke* broke box-office records for all Japanese features, at US$23.6 million (¥26 billion; *Uni Japan*, 2001). The generous share for domestic films had to wait until 2005 to be repeated. Meanwhile, in 2001 there was another boost for Japanese film, bringing the total revenue to over US$71 million (¥78 billion), the highest return in more than twenty years. Again, this was because Miyazaki's *Spirited Away* alone grossed US$27.3 million (¥30 billion), nearly 40 per cent of the total domestic film gross. There were just over 163 million admissions for the year. This was the highest number of admissions since 1983, at nearly 175 million. In 2005, another Miyazaki film, *Howl's Moving Castle*, brought US$17.8 million (¥19.6 billion) to its distributor, Toho, and grossed well over US$50 million. As the top grossing Japanese film of 2004, *Howl's* alone boosted the domestic take 24 per cent and helped achieve yet another record market share (41.3 per cent) for Japanese movies. That was surpassed in 2006, because of Ghibli's release *Tales from Earthsea*, directed by Miyazaki the younger from an Ursula Le Guin story. Studio Ghibli films have galvanised Japanese audiences and led the industry to a new era of domestic profits and popular cinema.

Box office is matched by prestige, which is somewhat unusual for animation, at least outside Japan. Unlike anime that began as manga and television serials, Studio Ghibli films stand alone as blockbuster features, with massive budgets and production schedules, starting with *Princess Mononoke*. Before that, Miyazaki films were made on more slender resources. His films appeal to audiences by having intriguing characters, inventive, careful storytelling, as well as high budgets and production values. And when the object is the entire Japanese population, there are phenomenal rewards to be won, as distributors like Warner Bros. and Disney know well. Ghibli's hallmark is meticulous craftsmanship, unlike many other anime such as the *Pokemon*, *Doraemon* and *Crayon Shinchan* series – low-budget, if charming, that work mainly as links in calculated media-merchandising chains.

Note the spikes in the Japanese box office in 1997, 2001 and 2004: these are due to the respective Ghibli features, *Princess Mononoke*, *Spirited Away* and *Howl's Moving Castle*. Yet Ghibli pictures are not alone; animated features regularly appear in Japan's top ten. In 2004 there were five animated films, including *Howl's Moving Castle* at number one (Schilling, 2005a: 5). The Ghibli brand looms over all others, and does so within an anime-rich environment. The disproportionate Ghibli is marked further by anime's overall saturation in Japanese media. In both reputation and in box office, Ghibli animations are exceptional, massive and top-heavy, like some of its characters. The ever-present commercial animation and comics in Japan provide a necessary background for the striking figure made by Ghibli movies. Of course, Miyazaki's films are also honoured worldwide, including in the US. *Spirited Away* won an Academy Award for Best Feature Animation, and Miyazaki himself received a career Golden Lion award at Venice, an unprecedented honour for an animation director. But only in Japan are his films loved so widely; they are marketed and received as blockbuster entertainment for the masses.

If the Ghibli films are unconventional, they are exceptions that prove the rule: the ultra-commercialism of Japanese media. In an industry known for heavy reliance on formula, anime is egregious, with endless serials relentlessly recycled from TV, manga and videogames. This makes Ghibli/Miyazaki even more remarkable, with their literary flavour and limited release; production is held to one Miyazaki picture every three years. Their painstaking quality, narratives and themes carry a kind of extravagant paganism. Ghibli's multiculturalism opposes Japan's insular, hidebound commercialism, with its attendant conformity and calculated rationalisation. Ghibli films have a distinctive taste since many stories are borrowed from European children's literature: Ursula Le Guin, Diana Wynne Jones, Lewis Carroll, Robert Louis Stevenson, Jonathan Swift, Norse mythology and, pre-Ghibli, the directors' television adaptations of *Heidi* and *Anne of Green Gables*. The visual style of *Howl's Moving Castle* is indebted to nineteenth-century French illustrator Albert Robida, 'a mixture of scientific and magical thinking,' says Suzuki Toshio, producer and company president (Schilling, 2003: 19). Ghibli's co-founder Takahata Isao graduated in French literature from Tokyo University, Japan's top institution, while Miyazaki himself attended Gakushuin University (the elite Peers School) gaining a degree in political science and economics (Mes and Sharp, 2005: 114). These lofty backgrounds are quite removed from that of the workforce in the frenetic world of commercial animation, comics and advertising.

Studio Ghibli's *Howl's Moving Castle* (2004)

The Ghibli line offers sincere, often didactic, humanism, at odds with received ideas in the Japanese media marketplace. Paradoxically, this gives the studio output tremendous commercial power. Running at cross-purposes to most Japanese audiovisual entertainment, Ghibli promotes environmentalism (not apocalypse), gender empowerment (not stereotypical sex roles), mysticism (instead of materialism), with a tendency to laugh at authority. These themes and motifs clash with the baggage carried by majority Japanese pop culture, with its array of hard-sell tricks. It should be stressed that despite this Miyazaki has spent over forty years in the animation industry and his partner, Takahata, even longer. Miyazaki movies travel well to other audiences, particularly in Europe, though technically they are not up to Disney or Pixar polish. Instead, Ghibli clings to a two-dimensional, handmade look, even if its capacity for digital animation has been vastly upgraded. In the West, Ghibli films are handled as art cinema, with matching box-office results, and this has been disappointing to the studio. They are easily outstripped by the 'catch them all' marketing of *Pokemon*, especially in the US (Table 3.2).

Miyazaki/Ghibli makes anime 'pagan' by assuming a childlike mysticism, even when narrating relatively dark tales as seen in *Princess Mononoke* and *Nausicaa* (1984). This special 'dissidence' sets them apart from most other anime, and constitutes a real distinction. Whether Ghibli's cultural apartness explains its enormous commercial success is difficult because it seems contradictory, i.e. commercial power flowing from apparently extra-commercial aims. It would be nice to think so, but Ghibli is not unique. Other serious anime rival Ghibli's in conceptual ambition and scope such as Oshii's Production I.G, Otomo Katsuhiro's *Steamboy* (2004), Anno Hideaki's *Neon Genesis Evangelion* (1995), Satoshi Kon's *Perfect Blue* (1998) and *Millennium Actress* (2001). And these do not command anywhere near Ghibli's box office and public respect.

Factors in Ghibli's favour are the following: a long gestation in Toei animation studios, from the 1960s, that allowed the two film-makers to refine their story-

In US$ million

Countries	*Princess Mononoke* (1997)	*Spirited Away* (2001)	*Pokemon: the First Movie* (1999)
US	2.4	10.1	85.7
UK	0.0004	1.6	19
France	3	8	12.5
Germany	0.4	2.2	14.4
Spain	0.6	1	5
Australia	0.09	0.5	5

Source: *Screen International* (2004: 21).

Table 3.2 International Box Office, Miyazaki and Pokemon

telling and design skills, as well as commercial acumen. In fact Takahata is not really an illustrator or panel designer, but concentrates on stories only (Mes and Sharp, 2005: 113). When Toei animation decided to compete with Tezuka Osamu's *Astro Boy* in the 1960s, it turned to Takahata for direction of the black-and-white cartoon *Ken the Wolf Boy* (1963). In the early 1970s, the two men left Toei to pursue more ambitious projects, such as *Lupin III*. Adapted from a manga character of the late 1960s, *Lupin III* became one of the most successful anime for its sponsors, leading to numerous television and movie spin-offs. One of these, *Castle of Cagliostro* (1979) was Miyazaki's debut as a feature direc-tor (Mes and Sharp, 2005: 116). Beyond anime, Miyazaki also published manga epics; for instance, *Nausicaa of the Valley of the Wind* came out in *Animage* mag-azine, and this brought investment from the publisher, Tokuma Shoten, for a groundbreaking feature animation in 1984. Tokuma Shoten also provided the capital to found Studio Ghibli. Before forming Studio Ghibli in 1985, both Miyazaki and Takahata had television work, pilots, shorts, features and long experience, plus setbacks, in Japan's commercial industry.

Another factor that favours Ghibli is auteurism, an author-name deployed and branded as the strongest in world animation. The Miyazaki-Ghibli name is an attraction for anything the company backs, much like Tezuka Osamu in the 1960s and 1970s, and Walt Disney itself. Ghibli also has strong producer con-tributions, with clear division of labour between Miyazaki, the flagship talent; Takahata, who specialises in discovering and refining stories; Suzuki, the man-aging director who crafts the look and sales point of every Ghibli feature; and other directors such as Morita Hiroyuki, who takes the helm on company pro-grammers between the big Miyazaki offerings. In 2002, Morita's *The Cat Returns,* a spin-off of the 1995 Miyazaki hit, *Whisper of the Heart,* was in the box-office top ten. As noted, *Tales from Earthsea* was directed by Miyazaki's son, Goro. It was among the top earners of 2006, at US$65.4 million (Gray, 2006b). Ghibli films are also handled by the most powerful distributor in Japan, Toho, ensuring major exposure for its star product. Abroad, Ghibli is released through Buena Vista International (Disney), a special detail assumed by John Lasseter, the acclaimed animator for *Toy Story* at Pixar and a Miyazaki devotee. Overall, the proof lies in successful branding of Ghibli as a trusted product with strong ethical and entertainment values. Only in Japan, however, where anime, comics and graphic design are such dominant forms of visual communication, could the Ghibli line earn its overwhelming returns and prestige.

CONCLUSION

In this chapter we briefly covered the power of television and video, especially as it underwrites Japanese screen industries and East Asian entertainment enterprises overall. This is a prelude to the next chapter, which describes pan-Asian co-production as an emerging business force. Because it catalysed East Asia's media industries, Japanese television and anime served large populations outside its own market, and further whetted appetites for large-screen entertainment. The power of small screens is not just their size, but their long reach, ability to focus opinion and magnify desires. Television extends far from commercial entertainment and information into art cinema, animation and non-fiction forms. It frames advertising, political discourse and publishing, not just screen entertainment. Many annual rituals on cinema screens owe their existence to television ancestors, and these are not limited to Japanese audiences. Rather, the small screen's extent is apparent all over East Asia and, with anime, around the globe as seen with Studio Ghibli. Due to its influence, Japanese television should be studied with greater critical precision, and here we have only signalled its generative capacities for screen industries in East Asia and the world. Japanese television is not just for Japan, but yields bumper harvests in multiple, widely scattered markets.

NOTES

1. In January 2005, the exchange rate was ¥103=1US$; in January 2006 it was ¥115=1US$. The 11 per cent depreciation of the yen explains the discrepancy, i.e. a smaller market share of slightly bigger revenue (37.5 per cent market share=US$76.7 million, as opposed to 41.3 per cent market share=US$71 million).
2. Thanks to Professor Michael Baskett at the University of Kansas, formerly acquisitions manager and assistant director working in the Japanese film industry.

4

Pan-Asian Cinema: Finance, Marketing, Distribution

During Christmas 2005, a Hong Kong–China co-production, *Perhaps Love*, premiered in five Asian cities – Shanghai, Beijing, Hong Kong, Taipei and Kuala Lumpur. Directed and co-produced by pan-Asian advocate Peter Chan Ho-sun, *Perhaps Love* packages Asian talent and capital from around the region. In all respects the film exemplifies a pan-Asian business plan, building a talent pool from Hong Kong, Japan, China, South Korea and India. Through casting, language, location and genre, the film sought and found audiences in several territories.

Pan-Asian cinema takes various forms: talent-sharing, cross-border investment, co-productions (which may be unofficial, or backed by formal treaties), and market consolidation, through distribution and investment in foreign infrastructure. For producers and audiences alike, pan-Asian is an emerging trend. As the ultimate tactic East Asian screen industries employ to sustain commercial markets, no Asian player, big or small, can overlook it. Everyone wants to play the pan-Asian game, including Hollywood. Several factors encourage more pan-Asian operations. First, the decline of individual national cinemas – in Taiwan, Hong Kong, China and Japan – necessitated investment schemes to amplify market potential and spread the risk. The years 2005 and 2006 saw historic lows in Hong Kong production, at 55 and 51 releases respectively, leading some industry figures to predict a brain drain, with talented young hopefuls moving to China and elsewhere to seek better opportunities (Tsui, 2005).

Next, mainland China opened up in the late 1990s, creating appetite for content and a new wave of co-production. Both Taiwan- and Hong Kong-based projects registered under mainland licences for exemption from Chinese import quotas. CEPA, the Closer Economic Partnership Arrangement, formalised this joint venture process in production and exhibition, and was phased in between 2004 and 2006. Under CEPA, intra-Chinese co-production is developing rapidly as one form of pan-Asian cinema, claiming core Chinese-speaking markets and, from there, venturing further afield into other Asian territories.

A third factor is institutionalisation of regional confabs. South Korea was the first to get these underway as a reliable model of co-financing and marketing.

These meetings were seized as a chance to revive East Asian screen industries overall. As described in our first chapter, the Korean film industry made a healthy recovery that helped galvanise the efforts of its Asian neighbours. A seminal place to form regional alliances between film-makers, investors, government agencies and international press is the Pusan International Film Festival (PIFF). It presents itself as a centre for pan-Asian co-operation as well as an Asian cinema showcase. In 1998, PIFF set up the Pusan Promotion Plan to operate a funding platform for works in progress. Not content with a market, rich screenings and Asian retrospectives, it also formed a collective of Asian film commissions, AFCNet, promoting Asian locations for international productions (see Chapter 6). This is not so much for Western productions as for Korean neighbours, initiating a 'pan-Asian network of film commissions leading to increased information-sharing across borders [and] expected to give film-makers in Asia an added layer of support' (Paquet, 2004a).

Hong Kong followed Pusan's lead with the Asia Film Financing Forum (HAF), a co-production market organised by the Hong Kong Trade Development Council and Hong Kong's Motion Picture Industry Association (see Chapter 6). In 2006, HAF selected twenty-five Asian film projects for over 500 producers, buyers and distributors to consider: ten from Hong Kong, with three from China and Taiwan, plus projects from Japan, Singapore, South

One Missed Call, Kadokawa-CJ Alliance

Korea, Thailand, and one from Iran. Honorary advisor Wouter Barendrecht commented, 'This year's selection is by far one of the broadest spectrums I've seen in terms of genre, budget and creative talent. The 2006 projects illustrate the excitement of Asia's finest commercial and artistic filmmaking' (Wong, 2006a).

In corporate jockeying for position, once-keen competition has turned to co-operation and regional consolidation. In late 2005, the Kadokawa Group, a giant media conglomerate, announced collaboration with Intercontinental, Hong Kong's film and video distribution giant. With partner Asmik Ace, Kadokawa also invests in and co-produces with Korea's distribution and exhibition company, CJ Entertainment. CJ's Catherine Park, head of international sales, says that 'international co-productions are now the main focus at CJ', especially those with Japan and mainland China (Paquet, 2004a). A result is *One Missed Call: Final*. Under the new deal with CJ, Asmik Ace is to produce the third instalment of the hit J-horror series *One Missed Call* (dir. Miike Takashi, 2003) (Kawamoto, 2005), a Kadokawa literary property. In a first for a Japanese firm, Kadokawa has set its sights on China, partnering with Hong Kong-based Sun Wah Group to establish twenty multiplexes in the PRC (Schilling, 2005c). Not to be outdone, CJ's exhibition chain, CJCGV, signed a joint venture with the state-owned Shanghai Film Group, to build multiplexes in China too. And, through Kadokawa's deal with Intermedia Film Equities, the original property was shopped to American directors for an English-language remake, scripted by Andrew Klavan (Kay, 2005). Significantly, mainland Chinese distribution remains firmly under China Film Corp, the state monopoly on film imports and distribution.

For pan-Asian cinema, the object is to co-produce films to satisfy audiences across the region. As one journalist pointed out in 2001, one reason for the drop in movie attendance was that local industries failed to provide blockbusters for their own audiences. Because Asian productions cannot match Hollywood in delivering state-of-the-art spectaculars, a possible alternative is pan-Asian films that will sell 'from Bangkok to Tokyo' (Beals, 2001: 57). In this chapter, we chart the history, patterns, practices and key players of pan-Asian cinema. We also include case studies on companies and individuals that contributed to pan-Asian formations. Pan-Asian cinema is not a mere device or alliance for cost saving. It has evolved into a regional consolidation that deepens the revenue pool, which is a necessary condition for sustaining the East Asian market.

PAN-ASIAN IN HISTORY

One might think that pan-Asian co-production imitates pan-European cinema, operating with mixed results since the 1980s (Jäckel, 2003: 67). But that is persuasive only if pan-Asian cinema is seen as a novelty, a new strategy borrowed from the Europeans. In fact, pan-Asian cinema can be traced very far back, as early as the 1940s during the Pacific War, but pan-Asian ideology appeared still earlier.

Contemporary regional alliances include the European Union, a supranational alliance intended to balance postwar American hegemony, and NAFTA (North American Free Trade Agreement), a continental free trade zone set up by the US in the 1990s. In Asia, late 2005 saw a contentious WTO meeting held in Hong Kong; meanwhile, a new East Asian summit of sixteen nations took place in Kuala Lumpur. Discussions there centred on the future of ASEAN, the association of ten Southeast Asian nations, and whether its progress in trade, politics and culture may be decided by core members, or a new coalition including Japan, China and South Korea (ASEAN plus three), or the APEC (Asia Pacific Economic Corporation) consortium incorporating other Asia-Pacific powers like the US and Australia. Pan-Asian dreams, though, go back to the nineteenth century and before.

Historically, intra-Asia trade relations, as well as religion, science and cultural exchange, stretch back centuries and exist alongside more naked territorial ambitions that sometimes escalated into armed conflict. The pan-Asian idea was further cultivated since the nineteenth century, responding to Western imperialism. Okakura Kakuzo, the acclaimed Japanese aesthetician, declared in 1904 that 'Asia is One', though the unstated proviso was an Asia free of Western encroachment, consolidated under Japanese headship (Okakura, 2005: 1).

In general, Japan led in a wedge-shaped formation, with East and Southeast Asian flanks winging their way into twentieth-century regimes of production, consumption and entertainment. Not only did Japanese modernisation galvanise its neighbours with its nineteenth-century Civilization and Enlightenment programme (*bunmei kaika*), it also brought overweening hubris, and then nuclear apocalypse, for the whole Pacific as well as for imperial Japan itself. Following the American occupation, in the 1950s Japanese studios rebuilt themselves into large, vertically integrated conglomerates.

Capitalists in Chinese-speaking territories followed their example, and that of the American majors. Until China's Cultural Revolution, mainland and Southeast Asian viewers could watch genre pictures and filmed opera in their own languages and theatre circuits, where there were groups of diaspora Chinese. Chinese-owned studios like Shaw Brothers and MP & GI (a subsidiary of Singapore-based Cathay Organisation) integrated, organised and rationalised to serve multinational audiences throughout East and Southeast Asia. In Taiwan, independents produced thousands of *taiyu pian*, Taiwanese-language films, for locals and for dialect speakers around the region (Yeh and Davis, 2005: 19–25). Large companies and small would subtitle everything in Chinese characters, and sometimes English, to extend the pictures' range. Such efforts to reach far-flung markets gave them a head start in pan-Asian enterprise.

Given this structural advantage, Hong Kong-based Shaws and other firms tried to interest Japanese studios in co-productions and other forms of collaboration, with little success. Shaws wanted access to the enormous Japanese market, since Shaws was already the major distributor of Japanese films in Hong Kong and Southeast Asia. Though Daiei co-produced a lavish costume picture with Shaws, *Princess Yang Kwei Fei* (dir. Mizoguchi Kenji, 1955), Japanese studios had more interest in co-producing on Hollywood big-budget spectacles such as *Tora Tora Tora* (dir. Kinji Fukasaku /Richard Fleischer, Toei/Fox, 1970). More recently, Japanese investors brought Asian, especially Chinese, cinema to domestic audiences, signalling a different orientation from the anti-Western imperialism of the past. Chinese expatriates have long settled in port cities like Yokohama and Kobe, though these were enclaves, if not ghettos. Japanese immigration continues to block full assimilation by long-term Chinese and Korean residents. Media and culture functions as a kind of compensation. Contemporary Japanese consumers acquired a taste for Asian continental food, fashion, music and design, and movies, all marketed as *mukokuseki*, or 'borderless', literally no-nationality. It served as shorthand for exotica not of Caucasian provenance. In short, *mukokuseki* indicates consumption of bohemian Southeast Asian products.

In movies, Japanese directors offered stories of plucky Asian battlers in Japan: titles like *Beijing Watermelon* (dir. Obayashi Nobuhiko, 1989), *World Apartment Horror* (dir. Otomo Katsuhiro, 1990) and *All Under the Moon* (dir. Sai Yoichi, 1993). Higher levels of Japanese investment in Asia also supported the work of Taiwan directors. Team Okuyama of Shochiku and Pony Canyon, a subsidiary of Fujisankei Communications Group (see Chapter 3), supported Hou Hsiao-hsien and Edward Yang. The PRC's Fifth Generation films *Raise the Red Lantern* (dir. Zhang Yimou, 1993), *Farewell My Concubine* (dir. Chen Kaige, 1994) and *The Emperor and the Assassin* (dir. Chen Kaige, 1999) also received major funding from Japanese producers in the 1990s. Japanese funding signals a recognition of regional quality that predated Western awareness, especially given the parlous state of Japanese domestic production. On a smaller scale, public broadcaster NHK and Office Kitano have consistently supported Chinese and Asian independents like those of Fruit Chan, Wu Wenguang, Duan Jingchuan and Jia Zhangke (see Chapter 3).

PAN-ASIAN CLUSTERS

With all this background, a network of regional production and distribution emerged, tightly connecting East Asian, Southeast Asian, Australasian and European agents. Noting this regional activity, Hollywood scouted scripts, talents, and story ideas for export and sometimes remakes in the US (discussed in Chapter 5). Many strands of pan-Asian co-production are based primarily in one country; others have dual or multiple bases; they may be tiny independents, large studios, or specialty arms of multimedia firms and government-backed initiatives. All are highly mobile and play key roles as delegates to trade fairs, markets and international festivals, institutions without which co-production activities would be almost impossible (see Chapter 6). The different clusters can be sorted by their primary markets, motivations and activities. They include:

(1) Euro-Asian alliances, including Fortissimo; Block 2; Celluloid Dreams; Paradis; Flach Pyramide; Sud Fond/Hubert Bals: various kinds of European funding aimed to support developing industries and often not-for-profit.

(2) Intra-Asian co-producers, including Hong Kong Applause Pictures; South Korea's Sidus, Show East and CJ Entertainment; Japan's Kadokawa; Singapore's Raintree-MediaCorp: predominantly commercial funding from big corporations, by and for Asian markets.

(3) Pan-Chinese co-producers: Media Asia; Jackie Chan's JCE Group; Bill Kong's Edko/Elite; Huayi Brothers; China Film Corp; Shanghai Film Group: commercial funding between Chinese-language markets, used to expand and consolidate ethnic Chinese audiences Asia-wide.

(4) Pan-Asian programme packagers, such as Arc Light; Y2K; NHK: funding from both Europe and Asia, straddling commercial, cultural and educational intent.

(5) Hollywood–Asia ventures: Columbia Pictures Film Production Asia (*Crouching Tiger*; *Kung Fu Hustle*) established in Hong Kong, then moved to Beijing; on the mainland, the first-ever tie-up between Warner Bros.-Asia and Hengdian HG, partnering with the state-owned China Film Corp to form Warner China Film HG Corporation (Liu, 2006). Hollywood–Asia linkages inject American finance, know-how and marketing into local production to boost standards and regional branding. For Warners' Chinese partnership, the arrangement mediates between public and private ownership. This crossover entails productive ambiguity, or détente, between state-run enterprise and commercial objectives. But in late 2006 Warner Bros. pulled out of its partnership with the Shanghai Film Group due to changes in the Chinese government rules on foreign ownership.

While these clusters may overlap, we can further clarify the difference between groups (2) intra-Asian, (3) pan-Chinese co-production and (4) pan-Asian packagers. The classification marks differences in size and location of audiences. Groups (2) and (3) are commercially oriented, and the difference between them is that (2) includes multi-language markets within Asia while (3) is mainly Chinese, addressing markets that span different Chinese-speaking areas. Groups

(2) and (3) may operate interchangeably. These are both focused on East Asian audiences, and quite indifferent to Western reception. Media Asia's action films *Gen-X Cops* (dir. Benny Chan, 1999), *2000AD* (dir. Gordon Chan, 2000), *Seoul Raiders* (dir. Jingle Ma, 2005) and racecar film *Initial D* (dir. Andrew Lau and Alan Mak, 2005) are exemplary. Pan-Asian programmes (Group 4) aim at export potential outside the region, such as Arc Light's *Beijing Bicycle*, a snapshot of urban China that's part of a city series intended for viewing in the West; or the Y2K project, a so-called 'combined Asian' (Tsukeda, 2002) trilogy of independents *The Island Tale* (dir. Stanley Kwan, Hong Kong, 2000), *YiYi, a One and a Two* (dir. Edward Yang, Taiwan, 2000), and *All About Lili Chou-Chou* (dir. Iwai Shinji, Japan, 2001). These films reflect a conscious intent to represent 'Asia' to the West as well as to Asian viewers. That Media Asia's crime trilogy *Infernal Affairs* (2003) was admired in the West, and acquired for remake by Warner Bros., is incidental. The intra-Asian players of Group 2 are very profit-minded, seeking high returns from the widest market footprint. They are in and of Asia because they target commercial prospects within the region. While they may produce fine work, like *Infernal Affairs*, these already dominant companies are less concerned with initiating new patterns of industry structure or aesthetic renewal. While all five of these clusters are pan-Asian broadly speaking, their finance base, marketing and target audiences are distinct.

Two basic notions or modes of pan-Asian cinema can be identified: first, cross-border talent sharing at planning and production stage. This is exchange of production craft across borders and cultures. As Tsukeda Naoko of Pony Canyon says, an outcome of co-production is that regional crew and talent are gaining familiarity with each other's working methods. Pony Canyon's Y2K project assembled funding from financiers and local distributors whose interest in Asian film jumped after the *Crouching Tiger* phenomenon. Pony Canyon's plan, typical of pan-Asian co-production, secures international distribution and marketing before production is launched as well as actively seeking presale investments.

Second, consolidating markets through restructure of finance and distribution. In effect, this enlarges the pool for Asian popular cinema overall. Rather than just sharing talent, the second mode of pan-Asian cinema tries to manage globalisation by reorienting screen industry around the Asian region, a vigorous response to Hollywood's worldwide hegemony. Above all, pan-Asian strategies are attempts to use successful Asian films to reach a broader audience – within Asia. Success on Asian screens means interest will follow naturally from the West. As Peter Chan of Applause Pictures says, 'international success depends on domestic popularity. We need a new way to put Asia together as a market,' he continued, 'not out of any cultural idealism, but from sheer necessity' (Chan, 2005). There are pitfalls, however, in regionalising production that leads to bland, formulaic commodity films lacking taste, let alone substance (like 'Europ-udding'). At the TIFFCOM seminar in Tokyo, Bill Mechanic of Pandemonium Films said, 'What works is movies with a point of view – homogenisation doesn't work. But pan-Asian distribution – that could work' (Shackleton, 2006c).

Pan-Asian Nuts and Bolts

How does pan-Asian cinema work in practice? First, as co-productions. Since the 1950s, Asian audiences and film-makers have been curious about their neighbours' films. Interest in multinational co-operation between Asian film industries has continued, intermittently: taking directors, technicians or actors abroad, seeking profitable encounters between Hong Kong and Korean stars, or a Japanese cameraman sharing tips with Chinese counterparts on location or the set. An example: Shaw Brothers' co-production with a Korean firm (Namkung Yo's South Korea Entertainment Co.) on the multiple version *Love with an Alien* (dir. Wakasugi Kazuo, Tu Guangqi and Chun Chang-kun, 1958) in Eastman-color, using Japanese technicians. Its star, Lucilla You Min, became very popular in Japan and continued to make co-productions there in the 1960s for Japan-ese studios. Talent sharing and cross-fertilisation occurred as there was little direct competition, due to language barriers, different production scales and storytelling conventions. In the 1960s Shaws followed up its early experiment with a wholesale conversion to mass production. In 1960 it established its comprehensive Movietown studio, bringing in-house colour-processing labs, non-synchronised sound to facilitate dubbing in multiple languages, a widescreen format called 'Shawscope', developed by Japanese cinematographer Nishimoto Tadashi, and a stable of prolific Japanese directors hired to boost efficiency and quantity (Davis and Yeh, 2003). The results aimed at domination of Chinese-language movie audiences worldwide.

Contemporary pan-Asian film reaches out to every Asian consumer, consoli-dating distinct markets and audiences to create international blockbusters. The US has nearly 300 million people. The size of the domestic market is Holly-wood's bedrock. With this market, the US studios continue producing works with programmatic regularity, in both quantity and quality, and sustaining its glo-bal entertainment network as well. Box office outside the US, in Europe and Asia, was for a long time pure surplus. But now that international markets have grown in importance, Hollywood studios pursue foreign revenues directly. In addition to holding foreign markets with blockbusters and intensive publicity campaigns, Hollywood has undertaken production for its international viewers, with foreign-language pictures in numerous local markets. It now finances and produces – or at least sources out – local films for distribution in Spain, Italy, and Chinese market segments, like *Crouching Tiger* and *Kung Fu Hustle* (Columbia-Asia), or *Turn Left, Turn Right* (Warner Bros.). These pictures' industry roles, as benchmarks, genre updates and new localism, are discussed in other chapters.

Asian countries are smaller. But taken together, Asian moviegoers numerically approach the world's largest concentration of viewers, in North America. When combined, the Asian total population comes to over 250 million: Thailand 60 million; South Korea 50 million; Taiwan 21 million; Hong Kong 7 million; Singapore 3 million; Japan over 130 million. And this is before the massive population of China is accounted for.

If Asian pictures consistently satisfied the majority on home turf, intra-Asian box office would cover production costs (which are cheap compared to Europe and the US), leaving further returns outside Asia as surplus. In its various forms, pan-Asian cinema primes a regional market for regional films, expands the 'home-field advantage' and unites separated audiences. For Peter Chan Ho-sun, pan-Asian film is more than creative teamwork, but really 'a collaboration of different markets by trying to break through the market barrier, the culture barriers, and the language barriers so [that] we have enough population to sustain a healthy industry' (Chan, 2005). This is not just good business, but simple survival. One need only glance at the free-falling numbers in Chan's native Hong Kong to see that audiences there cannot sustain an ongoing industry. And so, integration with and assimilation into the Asian and mainland Chinese market is unavoidable, as argued below.

INTRA-ASIAN CO-PRODUCTION:
APPLAUSE PICTURES AND COMMERCIAL INITIATIVES

Hong Kong-based Applause Pictures best exemplifies pan-Asian cinema in the field and, in many respects, set the parameters of current pan-Asian co-production. As noted, pan-Asian cinema seeks out talent sharing as well as redistributing capital and markets. Its strategies are not altruistic, let alone ide-

Peter Chan Ho-sun, Applause Pictures

alist, but pragmatic expansion of contacts, connections and resources. The idea behind pan-Asian co-production is to build a networked market that's actively connected and co-operating rather than fragmented, isolated and antagonistic. 'Connectivity' has been an important business strategy in managing media globalisation (Li, 2003). Applause shows a transnational drive to connect and consolidate the whole Asia-Pacific market. The company was co-founded by Thai-Chinese writer-director-producer Peter Chan Ho-sun, the award-winning director of *Comrades, Almost a Love Story* (1996) and entrepreneur behind the UFO film group in Hong Kong. In 1998 he was recruited by Hollywood along with other Hong Kong talent at that time and directed Kate Capshaw in *The Love Letter* (1999). Chan soon repatriated to Hong Kong and is active in promoting pan-Asian projects. Lately he teamed up with Andre Morgan, former US partner of Golden Harvest, to form Applause-Ruddy Morgan, or ARM.

Applause initiates flexible production packages in order to recover markets lost to Hollywood. Its initial strategy was to invest in local Asian movies and directors capable of making commercial art films. Korea, China, Thailand, all these areas were carefully researched and underwritten by Applause. Another strategy is to repackage genre pictures to stimulate new interests in popular forms. In the first slate of Applause's pan-Asian projects, these two strategies were integrated. *One Fine Spring Day*, *Jan Dara*, *The Eye*, *Three* and *Three ... Extremes* all show commitment to trans-border co-productions with local talent, location shooting and new twists on genre. For instance, the Korean melodrama *One Fine Spring Day* had a production budget of US$1.5 million, co-financed by Sidus Pictures (one of Korea's largest production companies), Applause Pictures and Japan's major studio Shochiku (Russell, 2005) and was conceived and made for sale to Korean, Japanese and Chinese markets. The film features an all-Korean cast, a distinct K-drama flavour and is directed by a Korean director Hur Jin-ho with a track record in romantic melodrama.

With its Thai-language melodrama *Jan Dara* (dir. Nonzee Nimibutr, Thailand/Hong Kong co-production, 2001), Applause embarked on a more audacious strategy. The film is based on an autobiography banned in Thailand for years for its sexual content and illicit liaisons. Sex is taboo in most Asian cinemas and this element helped generate heat about the film. To add to the publicity, Applause included nude scenes of Hong Kong actress Christy Chung to entice Chinese audiences. Although the film had trouble clearing censors in Thailand, it was eventually released with revisions. In Hong Kong the film was classified Category III (adults only) but, because of its notoriety, it attracted many adults who rarely set foot in theatres.

In these two cases, Chan says, the pan-Asian work was embryonic, 'not real collaboration or real co-production'. However, the next step in that direction was to produce a genuinely multinational film. This was the source of omnibus horror film *Three*, and here the business model is clearest. *Three* (dir. Nonzee Nimibutr, Kim Kee-woon, Peter Chan, Thailand/South Korea/Hong Kong co-production, 2002) and sequel *Three … Extremes* (dir. Miike Takashi, Kim Kee-woon, Fruit Chan, 2004) are both comprised of short films from three different countries, styles and directors. In the sequel *Extremes*, the Thai section was replaced by a Japanese contribution from Miike Takashi, a cult film director known for stories of Asian migrants and cross-generic experimentation, horror-gangster shockers like *Ichi the Killer* (2001) and *Gozu* (2003). The objective for these two co-productions was to disseminate the risk. Moreover, the material and market is tripled: three directors, three stories and three territories. The last segment for these two films, *Three Go Home* (dir. Peter Chan) and *Dumplings* (dir. Fruit Chan) were spun off into feature-length horror films of their own. Both films received several film awards from Hong Kong and Taiwan for their new treatments of horror. The recognition shows that Applause's pan-Asian strategy of repackaging genre also pays off in prestige, an important value added to the company's visible branding.

Horror stands out in the Applause slate, a response to the huge success of J-horror. Low-budget J-horror was a germ in the sleepy Japanese film market in the late 1990s and spawned an international J-horror trend (see Chapter 5). Seeing the surprising payoffs of Japanese horror, Applause seized the chance to rework traditional Chinese materials into a new type of 'C-horror' for Chinese-speaking audiences. The result was *The Eye* (dir. Oxide and Danny Pang, 2002, Hong Kong/Singapore/Thailand co-production), and by far Applause's most commercially successful film.

Horror genres translate well. At the same time, each segment has regional variations. In *Three*, each part is dramatically different, one being a classic ghost story, another a sadomasochistic psycho-thriller and the third an unusual exploration of the social uncanny. *Three*'s Chinese title, *san geng* (three bells, 11:00 pm), is a specific time of night. It conjures supernatural visitations, ghost stories, nocturnal chills. Chan stretches this folklore to embrace Asian genre, regional co-operation, collaboration and industrial alliance. So, Applause's *Three* points toward expanded, multiple production, consumption and a new type of pan-Asian cinema.

In bringing pan-Asian films to market, distributors must persuade exhibitors and then audiences that the entire package will appeal. The marketing campaign therefore must transcend national differences and sell it as mainstream, but Asian: genre fare not trapped in the foreign-language ghetto. Only then will the film attract enough attention – from journalists, critics, and the public – to open wide, on 150 screens, as *The Eye* did in Bangkok, instead of the fifteen to twenty screens normal for Hong Kong imports in Thailand. The result of this wider opening tactic was 80 million baht, the third highest gross for the year, and, says Chan:

> the first two were both Thai films. We were the third and we sold the film as Thai because there were the Thai elements, with Thai actors [and directors] in it ...
> That's just to show how different ways of distributing movies actually could impact on the local reception of the film. (Chan, 2005)

With Malaysia-born, Taiwan/Hong Kong-based actress Lee Sinjie, and Singaporean actors and Singapore co-financing (Raintree-MediaCorp), 'it had elements from everywhere, so everyone treated it as if it was their own baby, and it is that TLC in distribution that really helped the film break through' (Chan, 2005). *The Eye* was a box-office success in Hong Kong, Taiwan, Japan and went ahead to enter the top ten charts in European countries such as the UK, Italy and Spain. The film's global box office topped US$13 million (see Table 4.1), a handsome record for Applause.

In Hong Kong million dollars

Title	Hong Kong	Regional	Europe	US	Worldwide
One Fine Spring Day (2001)	0.42	27.88 (S. Korea)	N/A	N/A	28.30
Jan Dara (2001)	7.55	0.89 (Taiwan, S. Korea)	N/A	N/A	8.44
The Eye (2002)	13.7	74.5 (Taiwan, S. Korea, Singapore, Thailand)	8.49 (France)	3.97	100.66
Three (2002)	7.37	6.62 (Taiwan, S. Korea)	N/A	N/A	13.99
Three ... Extremes (2004)	5.90	2.56 (Taiwan, Thailand)	N/A	0.60	9.06
Perhaps Love (2005)	13.79	37.9 (China, Taiwan, S. Korea)	N/A	N/A	51.69

Sources:
Data compiled from Box Office Mojo ('South Korea Box Office', 'Taiwan Box Office', 'Thailand Box Office'), *City Entertainment* (2001–2006), *Korean Cinema* ('Korean Films Weekly Box Office'), Singapore Film Commission website, *TPBO WRETCH* (2002, 2004) and Zhu (2006).

Table 4.1 Box Office of Pan-Asian Co-Productions by Applause Pictures (2001–5)

The local is here redrawn in regional terms: Asian-made films for Asian audiences, the better to seize home-field advantage. By capitalising on East Asian familiarity with neighbouring cinemas, Chan hopes to 'build a unified Asian marketplace' (Kan, 2002). Though Applause pictures may have outside elements, these do not make them 'foreign'. However well this goes, the model is probably insufficient to sustain a real studio, which needs to produce thirty to sixty films annually. Chan's method, he says, can maintain at most four to five pan-Asian hits per year. To have a film industry, you need a system, not as pan-Asian novelties or one-offs, and only when that line is up and smoothly running can a pan-Asian industry, not just a market, continue.

How feasible is this? Can it rival Hollywood's market power, or is it just another kind of industrial and cultural homogenisation? Related issues for Applause are the transnational division of labour and the gaps between established and developing sectors. As a mature, if declining industry, Hong Kong takes the lead, a tutelage in promoting co-productions by helping new players like Thailand develop their industries. Thailand now has become the top production destination and post-production site for many international projects for low-cost labour, scenery, facilities and logistics. This may help Thai film-makers and audiences, but it also has knock-on benefits to investors, like those in Hong Kong. Therefore, Applause's activities raise issues about the distinctiveness of national cinemas, like regional consolidation, talent sharing, risk management and re-territorialising markets. The work of Applause showcases Asian market expansion, and possible crossover to Europeans and North Americans.

Perhaps Love, Pan-Asian Musical

For Christmas 2005, Applause released the original musical *Perhaps Love*. This marks a shift from modest pan-Asian ventures to a high-risk media event. *Perhaps Love* is a model of pan-Asian casting, interlocking market segments with differentiated performer–territory links. The film was backed by TVB, Hong Kong's leading broadcaster, Malaysian television platform Astro, parent company of Celestial Pictures, which in turn handled international sales. Its objective of a pan-Asian release is shown in the casting. It stars Takeshi Kaneshiro, a half-Japanese, half-Taiwanese actor with art-house credentials and commercial mileage in Japan, Taiwan, China and Hong Kong. Next was veteran singer Jacky Cheung, one of the 'Four Heavenly Kings' of Cantopop (see Chapter 2). With his strong voice, Cheung lends musical substance to the film. In 1997 and 2005, Cheung took his musical *Snow Wolf Lake* on the road, augmenting a prodigious recording career and screen appearances through the 1990s. Cheung's fan base is wider than Kaneshiro's, appealing to all ages throughout East and Southeast Asia. *Perhaps Love*'s femme fatale is mainland Chinese Zhou Xun, who began in television dramas, then crossed over to art film acclaim with *Suzhou River* (dir. Lou Ye, 1999). She appeared in the pan-Asian art films *Hollywood Hong Kong* (dir. Fruit Chan, 2002), the French co-production *Balzac and the Little Chinese Seamstress* (dir. Dai Sijie, 2004) and *Bao'ber in Love* (dir. Li Shao-hong, 2004). Finally, Korean television star Ji Jin-hee is cast as the narrator/ringmaster. He provides a frame, linking the main show-business story with the lives of ordinary, anonymous people. Ji's casting draws on his following in K-drama, particularly 2003's pan-Asian hit *Jewel in the Crown*, and the over-all cachet of Korean pop culture around Asia (Onishi, 2006).

The language of the film is Mandarin Chinese, the setting Shanghai and Bei-jing. *Perhaps Love* presents itself as a 'Shanghai film', with glamour, nostalgia and a touch of decadence. Physicality comes in African and South Asian faces appearing as dance extras, whose numbers were arranged by Farah Khan, a famous Bollywood choreographer. The Japanese term *mukokuseki* (bor-derless) may describe this splashy cosmopolitan musical, much like *Moulin Rouge* (2001) and *Chicago* (2002). Post-production complete, the movie opened in Shanghai in mid-November, followed by premieres in Beijing, Taipei, Kuala Lumpur and Singapore. In Hong Kong there was a triple premiere on 6, 7 and 8 December, with three successive sponsors to throw parties and gala benefits for charity. *Perhaps Love* continued its profitable run well into the New Year

Pan-Asian musical *Perhaps Love* (2005)

(HK$13.79m and RMB 29 million) and sparked catty radio chat – from Sandra Ng, Peter Chan's partner, who mocked the visual effects in the season's other big release, *The Promise*, directed by Chen Kaige (in the US, *Master of the Crimson Armor*). The latter's partner, actress Chen Hong, fired a riposte from Beijing, doubting *Perhaps Love*'s box-office boasts. *The Promise* was touted as China's most expensive film ever with a production budget of US$35 million, while its Hong Kong box office was a paltry US$660,000 (HK$5.1 million). On the mainland, despite negative chat-room reviews, *The Promise* delivered, with strong returns of US$23 million (RMB 180 million).[1]

Like its Applause rival, *The Promise* boasts pan-Asian investment: top Korean distributor Show East co-produced, and it stars Korea's leading actor Jang Dong-gun (*Friend* and *Taegukgi*, see Chapter 1). Besides Jang there was Japan's 1980s heart-throb – Sanada Hiroyuki (*Twilight Samurai*, *The Last Samurai*) – as the haughty king, and Hong Kong stars Nicholas Tse and Cecelia Cheung. Established in 2003, Show East identifies itself as a major pan-Asian company. Its recent triumph was pan-Asian hit *April Snow*, whose star Bae Yong-joon is a huge idol in Japan. The film reaped over US$24.2 million and became the second top grossing Korean film of all time in Japan. Show East now has majority investment (nearly 55 per cent) from YeDang Online, a games/music entertainment portal whose cross-media interests will only intensify the pan-Asian ambitions of Korean production (Noh, 2006a). We see then that Hong Kong's Applause is just one of many aggressive pan-Asian enterprises.

PAN-ASIAN PACKAGERS: ARC LIGHT PICTURES, TAIWAN

Arc Light was formed in 1996 by Taiwan's eminent producer-critic Peggy Chiao Hsiung-ping. With French financial backing and talent scouting in Taiwan, Hong Kong and the Chinese mainland, Arc Light produced films that cross over between popular, local and international sales. Initially, Arc Light focused on non-fiction films for television and festival circuits. With the handover of Hong Kong to China in 1997, it co-produced a documentary series 'Hong Kong Stories' by directors such as Ann Hui (*As Time Goes By*) and Stanley Kwan (*Still Love You After All These* …). Arc Light also produced Taiwan director Hsu Hsiao-ming's *Homesick Eyes*, a portrait of Thai and Filipino migrant workers in Taiwan. Arc Light then assisted on French director Olivier Assayas' documentary *HHH: A Portrait of Hou Hsiao-hsien* (1997) about Taiwan's pre-eminent director Hou Hsiao-hsien.

Arc Light's films aim to attract specific, niche audiences: educated urban youth, those concerned with specific social issues, and film festival followers. To some extent these groups overlap. Efforts are made to cultivate loyal, niche markets at a time when Taiwan feature exhibition is completely dominated by

Peggy Chiao Hsiung-ping, Taiwan producer-critic

Hollywood imports. Since Arc Light has had major success at festivals, its courting of more popular audiences reaches across a divide, combining film festival
artistry with commercial appeal. This is part of a worldwide trend, post-*Crouching
Tiger*, for sales companies to make demanding foreign films more accessible or,
to put it another way, to make enjoyable, easy-to-digest art films. This is reflected
in the terminology, from segregated 'art house' films to 'specialty' product that,
with careful handling, can play anywhere. In Taiwan, film festival audiences
remain somewhat special, a congregation of cinephiles with a taste for unusual,
offbeat fare. One of Arc Light's earlier projects was Tsai Ming-liang's queer
musical *The Hole* (1999), co-produced with French company Flach Pyramide.
The Hole would never reach a large commercial public, but Tsai's more recent
work has, returning to the musical and exploiting audience curiosity with satirical porn (*The Wayward Cloud*, 2005). Peggy Chiao split with Tsai, after
producing two excellent but quite challenging films with him, including *The
River* (1997).

Arc Light then launched its six-film Tales of Three Cities series with Wang
Xiaoshuai's *Beijing Bicycle* (2000), Lin Cheng-sheng's *Betelnut Beauty* (2001),
Yee Chih-yen's *Blue Gate Crossing* (2002) and Hsu Hsiao-ming's *Love of May*
(2004). But Nelson Yu Lik-wai's Hong Kong project and Jia Zhangke's Shanghai project were withdrawn from the package.

The Three Cities series explored regional synergies with a slate of new urban
films. Like Applause Pictures, Arc Light's model seeks efficiencies of scale and
audience consolidation in the region. As Asian cities grow more cosmopolitan,

they also assert local cultural distinctions. A programme of stories connecting several films with strong regional flavour promotes both international and local recognition. The Tales of Three Cities series represents a larger 'footprint', if audiences see that the film belongs in a package ('collect all six!'). Viewers who like *Beijing Bicycle* or *Blue Gate Crossing* will be tempted to see the other instalments, if the product is properly branded and marketed as a series. In production, planning six films in a package allows risk management, by arranging finance for a whole product line, not just one film that stands or falls alone. Pressure on each is reduced if several films are included on the same finance-marketing platform. According to Chiao:

> Because we have six products, we can get a cheaper deal for production expenses. This makes it easier to get investment from overseas. If you say you have a package of six movies about the changes in Chinese societies, it's more appealing to foreign investors. (Yu, 2001)

Arc Light's Tales of Three Cities programme is highly attractive to Euro-American festivals and Japanese art houses. This distinguishes Arc Light efforts from the pan-Asian projects of Hong Kong-based Applause, which court mainstream Asian audiences, rather than Western niches.

EURO-ASIAN ALLIANCE:
FORTISSIMO OF HONG KONG/AMSTERDAM

A major sales company based in the Netherlands and Hong Kong, since its founding in 1990, Fortissimo has become one of the premier firms handling pre-sales and distribution of art films in Europe and Asia. Fortissimo's catalogue contains over 200 films – about 60 per cent of which are Asian – and is expanding by about a dozen per year. It has positioned itself as an important gatekeeper, promoter and broker of film circulation between East and West.

Founder Wouter Barendrecht was a festival programmer and architect of Cinemart, the market that runs during the Rotterdam Film Festival. Asian films and films from developing countries are Fortissimo's special brief, especially since opening the Hong Kong office in 1997, an expansion prompted by Barendrecht's friendship and business partnership with Wong Kar-wai. The company has embarked on more English-language films, especially independents from Australia and Asian films with higher budgets. Tsui Hark's martial arts epic *Seven Swords* (2005) was budgeted at US$18 million, Fortissimo's biggest budget to date, but more typical is its funding and production of Thai director Pen-ek Ratanaruang's noir-flavoured *Invisible Waves* (2006) and *Last Life in the Universe* (2003). The latter was actually a co-production between Thailand, Singapore, Hong Kong, Japan and the Netherlands. The company also invested in Zhang Yang's *Sunflower* (2005), and co-ordinated projects with other co-production companies such as Applause (*Three* and *Three ... Extremes*). Like Applause, Fortissimo is drawn to multicultural, hybrid projects that play festivals, but also have high entertainment value. All Fortissimo's projects are designed for festivals, where many receive awards and therefore critical and, it is hoped, commercial interest. Fortissimo is one of those companies actively blurring the institutional and artistic distinctions between the so-called art cinema and box-office success. All of the company's product, marketing and finance activity is 'auteur driven'.

Most importantly, Fortissimo has become active in production, not just sales, marketing and distribution. Just as it crosses between regions and cultures, it is liaising with major studios like Paramount Classics and Warner Bros. Fortissimo has good contacts with funding agencies, especially the 'lead banker Royal Bank of Scotland, which provides both project financing and gap financing'. Barendrecht says that despite forays into production, sales remain its core business: 'It's natural that sales agents begin to act more as executive producers. The longer they are selling, the better they know the markets; the better their relationships with film-makers and banks, the greater the trust' (George, 2005). Fortissimo's financial resources do not come from the region, where banks seldom invest in feature films. Like most other Hong Kong companies, Fortissimo is assessing greater exposure and activity in mainland China, with investment and international rights to Wang Xiaoshuai's Cannes prizewinner *Shanghai Dreams* (2005), Jacob Cheung's *A Battle of Wits* (2006) as well as projects in Latin America.

CEPA, THE CLOSER ECONOMIC PARTNERSHIP ARRANGEMENT
Implemented in January 2004, CEPA affords concessions to Hong Kong films allowing them easy access to the mainland. Its purpose is to lower trade barriers, and phase in measures to reduce obstacles to Hong Kong Special Administrative Region (HKSAR) imports, like films, video, television programming and cinema infrastructure. All told, CEPA aims to liberalise eighteen sectors, including media production, exhibition and promotion. In 1993, the PRC film industry was in trouble, desperate for audiences who had abandoned theatrical attendance since the late 1980s. Socialist propaganda and award-winning art film-makers could not keep the industry afloat. So authorities used incentives, letting distributors and exhibitors show imported films. These were carefully limited and screened for content. At first only ten foreign pictures were allowed, then with WTO access in 1999 the annual quota was raised to twenty. Since this included all foreign pictures, Hollywood movies dominated: *Titanic* was a big

hit, but *The Fugitive* (dir. Andrew Davis, 1993) and *True Lies* were the first. Any Hong Kong prospects had to compete with these, so they were likely to be Jackie Chan vehicles shown during Lunar New Year (Chapter 2). If Hong Kong producers wanted to export to China, they needed to form joint ventures with state-run distributors and studios. Ever since reunifying in 1997, Hong Kong SAR companies fought for permission to access the mainland.

CEPA is designed to give Hong Kong firms a leg up, but it appears that screen industries are among the less successful of those involved. When key conditions are met, Hong Kong movies are exempt from the annual quota of foreign films now allowed into China. Under CEPA, they count as domestic Chinese releases, and are therefore not subject to a box-office cap of 13 per cent, as prescribed by the China Film Corp, the country's main importer of foreign films (Liu, 2006). As mentioned, Hong Kong movies were subject to the annual quotas for foreign imports and thus competed directly with Hollywood and other Western films from 1994 to 2000. Though the quota was doubled, Hong Kong cried foul; officially China since 1997, HKSAR film exports deserved a head start. CEPA, as an expanded trade zone between Hong Kong and China, offers preferences to Hong Kong productions. But to be eligible, a joint partnership with Chinese companies was required and Chinese counterparts would have to comprise more than 51 per cent of the joint ownership. In later rounds (2005 and 2006), these rules were relaxed or phased out, as follows.

Under the terms of CEPA (I, II and III), concessions are gradually liberalised:

– Hong Kong-Chinese mainland co-productions will be exempt from the foreign film quota
– the ratio of Hong Kong workers in co-productions will go up from 50% to 70%
– co-productions no longer need to be filmed completely in China and stories need not be China-related (although one-third of the cast must be Chinese, in effect stipulating material that can be covered)
– Hong Kong investor stakes in cinemas in China to go up from 50% to as high as 90%
– Hong Kong investor stakes in audio-visual companies in China to go up from 50% to 70% (*FILMART 2004 Brochure*)

Relaxation of access rules requires adjustments in content to cater for mainland Chinese audiences, and to satisfy censorship, which stipulates 'the plot or the leading characters must be related to the mainland.' Although this has been officially relaxed, Hong Kong films must still have a significant mainland connection if they are to succeed. For instance, the third instalment of *Infernal Affairs* received PRC endorsement with the casting of mainland actor Chen

Daoming (who played Emperor Qin in Zhang Yimou's *Hero*), bringing a cross-border perspective to the story. Beijing director Feng Xiaogang was hired to make the Media Asia caper *A World Without Thieves* in 2004, starring the biggest cross-straits talent: Taiwan's Rene Liu, appearing with Hong Kong star Andy Lau and Ge You, a popular star on the mainland and a fixture in Feng's post-socialist comedies (see Chapter 2). Though not because of CEPA, Hong Kong stars now appear often in PRC films, with Andy Lau in Zhang Yimou's *House of Flying Daggers* (2004), and both Cecilia Cheung and Nicholas Tse in Chen Kaige's fantasy *The Promise* (2005). Hong Kong directors also work in China: Jacob Cheung's pan-Asian *A Battle of Wits* (2006, starring Andy Lau and Korean Ahn Sung-ki) and John Woo's forthcoming *The Battle of Red Cliff*. The result is a more porous connection between the PRC and HKSAR film industries. The ardour seems greater for Hong Kong producers though, with access to possibly huge demand, and revival, perhaps, of its own moribund industry.

There is worry too that Hong Kong audiences will be sidelined in favour of entertainment made for the mainland; local tastes aren't always commercially adaptable to Chinese moviegoers, or censors. Worse, the biggest producers in Hong Kong – Media Asia, China Star, Emperor and Gold Label – are enlarging their share of the local market: 75 per cent in 2005, according to Media Asia's John Chong (Tsui, 2005). For producers, there is incentive to avoid locally specific stories and go for the larger mainland market; for small, local storytellers, the barriers to entry have become higher. In this, pan-Asian cinema may sacrifice minority or local taste to the larger market. Director Alan Mak (dir., *Infernal Affairs*, *Initial D*, *Confession of Pain*) said:

> A lot of investors had ruled out Hong Kong as a major market when they agreed to back a movie. This is something we don't want to happen – how can we just abandon the locals? And I believe audiences want to see Hong Kong movies with Hong Kong traits. (Tsui, 2005)

China, meanwhile, looks westward in its own co-production plans. Lai Peikang, president of the China Film Co-production Corp, says:

> The government has adopted this [co-production] policy so that Chinese companies can learn about different aspects of the film business, including production management, financing, marketing and international distribution. It should also help them gain access to overseas funding. Our aim is to increase the number of films that China makes each year and to make bigger-budget movies. China is a large market and there's room for a more diverse range of local films.

Lai refers here to co-productions with the West, which the government officially encourages to bolster local production in anticipation of WTO liberalisation. China has undertaken aggressive campaigns pushing for more multinational co-production treaties, which not only bring investment, but know-how and technology to the mainland film industry. There are a number of co-production treaties being contemplated and drafted, like that between China–Australia, and China–India, to bring 'a pooling of resources between two potentially giant markets' (Shackleton, 2005b).

With CEPA, Hong Kong films now face more stringent Chinese censorship if seeking mainland distribution. In *The Twins Effect II*, content was significantly altered. The first *Twins* was a spoof of Buffy-style vampire slayers, but since mainland audiences cannot have 'superstitious' entertainment, this was eliminated for the sequel. One mainland director suggested all horror films should end as a dream sequence, so that they can get through the censor board. Along with superstition and supernatural themes, politics – 'cultural revolution stories are absolutely no-no' (Liu, 2006) – organised crime, nudity, homosexuality, violence and lasciviousness – all are prohibited by mainland censors. It should be remembered that Hong Kong studios have long been producing multiple versions of films to pass censorship in different environments, as in Malaysia, Singapore and Taiwan. The PRC presents new challenges for these familiar dilemmas. The first *Infernal Affairs* film was banned for triad themes while the third was co-produced by the Chinese and thus became an anti-crime morality tale. Unpredictable Chinese censorship means Hong Kong film-makers must work harder to justify helpings of erotica, violence and many kinds of humour. Another triad movie *Jiang Hu* (with two Heavenly Kings Andy Lau and Jacky Cheung) was banned outright in 2004, betraying a bitter dispute between producers and censors over the finished product, alleged to have deviated from the approved script. The writers and film-makers of *Jiang Hu* did everything right in pre-production, qualifying for mainland distribution, but when the film was confidently submitted for screening approval, the censors struck. Its dark, choreographed violence and politically ambiguous ending caused its demise, though producers maintain that they got all the necessary approvals.

Film and video distributors are not entirely sure whether CEPA can really help the Hong Kong industry. Piracy is a big problem leading to revenue loss at point of sale while requirements for joint venture and revenue sharing with mainland partners are onerous. In theory, CEPA opens a vast operating theatre for Hong Kong producers, and for multinationals prepared to partner with mainland organisations at high levels. In practice, there are still obscurities and red tape, and many hurdles to clear. One company successfully running the race into China is Media Asia.

MEDIA ASIA, PAN-ASIAN OR PAN-CHINESE?

To be eligible for CEPA, there are stipulations involving the company's business, domicile and the nationality of staff members. The business must be officially certified as a 'Hong Kong Service Provider' on both sides of the border. The documentation must be submitted and approved by authorities in Hong Kong and the mainland. Media Asia is one of only six Hong Kong media companies that qualified as a Hong Kong Service Provider under the treaty terms. Golden Harvest was another.

Media Asia Group started life in 1994 as a film distribution division of the Star TV satellite service. It split from Star TV when the successful channel was sold to Rupert Murdoch's News Corp. A group of executives, dubbed 'the seven samurai', agreed to work as independent distributors of Star's film library. The founding partners included Jerry Liu, Wellington Fung, F. K. Ma, John Chong, C. Lo Chen, Nick James and Thomas Chung, a certified public account- ant. In its first year the firm distributed around 800 titles, on screen and video, but soon branched into production. It started a film fund to finance a whole slate of pictures, with risk spread over six to eight titles (Frater, 2004; Curtin, 2007). As managing director, Thomas Chung crafted a professional look to the production slate, with production costs rising to around 80 per cent of expen- diture. Meticulous calculating and rationalising of concepts led to carefully managed packaging, a rarity in impetuous Hong Kong film culture. Insisting on complete scripts with well-structured stories, the company signed formal con- tracts with personnel, got completion bonds, relied on insurance, marketing campaigns and other legal apparatus to present a professional, polished pack- age (Chung, 2002). This emphasis on solid business packaging, with full financial and legal disclosure, meant to attract outside investment, and promote confidence in the Media Asia slate. Outside interest soon materialised in the company's takeover by Peter Lam, who – as one of Asia's richest tycoons – made a move into Hong Kong's top production echelon. Bringing in one of Hong Kong's savviest producers, Nansun Shi, Lam green-lighted the hits *Elixir of Love* (dir. Yip Kam-hung, 2004), *Magic Kitchen* (dir. Lee Chi-ngai, 2004), and the all- important *Infernal Affairs* trilogy (Frater, 2004). Under Lam and his eSun company, which manages a talent stable, Media Asia opts for high budgets, closely overseen by line producers and auditors, over economies of scale in its picture-making. It usually produces between six and ten films a year, and dis- tributes 269 for third-party copyright holders. As of 2005 it held a library of twenty films produced in-house, and counts sub-distributors and licensees in over thirty countries worldwide (Media Asia, 2003).

Media Asia is one of the most active pan-Asian co-producers and regional col- laborators. It has tie-ins with Gaga Communications and Avex (Japan) and

Raintree-MediaCorp (Singapore). Its most important commitments, though, are China-bound, tying up with China Film Corp, a state-run conglomerate. And like Golden Harvest and Kadokawa/Sun Wah, it has begun the race to build multiplexes in mainland China, where the ratio of screens to population is negligible. According to *Screen International*, 'each screen in China plays to an audience of more than 240,000 people and the average person visited a cinema 0.1 times ... [while] in the US, each screen plays to 8,123 people and the average person visits a cinema 5.4 times a year' (Shackleton, 2006a).

An early draft of Media Asia's business plan saw cultivation of fresh audiences among affluent youth, who were not being supplied with movies. This production and marketing strategy led the aggressive push into pan-Asian production later by companies such as Applause and Show East. With *Purple Storm* (dir. Teddy Chan, 1999) and *2000AD* (dir. Gordon Chan, 2000), Media Asia enticed a young demographic away from its computers and games, courting them with pretty boy-and-girl characters fluent in a variety of cultures and environments. Their proficiency was not only linguistic, but included fashion, food and stylish travel as well as the latest technology, cars and weapons. These new cosmopolitan Asians, including Daniel Wu, Edison Chen, Eason Chan, Michael Wong, Nicholas Tse, Kelly Chen, Cecelia Cheung, Wang Lee Hom and Jay Chou, drew from a pool of privileged, English-speaking Chinese who, whatever their acting skills, seemed convincing in diverse settings. Many of these stars were North America born or raised. Examples of these cosmopolitan youth films are *Purple Storm*, *GenX Cops* (1999), *2000AD* and *GenY Cops* (dir. Benny Chan, 2000).

Pan-Asian adaptations appeal to this demographic, with a pointedly twenty-first-century amalgamation of commodity and entertainment values. Properties likely to appeal to young cosmopolitans include Japanese manga, comics avidly consumed far beyond their country of origin. Media Asia's *Initial D*, a Hong Kong film based on a Japanese comic, and destined for pan-Asian distribution, transcends what we've elsewhere called 'Japan Hongscreen', a bilateral connection between Hong Kong and Japan (Yeh and Davis, 2002). *Initial D* draws a large pan-Asian following around a big-screen translation of a Japanese popular source. The film does not dilute or smother the Japanese qualities of its origin, but trusts in its stylish characters and premise, rising above its manga-TV 'citizenship'.

Initial D is a key pan-Asian property, like Jacob Cheung's *A Battle of Wits*, based on a hit manga from 1995 and made into a Japanese television series in 1998. Gaga Communications and Avex Inc. bought the rights to show the film adaptation in Japan, and with access to the manga and television series, Gaga and Avex functioned as both seller and buyer – getting licence fees from Media Asia for adaptation rights; and buying distribution rights to the movie in Japan (Hopewell, 2004). This allowed full exploitation of Japanese market reception to both original properties as well as the Hong Kong-made film (Li, 2003). According to Nick Marumo of Gaga Communications:

> We'll release the film on more than 200 prints and work closely with Media Asia to produce a pan-Asian release. ... The whole purpose of this joint buy is to leverage the maximum marketing benefits from our experience with the *Initial D* products. (Kawamoto, 2005)

But the PRC, a market unfamiliar with the originals, needed special handling by distribution-marketing people. Despite its size, China may go out of step with pan-Asian pop cultural phenomena. *Initial D* works then as a wedge-shaped formation, starting life in Japan, then migrating gradually to other parts of East and Southeast Asia. In Hong Kong, awareness of Japanese popular culture runs high, and *Initial D*'s box office was number one there in 2005 with a box-office record of US$4.9 million (HK$37.8 million). Taiwan, as well, took excellent returns of US$1.25 (NT$40 million) due to the casting of Taiwanese pop star Jay Chou, whose movie debut was embraced by critics and by audiences. However, source material should not be overrated; it was Media Asia's robust campaign of saturation advertising and niche marketing that paved the way for the film's success.

On the fringes of this pattern, China needed considerable priming (see *Initial D* section, below). Marketing the film was touchy in a place that officially remains suspicious of Japanese imports. It was essential to avoid upsetting Chinese patriotic sentiments, language, humour, sexuality, etc. *Seoul Raiders*, Media Asia's weak sequel to Golden Harvest's *Tokyo Raiders*, was enjoyed by mainlanders – taking US$3.9 million (RMB 31 million) – which might be accounted for by the huge popularity of Korean pop culture overall in China (Onishi, 2006).

A disproportion between Hong Kong and mainland admissions was visible in Tsui Hark's over-inflated *Seven Swords*, earning US$1 million in Hong Kong (HK$8 million), but taking ten times that in China, US$10 million (RMB 80 million), despite rampant piracy. Some Hong Kong journalists lament this, as piracy's threat starts to recede, and insist 'probably the most defining development for local cinema in 2005 [is] a gradual watering-down of the streetwise edge of Hong Kong cinema in exchange for wads of [mainland] yuan' (Tsui, 2005). The box office for *Initial D* in China later came to US$8 million (RMB 64 million).

Initial D in China

Is it ironic that CEPA facilitates entry to Chinese markets using Hong Kong adaptation of Japanese pop cultures? Yet it was not seen as a Trojan Horse by authorities or the public. Media Asia's saturation marketing on the mainland included:

- providing exclusive news bulletins to a PR agency
- contracting with major sponsors to buy all the toys, prototypes and events in cities nationwide (premieres, car-racing shows, beauty contests and on the spot computer game events)
- recruiting 100,000 fans to sign a document supporting the film: generating hype (not protest)
- online contests, games and quizzes
- interactive SMS (short message service) campaigns and other e-marketing schemes.

The film was promoted in every way possible to bring it into the public eye, through games, toys, contests, press conferences and merchandise. Free videos featuring Jay Chou were supplied to KTV parlours, since Chou is one of the top crooners in the region and star of the film. Racing cars and stars were shipped over from Japan and Hong Kong for special events. With its drift-racing theme, 'Drift Girl contest' and 'Drift King' shows travelled the country from Guangzhou, Hangzhou, Chengdu, Shanghai and finally Beijing. Television and press monitored their progress, interacting with locals along the way. T-shirts, model cars and souvenirs for *Initial D* were distributed in lucky draws; special postage stamps (limited collectors' editions) and a colour picture book (in one week before the release, 300,000 copies were sold, raising more than RMB 600,000 in royalties). The campaign seemed meant not only to ignite interest in the film, but also to cover reactions of provincials for the enjoyment of urbanites used to such ballyhoo.

The campaign's biggest success was reaching gamers, online promotions, videogames and SMS. Media Asia hired the web designers of the *Kung Fu Hustle* game, whose software was a big success for China Film Corp's campaign for Steven Chow and Columbia-Asia.

Crucially, none of this promotional flurry was done under Media Asia's own name but through internet portal Taobao and other Chinese corporate sponsors. Another point was a close watch on American publicity and marketing campaigns, tracking public awareness as the release date approached. In Hollywood distribution, three-quarters of revenue comes from 'post-product' back-end marketing (merchandising, tie-ins, endorsements, etc.), according to Chen.

Initial D was promoted during a season of anti-Japanese sentiment, so official televised talk shows had to be curtailed. The campaign switched to Phoenix TV because this was more discreet, and doesn't have the status (and implicit approval) of CCTV, China's official broadcaster. Despite this, television coverage proved to be the most effective means of promotion, with 30 per cent of viewers getting information about the film from TV. Media Asia generated US$5 million (RMB 40 million) just for selling promotional rights to corporate sponsors, like Sina.net, China Mobile, games companies and associated subsidiaries, such as magazines and PR firms. This was money raised before a single admission ticket was sold (Chen, 2005). With a production budget of US$10 million, *Initial D* had box-office returns of US$14 million from Greater China (Taiwan, Hong Kong and mainland China) and another US$5.67 million from the rest of East Asia, including Japan. The film's worldwide theatrical sales amounted to US$21.4 million, only 0.6 million less than the total amount of Media Asia's previous three hits – *Infernal Affairs* and its sequels.

CONCLUSION

In this chapter, we reviewed the historical and contemporary aspects of pan-Asian film production, distribution and sales. We differentiated types of pan-Asian activity in terms of institutional agency, geographical spread, commercial v. educational aims and target viewers in Asia and the West. The hallmark of contemporary pan-Asian cinema is a push toward market consolidation, creating an enlarged, unified film market that sustains investment in medium-to-large scale movies and marketing. Nonetheless, it aids cultural diversity by ensuring local tastes and expectations are served. Such delicate balancing acts can be seen in the films of Applause, Fortissimo, Arc Light, Media Asia and others. Since Hollywood pictures are the default popular cinema, why can't Asian pictures also offer attractive talent, high production values and local ingredients, shrewdly marketed in multiplexes and publicity campaigns to become box-office hits? At the fore of pan-Asian cinema, Applause Pictures and Media Asia both use policies like CEPA and co-production treaties to take advantage of regional film investment. Meanwhile, Hollywood is entering the pan-Asian scramble for concessions and audiences, forming subsidiaries and partnerships to produce movies for local consumption. In the PRC, the process rapidly advances which, however, is often hampered by government bodies that want to make the rules (via censorship, distribution blackouts and copyright enforcement), yet benefit from partnerships with foreign commercial organisations. The vagaries of CEPA show how pan-Asian cinema often comes down to pan-Chinese schemes to bypass official PRC stipulations; whether this will inaugurate a phase of real liberalism in Chinese cinema, its markets and modes of expression, is an open question.

NOTE

1. Chinese responses to prestige picture *The Promise* were mixed. In late 2005 Hu Ge, a young Shanghai audio salesman and freelance sound-effects designer, caused a media furore. Like others, Hu Ge was disappointed with the film. He thought it was too simple, with simple plot, simple-minded characters and technical flaws. Yet it afforded him source materials for practising digital editing skills. Inspired by a CCTV legal programme, Hu invented a bizarre cat-and-mouse story centring on a steamed bun (similar to the opening incident in the film). Then he illustrated it with images taken from *The Promise*, combined with a hilarious hip-hop soundtrack. His twenty-minute video, entitled 'A Murder Sparked by a Chinese Bun', was completed on two computers in just five days. It circulated among friends, but soon gained tremendous popularity online in early 2006. Chen Kaige however was not amused. At the Berlin Film Festival, Chen loudly denounced the parody as immoral and vowed to sue for copyright violation. Did the video affect the box office of *The Promise*? Many admitted seeing the original film because they saw Hu Ge's spoof first. The online 'Bun Incident' indicates the gap between the high expectations raised by extravagant marketing and lukewarm viewer response. Chen Kaige's harsh reaction ('overreaction', to critics and netizens) reflects how desperate the veteran director was to reclaim his artistic and commercial credibility. (Courtesy Lake Wang Hu, Phoenix TV, Hong Kong.)

5

Genre/Nation:
Cultural Commerce and Signature Narratives

In 2003 Walter Parkes, of DreamWorks and producer of *The Ring*, had this to say about contemporary Asian film:

> There is more access to Asian cinema now than probably at any other time in film history. It is in many ways becoming a world market. Hollywood's voracious appetite will look wherever it can. For the last ten years, a generation ... has been growing up on *Pokemon*, Japanese anime, and manga, which may be causing certain sensibilities to evolve. (Frater and Kay, 2003)

Parkes's statement underscores the globalisation of Japanese, and Asian, popular cinema. More, it shows the importance of genre as a marketing tool, in contrast to its former role as support for product rationalisation in a studio system.

To pique interest in his remake, Parkes describes what he considers a lowering of barriers – cultural, trade and quality barriers – between regions: 'in many ways becoming a world market'. He believes young Americans will flock to a slate of remakes of Japanese pictures. So-called J-horror offers simple but unsettling stories, like *Ringu* (dir. Nakata Hideo, 1998) and its two sequels; *Chaos* (dir. Nakata, 1999), *Ju-On* (The Grudge, Parts 1 and 2, dir. Shimizu Takashi, 2002), *Pulse* (dir. Kurosawa Kiyoshi, 2001*), Dark Water* (dir. Nakata, 2002), *One Missed Call* (dir. Miike Takashi, 2003) and many others. Solid hits in Japan, these quality films delivered healthy returns on modest outlays. Although as horror films they are rather restrained, their domestic success attracted attention overseas, at least for a market already attuned to Japanese pop culture. Abroad, remade with international stars and big budgets they could become bona fide blockbusters. DreamWorks paid US$1 million to acquire (not merely option) the remake rights of *Ringu*. In its handling of the US$48 million remake, DreamWorks did the expected – not suppressing Nakata's Japanese source, already a cult film for Asian horror fans, nor playing it up. As we'll see, the American version of *Ju-On* took a different tack. In Japan, DreamWorks' *The Ring* was a modest success, earning around US$14 million, double the box office of the original. Internationally, its returns were huge: a worldwide gross of US$244 million on theatrical revenues alone. Parkes traded on the gap between an obscure Asian title and a bigger budget American film, and profited spectacularly. DreamWorks' tactic represents a transnational amplification of genre that feeds back to the East Asian source.

This chapter focuses on genres and nationality, and how they play complementary roles in the industrial and stylistic force of East Asian cinema. The growing visibility of Asian cinema is closely linked to innovations and updates of popular genres. By analysing Japanese horror and Chinese martial arts as our main case studies, we demonstrate Asian screen industries' productive revitalisation of old forms for new audiences. Our approach here is extensive and speculative, outlining key features of genre in relation to East Asian society. We identify genre elements that can travel abroad, while retaining distinctive cultural traits. While many lament the de-specification of Asia in its global diffusion, international exposure can facilitate production and consumption at home. In reconstructing national cinema through popular genres, East Asian screen industries effectively compete in the global screen trade.

GENRE/NATION:
ASIAN POPULAR FILM AND GLOBAL HOLLYWOOD

Unlike its B-movie reputation, a cult cinema catering to minority audiences ('trash cinema', 'Asian extreme', etc.), Asian popular film is translated to Hollywood for mainstream entertainment. This is abetted by 'genre/nation', the classification and alignment of genres with different countries. The process of cross-cultural translation is smoothed by a cottage industry of producer-brokers, like Roy Lee (Vertigo Entertainment) and Ichise Taka (Entertainment Farm), who sell remake rights to buyers like Parkes. Through Roy Lee, Bob Weinstein's genre outfit Dimension Films acquired options on hit Korean comedies such as *My Sassy Girl*, *My Wife Is a Gangster*, *Hi, Dharma*, *My Teacher Mr Kim* and *Jail Breakers*. In 2006, Lee's Vertigo Entertainment and Warner Bros. released *The Lake House* (dir. Alejandro Agresti), a remake of the Korean romance *Il Mare* (dir. Lee Hyeon-seung, 2000).

Roy Lee posits an alignment of nation and genre: 'Each country seems to have a speciality [sic] that the executives at US studios respond to. For South Korea, it is the comedy; Japan has the horror-thrillers; and Hong Kong has the action genre that is attractive for executives' (Frater, 2003a). Links between genre and nation are explicit, as genre/nation. Lee's sales strategy vividly connects genre and nation, assigning individual Asian countries to recognisable types, thus promoting the entry of domestic Asian hits. The idea of genre/nation also helps studio executives justify Hollywood's purchases of the rights. Sometimes sales people venture wildly optimistic comparisons to keep the pipeline flowing. Amanda Klein, of Primal Pictures, says, 'South Korean and US films are very similar in sensibilities, genres and subject matter' (Frater, 2003a). Although the Korean options have only just begun to materialise into films, Japanese properties have a track record, not only with horror, but also romantic comedy such as *Shall We Dance* (Miramax, 2004), from the Japanese film of the same name (dir. Suo Masayuki, 1997). Hong Kong's first remake was Martin Scorsese's *The Departed*, a Boston-set version of Media Asia's undercover policier, *Infernal Affairs* (2003–4, see Chapter 1). What is the long- and short-term significance of this East Asian genre dissemination?

To Hollywood executives, the advantages of looking to East Asian sources are manifold: low budgets suited to horror and comedies; a proven track record; distinctive, but ultimately translatable premises and favourable export prospects based on key genre/nation intersections. Japan is renowned for its quietly creepy horror pictures, far removed from American slasher films. Horror comes across poorly on the page or in a pitch. So in addition to showing overseas buyers finished products, these are 'concept horror' models, with finely honed premises or hooks (not to be confused with 'high concept'). Mike Macari, involved in the sale of *Ringu* to DreamWorks, says:

> The kind of Asian films that get remade have very strong concepts. Genre films are easy, they don't cost so much and make a lot of money. Also, pitching a horror concept is hard. If you are able to show one that works on screen, you can argue that it will work again. (Frater, 2003a)

This is consistent with director Sam Raimi's admiration for Shimizu Takashi's *Ju-On*, which Raimi's company bought and produced as an American remake. From an artistic viewpoint, Raimi pays tribute to Shimizu's tight control of camerawork, editing and suspense. He says *Ju-On* exemplifies J-horror's potential for subtlety, in contrast to over-the-top techniques of American horror pictures, including his own (*Ju-On* DVD commentary, Lions Gate Films, 2004). *Ju-On*'s remake prospects are strong because of its skilful handling of basic horror materials, rather than its dialogue or specific social context. The reasoning is, if it already works on an American viewer, then Japanese horror pictures will work just as well as an American remake.

Peddling his own DreamWorks picture, Walter Parkes hints at new market formations, via lower barriers to foreign entertainment. A key factor is the global explosion in media trade: a plenitude of cable, satellite and home-video platforms, not to mention extra-cinematic access points like music, games, comics, toys, even food. This unprecedented availability affords greater movement, with Asian cinema travelling beyond its usual homes and niches where it had been confined. Asian cinema moved in distinct stages: from domestic consumption within Asia, to diaspora audiences, cosmopolitan appreciation by connoisseurs and to new horizons of mobile, downloadable, potentially unlimited material on demand. With greater awareness and proximity to non-Western media come opportunities for alternative models of production, consumption and a chance for genuine global popularity.

Overall, exchange-values of genre in Asian films' circulation promote marketplace shifts. A senior buyer at Miramax insisted in 2003 that, *Crouching Tiger* notwithstanding, foreign-language pictures are inherently art house within the American market (Brodlie, 2003). But, in fact, the match-up of genre and nation is a way to move beyond art-house constraints: comedies with South Korea, action-thrillers from Hong Kong and mainland Chinese martial arts join the exodus of J-horror to potentially lucrative reincarnation in Hollywood. This alignment happens in the minds of risk-averse Hollywood executives, but it also means a greater discursive articulation of East Asian cinemas throughout the world. As shown in Table 5.1, the genre/nation idea brackets foreign (or national cinema) qualities in favour of genre, and this new articulation works on at least two registers.

Genre Habituation, Genres Contemporised

First, genre/nation shifts away from art-house typecasting of Asian cinema in world film culture. Asian 'genrefication' entails a move toward regular entertainment movies. No longer alien, they are likely to seek and reap large profits in multiplexes, not just in festivals and retrospectives. Now, martial arts scenes are used in American multiplexes to remind patrons to switch off their cell phones. One public service announcement opens with the titles, 'In a time of war ... an old enemy returns.' Thundering horses and a pair of duelling warriors follow images of calligraphy, then a beautiful Asian woman. As a swordsman balances on his enemy's outstretched blade, he pauses to ask, 'What's that noise?' (Faint beeping sound.) His opponent says, 'Must be coming from the audience,' and flips his adversary backward into the water. Then, there is a reminder to be considerate, and switch off mobile phones. Telephony and mobile phone manufacturers sponsor the spot. Martial arts have become truly domesticated if their once exotic appeal can carry such routine messages.

As this example shows, Asian films emerged from the ghetto of 'specialty' markets, though auteurs of exoticism like Wong Kar-wai, Kim Ki-duk and Tsai Ming-liang remain on festival circuits. Due to high visibility of the Hong Kong style, East Asian over-representation at festivals and cult aesthetics' infection of the commercial mainstream, these once-specialised markets have outgrown

Title	Prod Yr	Director	Remake Title	Remade Yr	Director
Japan					
Shall We Dansu?	1996	Masayuki Suo	*Shall We Dance?*	2004	Peter Chelsom
Ringu	1997	Nakata Hideo	*The Ring*	2002	Gore Verbinski
Ringu 2	1999	Nakata Hideo	*The Ring 2*	2005	Nakata Hideo
Ju-On	2002	Shimizu Takashi	*The Grudge*	2004	Shimizu Takashi
Ju-On 2	2003	Shimizu Takashi	*The Grudge 2*	2006	Shimizu Takashi
Joyu-rei	1996	Nakata Hideo	*Don't Look Up*	N/A	N/A
Kaosu	1999	Nakata Hideo	*Chaos*	2005	Jonathan Glazer
Kairo	2001	Kurosawa Kiyoshi	*Pulse*	2006	Wes Craven
Dark Water	2002	Nakata Hideo	*Dark Water*	2005	Walter Salles
One Missed Call	2003	Miike Takashi	*One Missed Call*	2007	Eric Valette
South Korea					
Il Mare	2000	Lee Hyeon-seung	*The Lake House*	2006	Alejandro Agresti
My Sassy Girl	2001	Kwak Jae-yong	*My Sassy Girl*	2007	Yann Samuell
My Wife Is A Gangster	2001	Jo Jin-kyoo	*My Wife Is A Gangster*	N/A	N/A
Marrying the Mafia	2002	Jeong Heun-soon	*Marrying the Mafia*	N/A	N/A
Old Boy	2003	Park Chan-wook	*Oldboy*	2008	N/A
Hong Kong					
The Mission	1999	Johnnie To	*The Mission*	2007	Peter Berg
Infernal Affairs	2002	Andrew Lau	*The Departed*	2006	Martin Scorsese
The Eye	2002	Oxide and Danny Pang	*The Eye*	2007	Xavier Palud
The Eye 2	2004	Oxide and Danny Pang	*In-Utero*	2007	N/A

Sources:
Information compiled from *Han Cinema*, Hong Kong Film Archive website, *Kateigaho International Edition*, *Midnight Eye* and *The Internet Movie Database*.

Table 5.1 Asian Films Remade or Acquired for Remake in the US

their base. They expanded and multiplied, like film audiences everywhere, into fragmented tastes, along with finer differentiations, more subcategories, and more choices across distinct markets. J-horror soon begat Korean K-horror, while Thai- and Chinese-flavoured horror vehicles were successfully made and marketed by Applause, Fortissimo and other pan-Asian production houses (see Chapter 4). Overall, prospects for foreign films have widened, becoming articulated and more competitive. While genre/nation alignments are simplistic, reducing whole national cinemas to a few signature films, they helped break out from geographical and market niches, and not just for buyers in the West. Led by Chinese martial arts, Japanese horror and South Korean hits, East Asian cinema engages and energises global screens via signature genres. East Asian cinemas rely on genre pictures to revive the home industry and protect their market share from Hollywood. 'Japan wants to do what South Korea has done so successfully: go head-to-head with Hollywood at home while creating a boom abroad,' writes Mark Schilling (2005b). For Hollywood, these genre triumphs are not a threat as they attract and stimulate demand overall. Genres provide a brand of taste distinction, a safety net and a representative agent for national film industries.

Second, this genre/nation development has an extensive history. Genre has worked for years as the leading edge in global circulation of East Asian cinema, pace 'great directors' historical accounts that privilege the masters at genre's expense. Genres carry directors, providing entry to the reception of films across a cultural divide. Genres are the first stop on the road to familiar pleasures. Genres are also an essential vehicle for stars. Recall kung fu, the only type of Chinese film that could enter the US market in the 1970s. Despite his charisma, Bruce Lee's stardom demands the generic conventions of martial arts. When they have track records and reputations to uphold, only then may stars, and sometimes directors, shrug off genre constraints but, even then, genre works well as a marketing tool in promotion, export or auxiliary sales.

Akira Kurosawa received the Golden Lion at Venice for his *Rashomon* in 1950. In this sensitive postwar period, the prize opened doors to Asian cinema's acceptance beyond its home field and the Asia-Pacific region. It also signalled recognition of an indigenous genre – *jidai geki* (period drama) – that could be appreciated outside its linguistic and cultural bounds.[1] *Jidai geki*, in the hands of another studio director Kenji Mizoguchi, displayed meticulous *mise en scène*, with camerawork that incorporated traditional theatre and architecture. Mizoguchi's extravagant staging and historical fatalism stunned European critics. His penultimate film *Ugetsu* (his seventy-seventh), a period ghost picture, won the second prize at Venice in 1953. Henceforth, Japanese cinema was identified with *jidai geki*, though other directors were making their best films in other genres.[2] A decade later, studio director Ozu Yasujiro's family melodramas (called 'home dramas' in Japan) were belatedly discovered by Anglo-American critics, and posthumously celebrated. In 1975 *A Touch of Zen* (dir. King Hu, 1971–2), a Hong Kong/Taiwan production, was honoured at Cannes for its distinctive treatment of martial arts, resonating with the countercultural interest in Buddhism. It received a special technical grand prize for its distinction from the craze for hardboiled martial arts as epitomised by Bruce Lee, Jimmy Wang Yu, *et al*. *A Touch of Zen* was not a typical martial arts film at all. Like Ang Lee, King Hu used a genre associated with lowbrow action to explore transcendental ideas like Buddhist enlightenment. East Asian cinema found a way to the world by sometimes unexpected uses of genre, not just by name directors.

But there are differences between the past and the current reception, normalisation and co-optation of East Asian genres. Now multilaterally diffused, genre/nation allows for more national differences within the region. There's a tendency to enlarge and diversify regional and global demand, showing a 'voraciousness of the market', in Parkes's phrase. Hong Kong film *Throw Down* (dir. Johnnie To, 2004) uses judo, a Japanese martial art, as exercise in noir style, male bonding, and tribute to Kurosawa a half century later. Kurosawa's first film *Sugata Sanshiro* (1943) glorified judo as a national sacrament, while *Throw Down* is a character study that substitutes judo for customary gangster and kung fu action. In addition, judo works as an exciting choreographic principle in the film's design, at the expense of a compelling narrative of competition. This would have frustrated viewers primed by its Chinese title, *Judo Championship* (Roudao longhu bang). A more conventional genre entry, *Fearless* (2005), is a lunar New Year picture starring Jet Li, whose martial artistry comes with a nationalist ethos of Asian resistance to nineteenth-century European hubris. This biopic of a famous martial artist named Huo Yuanjia typifies patriotic glorification of its subject (Li was inspired by Mel Gibson's *The Passion of the Christ*, 2004), while attracting a lawsuit from Huo's descendants. Chinese audiences do not always follow the prescribed reverence for official culture, but the film's healthy box office was perhaps a compelling factor in the suit.

Generally, the pattern is that each industry may wrap itself in a signature genre, a sort of branding in global projection: 'each country seems to have a speciality.' Genre/nation is now directed both outward and inward, unlike many Japanese films of the 1950s and Taiwan of the 1980s, made primarily for foreign festivals. Mainland China, too, broke onto festival circuits largely on the robust, exotic appeal of the actress Gong Li, in films by the now mainstream directors Zhang Yimou and Chen Kaige. Today, domestic success may promise potential breakout to the region or the whole world (perhaps as a remake), because commercial norms are internalised, thoroughly saturating theatres of the globe.

A domestic hit may become a runaway international success because, after years of Hollywood domination, Asian films have recovered local appeal (see Chapters 1 and 2). Complementing this is an explosion of film festivals – no longer the preserve of the art cinema – and, crucially, festival/cable offerings, allowing greater familiarity with cinematic diversity and experimentation (see Chapter 6).

JAPANESE HORROR AND ITS PAN-ASIAN REVERBERATIONS

Historically, Japanese studios stood on solid genre foundations, with swordfight-laden period films (*jidai geki*), gangster pictures (yakuza or *ninkyo eiga*, chivalry pictures), melodramas and comedies (*kigeki*). Toho was known for its period films, Toei for yakuza, which appealed to students, and competed with Nikkatsu in the 1950s and 1960s for the rebellious youth market (known in Japan as the *après guerre* generation). Since the 1930s Shochiku was specialised in modern-day comedies, romances and women's pictures, and its longtime chairman Kido Shiro was actively promoted the so-called 'home drama'. As mentioned, Ozu was a stellar 'home drama' director for Shochiku. By the 1970s these distinct categories were in disarray because the studios, as cogs within entertainment and transport conglomerates, cut back on production in favour of other activities.[3] It was this disaffiliation of genre pictures that opened the door to more experimentation in horror genres, particularly in straight-to-video work.

Japanese horror films have a long history, tapping ghost tales and Buddhist sermons from the Edo period. They are traditionally low-budget, summer offerings without much ambition. Japanese horror has lately become more serious, at least compared to most international counterparts. Still low budget, with minimal effects, J-horrors plumb emotional depths rather than showing bodily mutilation. Gory special effects and rampaging monsters are infrequent, despite Godzilla and his reptile cousins. Contemporary Japanese horror is intimate and restrained, working on social, emotional and conceptual registers. Japanese concept-horror films have a simple, incisive premise. These shock, but do so in a piecemeal way, wherein evil's full extent dawns gradually. *The Ring* (*Ringu*, 1997): lethal videotape kills viewers a week after being watched, announced by the ring of a telephone. In this story, some of our most trusted devices inexplicably turn on us. *The Grudge* (*Ju-On*, 2002): Japanese house haunted by furious ghosts who turn their rage on anyone who darkens its door. *Pulse* (*Kairo*, 2001): the dead mingle and multiply in cyberspace, possibly eliminating humans (2006 remake by Wes Craven). *Chaos*: a clerk gets involved in a kidnapping and murder, then tries to figure out the sequence of events that dragged him into his predicament (optioned by Universal). *Premonition*: a newspaper that predicts the future. Japanese concept-horror is less *Texas Chainsaw* than *Blair Witch Project*, with small hints of incremental, anticipated dread. It is more intellectual, even aloof, unlike mainstream horror excess. Despite its scary mandate, Japanese concept-horror is subtle, with a variety of possible social causes for its disturbances. It therefore has an uncommonly topical element. Threats themselves are dispersed, not concentrated within a single malevolent being; ambient, seemingly random, and not completely disembodied, but resembling hazards pestilential, environmental, electronic, and social – fuelled even by rumour. Titles like *Pulse, Chaos, Charisma, Infection, Prophecy, Loft, Premonition, Parasite Eve, Cure, Sleeping Bride*, and *Reincarnation* indicate the films' hypodermic effects.

Why did horror become a flagship genre for contemporary Japanese film? Other genres should qualify, given the industry's unmatched productivity. Like the rest of East Asia, Japan is an affluent, postmodern country yet also remains somehow 'primeval'. Cutting-edge design, technology and fashion mix with compulsive fears of impurity and disorder, so Japanese phobias resonate with much refinement and deviance. In a comment on novelist Haruki Murakami, a Waseda University critic mentions 'the off-kilter, weird and uncertain feelings that remain in Japanese society' (Plate, 2006).

Still other factors justify the alignment of Japan with the horror genre. Consider this list from the 1990s (Table 5.2) when real-life horrors flourished in Japan. While selective, these events are a media *fin de siècle*, hints of rising unease about a grim millennium.

Economic bubble burst in the early 1990s
Kobe earthquake, 1995
Tokyo, Aum shinrikyo sarin attacks, 1995
Death of Atsumi Kiyoshi (beloved movie star, Tora-san), 1996
Death of Itami Juzo (by suicide), 1997
Hase Jun beheading case, 1997
Coup d'état at Shochiku studio, 1997
Festival prizes: Imamura Shohei's *The Eel* and Kawase Naomi's *Suzaku* at Cannes; Kitano Takeshi's *Fireworks* at Venice, 1997
Nagano Olympics, 1998
Death of Akira Kurosawa, 1998

Table 5.2 Disruptions in the 1990s, Japan

The new Heisei era in 1989 immediately brought a decade of severe economic and social dislocation. The stock market's plunge underlined the precariousness of high growth and the vulnerability of corporate social foundations. Prosperity was visible on paper only, without security and better living standards for the public. Paper riches also failed to provide much stimulation to the film industry, with the 1980s proving a nadir in both quality and quantity. In 1986 there were just twenty-four studio-made Japanese films (*Pacific Friend*, 2002: 19), this from an industry that for decades was among the top three film-producing countries in the world. The only bright spark was the work of Itami Juzo, whose satires lampooned the excesses of executives, bureaucrats and gangsters. Itami killed himself in 1997, hounded by tabloid charges of sexual impropriety.

Apocalyptic events like the sarin gas attack on Tokyo's mass transit system by a violent cult, the Aum shinrikyo, alternated with quiet atrocities like the Hase Jun case. In an affluent suburb, eleven-year-old Jun was beheaded. After placing the head on the school gate, the killer taunted police for days with riddles published in the local paper. It turned out to be a fourteen-year-old playmate and neighbourhood bully. Such senseless cruelty prompted much anxiety over public morals, but events like these made Japanese society not just threatening, but more dramatic. Crime, corruption, delinquency and outright menace became plausible as topical premises, and the phenomenon of *kireru* ('to snap') was widely remarked on. Though usually related to the pain of downsizing, *kireru* could infect anyone, even a schoolboy, whose patience was stretched beyond endurance by the pressures of living.

Kireru – running amok in the 1990s – was a touchstone image with the loss of lifetime employment and faith in public security. At Shochiku, the Okuyama faction, father and son, were sacked from the board in a shock rejection of their autocratic style. A sudden relapse to more consensual, conservative management meant innovations like Shochiku's Cinema Japanesque series, including auteur prizewinners *The Eel* (dir. Imamura Shohei, 1997) and *Sonatine* (dir. Kitano Takeshi, 1993), were doomed. These successes, despite global acclaim, brought little financial reward. The venerable, longsuffering Shochiku had had enough. The company had been losing money with the end of its signature Tora-san series, directed by Yamada Yoji. The forty-eight-episode series ended in 1996 with the death of Torajiro, played by the irrepressible Atsumi Kiyoshi. At the end of 1997 Shochiku recorded almost US$10 billion in losses. The *kireru* complex has great resonance in an over-regimented, hypertensive society beset by corporate–government collusion. This doesn't explain why J-horror made a smooth journey to US-made versions. Maybe Japanese concept-horror (like anime) is a recombinant narrative pattern with technological, millenarian resonance. Unlike classic ghost stories, J-horror films are not overwhelmingly supernatural but pull toward 'paramedical' impulses. Intriguing twists on the *kireru* idea are the art films *Eureka* (dir. Aoyama Shinji, 2000) and *Distance* (dir. Kore-eda Hirokazu, 2001); both explore post-traumatic stress, though neither are popular genre films. Going postal in a conformist society is a rich narrative lode for serious contemporary Japanese cinema and fiction, in many genres.

Slightly different are the films *Tomie*, *Uzumaki* ('whirlpool'), *Shikoku* ('deadland', wordplay on Shikoku, one of the Japanese home islands) and Korean films

Tale of Two Sisters and *Whispering Corridors*. These all resemble American horror, and feature high-school students' elaborate codes of exclusion, caught in hysterias connected to evil spirits. Alternatively, they may be self-generating delusions and paranoia. The lines between individual, social and environmental psychosis are porous. This makes the terror highly contagious. Merely seeing or hearing another person in terrible fright is enough to pass on the curse. But these films are surprisingly tender toward emanations of monstrosity, and they often reflect (being the fruit of) contemporary social problems: neglect, loneliness and ostracism. Monsters are symptoms, taking on scapegoat roles in a group-oriented conformist society. This vents expressions of cruelty toward social pariahs, and also pity and empathy, and much-suppressed paroxysms of revenge that monsters finally unleash. Like *The Ring*, Hideo Nakata's film *Dark Water* was remade in America (through Lee's Vertigo Entertainment) and it too explores truncated love in the family, centring on a single mother and the desolation of a child who loses her. Nakata has remarked on his ambivalent feelings toward horror and the film industry.

> I like the image of females who try hard to compete and live [out] their lives. At the same time, such females are the ones who contribute most to the family, though it may be a stereotyped image. Although it is not the melody of my works, 'broken family' has been the common base. As I get to know that, I'd like to make a film which focuses on it. But I know it would be difficult for me ... (Muzushi, 2002)

Nakata claims to have no special love or affinity for horror, having used it as a means to fund his independent documentary on the American director Joseph Losey. With the breakout success of *Ringu*, he was involved in numerous business negotiations over US projects. Nakata was even appointed to an agency screening projects suitable for American remakes. He was moved by a sense of abandonment and separation on his removal from a nurturing, but stifling, environment: the movie studio. For seven years Nakata had laboured at Nikkatsu, working as assistant on low-budget porn films, but then the company went under, and he left to go freelance. Rather than emancipation, he felt deflated, almost as if he had been dismissed. But Nakata's alienation from collective belonging prompted a determination to tell stories of thwarted desire, like those of Japanese graduates facing unemployment in a post-bubble economy. Losing control, disillusion, superfluity, abandonment – such turmoil became common currency in Japanese concept-horror. Accordingly, horror genres in Japan epitomise a social darkening, especially among the young. Japanese popular film is by now suffused with *kireru*, the breaking of spirits pulled too far.

Nakata also fears abrupt truncation in his own film projects, wherever he is working. This happened once in Japan; a producer suddenly pulled the plug, and the whole film was off. Even the reason for its cancellation was obscure. In the intensely capitalist, high-turnover Hollywood there is even more reason to fear creative emasculation: 'In the US, for example, if the movie star says, "Who's this Nakata?" a new director like me will be fired, as simple as that. I've heard that something like this frequently happens' (Muzushi, 2002). Nakata has no illusion that he is indispensable, or that a move to Hollywood spells greater security.

Ju-On v. The Grudge

Shimizu Takashi's *Ju-On* was sold to and produced by Sam Raimi and Rob Tapert's Ghost House Pictures, and *The Grudge* was its debut project. Raimi and Tapert, along with Ichise Taka of Entertainment Farm, were producers; Ichise also produced the original, along with *Ringu* and many other J-horror pictures. Roy Lee and Doug Davison, perennial remake brokers, received executive producer credits. Senator International (part of a German conglomerate) provided the finance, through Nathan Kahane. Ichise is a key figure here because he had a slate of J-horror pictures sold to Lions Gate Films, which successfully released *Ju-On* theatrically. Raimi saw it in Los Angeles and was very impressed by its meticulous direction and the strong effect it had on audience. In Japan, *Ju-On* was also successful, earning US$4.2 million on 120 screens. It was prefaced there by two instalments made for video. When the *Ju-On* remake deal was done, Ghost House and Senator were able to pre-sell distribution rights to twenty-seven territories worldwide, including Columbia in the US. This generated several million dollars for Senator up front, funds that could be spent on production. Compared to *The Ring*, *The Grudge* was low budget ($10 million), earning $40 million in its opening Halloween weekend and eventually a worldwide gross of $187 million. Though the Japanese *Ju-On* was considered a success, it brought in just US$3 million worldwide for Lions Gate Films (Box Office Mojo). The enormous box offices of J-horror remakes are given in Table 5.3.

How was this project different from *The Ring*? At DreamWorks, Gore Verbinski was hired to direct Naomi Watts in the lead and the story was removed from Tokyo to Seattle, USA. In such remakes, there are key substitutions in casting, location, and director. These reconstitute an original work to address and play in a brand new market. With high regard for the original, Ghost House decided to transpose, not substitute, many of the elements that made the Japanese film compelling. Thus, there was some translucence, with Japanese source material hiding behind American transposition. Using the same director, Takashi Shimizu, and the same setting, *The Grudge* preys on its source, with echoes and recollection, not just reconstruction of the original. Of this decision, Raimi said:

Title	Prod Yr	Director	Worldwide Box office/US$
The Ring	2002	Gore Verbinski	249,348,933
The Ring 2	2005	Nakata Hideo	161,451,538
The Grudge	2004	Shimizu Takashi	187,281,115
The Grudge 2	2006	Shimizu Takashi	59,209,234
Chaos	2005	Jonathan Glazer	*1,063,601
Pulse	2006	Wes Craven	25,350,824
Dark Water	2005	Walter Salles	49,483,352

Sources:
Data compiled from Box Office Mojo website ('Movies').
*US and France box office only.

Table 5.3 Worldwide Box-Office J-horror Remakes

> My goal was in trying to preserve what [Shimizu] had done. I had a hand in the casting, I had a hand in the script, along with my partners and a hand in the editing, choosing the sound designer, the composer ... And, you know, lining up the proper mix and trying to, if necessary, protect the vision of the director from outside influences that American commerce in the film business seems to impose upon filmmakers. (Otto, 2004)

The same house, neighbourhood and background characters provide some indexical connections. The production strategy highlights the process of cultural and industrial sifting needed to get the remake across. The original story never does specify the root cause of the grudge. Perhaps it is a generic syndrome typical of an increasingly impersonal, automated society like Japan. For unknown reasons, the Japanese family committed multiple murder and suicide. Obscurely, the house produces ghosts who attack those who approach, who enter the orbit of the grudge. Thus, a connection emerges between congestive heart failure within the Japanese family and intense peer pressure among high-school girls.[4] A remake that echoes its source evokes the traces carried from earlier lives. In effect it reincarnates another presence, which is not only appropriate to a horror film but also promotes haunting, cross-cultural effects. These contact points provide a synapse or connection through which seeds of fear may travel.

The Grudge's protagonists are American, yet their story happens in the Japanese capital, a typically Japanese but foreign neighbourhood. Tokyo's famous sights and five-star facades are absent. *The Grudge* lurks in quieter, everyday Japan, a place of ordinary confusions and problems. The Americans in the haunted house are on an extended overseas contract, a reluctant diaspora of computer technicians serving global markets. A telling scene in a Japanese market has Jennifer, the American wife (Clea DuVall) examining some instant noodles. She cannot decipher anything about the package, not even a picture, so she discreetly tears the label for a peek. Her helpless behaviour infantilises her, but she also realises this, conveying vulnerability and chagrin. This is in tune with the picture's genre, perhaps more even than the all-Japanese original, given its strange cultural mixture.

Shimizu's American remake adds diabolical hints about monoculture blithely inhabited by most Japanese, to them ubiquitous and invisible. To American outsiders, it is palpably menacing. In *The Grudge*, Japan is bland, pedestrian, routine, a rejection of postcard views, insidiously alienating and depleting. Steven Susco's script is also less episodic, weaving various strands that link the victims. On the mechanics of remaking the original Japanese film, Susco said:

> In this case, what was difficult about it was also what was good about it, which is that we had three separate films from which to pull material and then while the script was being developed we ended up having a fourth film, as well (to draw from). It was certainly difficult to figure out what we wanted to use out of all that material, but it was beneficial to have that much material. For me, the biggest challenge was to try to find a way to keep the essence of what Takashi was doing with his movies and, at the same time, trying to layer in my own original ideas, especially since Takashi was going to direct my version. I wanted to be very, very respectful and give him the kind of script that he wanted to make. This was a story that he has directed four different permutations of and I was going to be writing the fifth essentially that he was going to direct. So there was this question of how much do I want to keep in there from his original films versus how many new original ideas do I want to try to find so that he is not shooting the exact same scenes that he shot before? At the end of the day, the process was more exciting and creative than it was daunting. (Grove, 2004)

It's also more frankly sexual, with the star Sarah Michelle Gellar enjoying active relations with her Japan-struck mate (Jason Behr). The cross-cultural infatuation with an American teacher leads to the Saeki family tragedy, and in turn initiates the grudge itself.

Another parallel is with Shimizu's own experience of the film industry. When beginning as an assistant director in 1990, he was bullied on the set, which was 'a common way of showing new players how low down the food chain they were,' explains Shimizu (Ryall, 2006). As noted, such experiences lead to the *kireru* complex, symptomatic of regimented, hierarchical workplaces. At the time, the apprentice system in the Japanese film industry was practically extinct, already yielding to independent, self-reliant modes of production.

J-horror was not just attractive to Hollywood but was regionally successful. For a long time, Japanese cinema was eclipsed in East Asia but J-horror began to multiply in the box offices of Taiwan, Hong Kong and even South Korea. In Taiwan, for instance, *Ringu* earned more than US$1.58 million (NT$50.8 million) and nearly NT$27 million for the sequel. Box-office records like these were usually taken by major Hollywood releases. Soon, other film-makers and producers capitalised on J-horror and began to make horror films with local characteristics. Peter Chan's Applause Pictures based its business plan on the economy and popularity of horror (see Chapter 4) with two ghost series: *The Eye* and *Three*. Hong Kong auteur Ann Hui's *Visible Secret* (Media Asia, 2001) and its sequel (2002) exploited it too. Mavericks Johnnie To and Wai Ka-fai (see Chapter 2) made *My Left Eye Sees Ghosts* (One Hundred Years of Film, 2002), a touching revival of Chinese ghost tales. There were many South Korean spin-offs, the so-called K-horror wave. Taiwan also came up with horror thrillers *Double Vision* (dir. Chen Kuo-fu, Columbia-Asia, 2002), *The Heirloom* (dir. Leste Chen, Three Dots, 2005) and *Silk* (dir. Su Chao-bin, CMC Entertainment, 2006).

According to Winnie Chung, managing director of Golden Scene, J-horror was a new business opportunity in Hong Kong. At a time when local films showed a visible decline in both creative energy and audience support, distributors needed to explore fresh content to keep audiences at the cinema. Chung had been publicist and distributor at Golden Harvest. Aware of the *Ringu* phenomenon, she wanted to acquire Nakata's film for Golden Harvest. But the company was unsure. Chung decided to press ahead anyway, without company support. *Ringu*'s impressive US$4 million take in Hong Kong afforded Chung her own firm standing in the business. Horror pictures have since been the house specialty for her Golden Scene. The company's wide distribution slate was enabled by the success of J-horror's distinctive signature. After *Ringu*, Golden Scene collaborated with Applause Pictures on marketing its first pan-Asian horror, *The Eye*, which recorded solid box office of over US$1.68 million (HK$13 million). Golden Scene is now established as the leading independent distributor and publicist in Hong Kong and owes its success to the popularity of horror films. The case of Golden Scene shows J-horror's impact on a pan-Asian and international scale, reverberating around the globe.

MARTIAL ARTS, MEGA GENRE

Another genre that has proven itself even more expansive in East Asian screens is martial arts, the definitive Asian genre.

'Mega genre' is more than genre; it is, rather, a super-category. Martial arts personifies East Asia itself for many Westerners, and to many fans in the region. In Chinese-language film, martial arts are not easily constrained. They are everywhere, and they often appear without warning, in places high and low. With weapons or without, martial arts infiltrated other narrative vehicles: mystery, thriller, soft porn, sports, horror/ghost, cooking and gambling films, and of course comedy. This partly explains why martial arts, as genre and as action style, continues as a staple of Chinese screen industries. Like Japanese *jidai geki*, they have a long history, periodically waxing and waning. We might call Chinese martial arts vernacular, part of the everyday expectations of audiences, whatever the genre. Its diversity is sustained, unlike *jidai geki*, through wide genre applications – in comedy, fantasy, even melodrama – as well as the martial arts genre proper. It is not only cultural factors that explain Chinese martial arts' adaptability, but industrial ones. Unlike *jidai geki*, martial arts was transformed and repackaged as a brand-name by Hong Kong and Chinese diaspora film-makers. So far, only three Chinese-made films have reached genuine global success (with over US$100 million). These are *Crouching Tiger, Hidden Dragon* (2000), *Hero* (2002) and *Kung Fu Hustle* (2004) – all are martial arts pictures. Martial arts' ready serviceability, their sheer quantity and genre tie-ins with Chinese vernacular culture qualify this style as 'mega genre'.

A Historical Overview

Martial arts, like opera film, belongs to national popular culture. One of the first Chinese martial arts films was *Burning the Red Lotus Temple* made in Shanghai, 1928. This was not an original story, but based on popular martial arts fiction of the same title. The screen adaptation of popular serials published in newspapers and magazines almost guaranteed good returns at the box office. This film went to become the first Chinese film serial, with over a dozen instalments. Dubbed 'shengguai wuxia pian' (magic spirit picture; Zhang, 2005: 55), *Burning Temple* illustrates the fusion of the supernatural with martial arts, paving the way for martial arts' adaptations, proving its flexibility for transfiguration and border-crossing. Embedded in popular fantasy, martial arts was judged sensational and inappropriate by the authorities of the just-formed Republic of China. Beginning in 1931, the right-wing Nationalist government banned further production for several years to protect the masses from excessive exposure.

After the civil war, the PRC Communist Party was even more suspicious of martial arts' fantastic, superstitious charm. Between 1949 and the late 1970s, the genre almost vanished from the mainland, like most samurai pictures during the American occupation of Japan, 1945–52. The ban, however, did not stop Chinese film-makers returning to their sources. Martial arts survived and flourished by migrating first to Hong Kong and later emerging in Taiwan. In Hong Kong, from the 1950s to the 1970s it was a staple for both independent and major studios and for both Mandarin- and local Cantonese-language produc-

Donnie Yen in *Iron Monkey* (1993)

tion. For example, the Wong Fei-hong series entertained Cantonese-language audiences throughout the whole region. Overall, 127 Cantonese-language martial arts features were completed in the 1950s and 250 pictures were released in the 1960s (Yu, 1997: 31, 38). Shaw Brothers, Hong Kong's leading studio of the 1960s and 1970s, with its in-house Fordist mode, took the rationalisation of martial arts to great lengths and produced hundreds of boilerplate action films. Golden Harvest capitalised on rival Shaws' weakness by offering an independent producer contract to a talented martial artist just returned from the US. With Warner Bros., it backed Bruce Lee to reach a huge international audience through several kung fu pictures, representing a major diversification of martial arts. According to Hong Kong critic Sek Kei, Lee rejuvenated Hong Kong film through his fusion of Cantonese and Mandarin cinemas, the impact of television and his enormous appeal to Western viewers that took Hong Kong films onto international platforms (Kwok and Ng, 2006: 79). After Lee's premature death, Golden Harvest promoted Jackie Chan and made him a regional star via a series of kung fu slapstick comedies.

In East Asia, martial arts' proliferation and predominance is due partly to the genre's organic tie to vernacular cultures. Popular martial arts fiction, folk legends or historical figures were ready source material to the industry. In Taiwan, martial arts was the leading film genre in the 1970s, and the basis of a profitable export industry. Martial arts' industrial significance in Taiwan is shown by the fact that more than half of the releases in the late 1970s were martial arts (Yeh, 2006: 163). *Crouching Tiger, Hidden Dragon* is an adaptation from a serialised novel of the 1930s. As noted, Hong Kong's Wong Fei-hong exemplifies martial arts' attachment to durable folk legends. The Wong Fei-hong series ran continuously for nearly eighty instalments between the late 1940s and 1970s. In the 1970s, Taiwan writer Ku Long was known for his prolific fiction and a touch of intrigue, mystery and eroticism. He was signed by Shaws to help launch the second wave of martial arts film. In the 1990s Hong Kong director Tsui Hark and Jet Li remade Wong Fei-hong and created a five-picture series. Spin-offs from this numbered at least a dozen. In the twenty-first century we have *Fearless* (Ronny Yu, 2005), a biopic about Huo Yuanjia, the early twentieth-century founder of the Chinese Jingwu Athletic Association. *Hero* (2002) is also loosely based on a historical figure, Jin Ke, whose failed assassination of China's first emperor was considered a political lesson. *Hero* boasts not only educational but fine production values, duly noted by Disney: 'The great thing about *Hero* is that it does deliver all things to all men and women,' said Daniel Battsek of Buena Vista International. 'When we first showed it at screenings to all audiences, people took what they wanted from it. If they wanted a beautiful, sensitive, artier movie, it delivered; if they wanted phenomenal fight sequences, it delivered as well' (Minns, 2004).

Because of their vernacular roots, martial arts proliferated, and became a recognised national genre aligned with cultural China. Even when it waned in the cinema, it was easily reproduced and brought to television. In the 1980s when Taiwan and Hong Kong cinema shifted to art films, gangster and gunplay thrillers, martial arts was resilient. In Taiwan and Hong Kong, martial arts primetime drama was tremendously popular. Hong Kong martial arts television series were a sensation in Taiwan in the late 1970s and marked the first time Hong Kong television found a lucrative market outside the territory (Curtin, 2007). Martial arts was a staple of TV production in both Taiwan and Hong Kong, in both independent and studio sectors until the late 1990s. When Hong Kong and Taiwan audiences no longer enjoyed TV martial arts, it found new life on the mainland. Film and television do not exhaust its fertility, as it proliferates electronic games, comics and popular fiction. Martial arts is an indomitable genre, just like its heroes. But what makes it so recognisably Chinese lies in its stars, not just the large production numbers. These performers are loved in Chinese-speaking areas and around the world, far beyond any crossover of Japanese martial arts stars – Toshiro Mifune (Kurosawa's leading man) would be nearest, and he is no match for the popularity of Chinese martial artists.

Stars and Genre: Bruce Lee, Jackie Chan and Jet Li

Each of these stars carries a specific national/ethnic trajectory, as well as their own distinct star persona. Bruce Lee, the magnetic pole of martial arts, was born in Hong Kong to a movie family, and even appeared in Cantonese films as a child.

He spent his youth in the US and there bitter experiences in television drove him back to Hong Kong. With Golden Harvest and American distribution, he conquered the world. There was a time when Bruce Lee was the biggest movie star on earth, universally appealing to every nationality and race. As a performer Lee radiated magic, perhaps confirming authorities' earlier fears of martial arts superstition. Audiences familiar with martial arts were enthralled, as were those in the West and beyond, all utterly taken by Bruce Lee's feral charisma.

Lovable Jackie Chan represents Hong Kong and, particularly, traditional folk arts of opera, acrobatics and elaborate stunt work. Bringing comic elements into martial arts gave Chan appeal in Hong Kong at a time when people were confronted with prospects of rejoining the mainland. He was also embraced in Japan and, eventually, the US. Like Bruce Lee, Chan appealed to African Americans and other minorities though he lacked Lee's anti-establishment attitude. The Jackie Chan style, as indebted to Buster Keaton as to Peking Opera, opposes the ferocious Bruce Lee persona. While Lee portrayed himself as a deadly Chinese hero, Chan belongs to everyone – funny, endearing and nearly harmless (in his early films, no one, not even villains, gets killed). Jet Li is the 'civil servant' of the three stars. As a bona fide champion of Chinese *wushu* while still a teenager, he soon made an impression in the Hong Kong film industry, starring in *Shaolin Temple* (1982). Unlike Lee and Chan, Jet Li exploited the European market, joining Luc Besson for *Kiss of the Dragon* (2001) and *Danny the Dog* (2005). Between these films, *Lethal Weapon 4* (1998, his first American film), *Romeo Must Die* (2000), *Hero* and *Fearless*, Li eventually won European not just pan-Chinese acclaim. All three stars remain internationally recognised, with great longevity in physical training and dramatic roles. Like genre/nation itself, each star has a provenance connecting them to their respective industries: the Hong Kong show-business diaspora (Lee), acrobatic folk opera (Chan) and mainland athletic gymnastics, or *wushu* (Li).

Both Bruce Lee and Jackie Chan share some common virtues with respect to martial arts: they are both unsurpassed in hand-to-hand combat, in superb condition and renowned for sheer inventiveness in choreography and set pieces. Not even auteur masters like King Hu or Zhang Che can rival their matchless exuberance of form and movement. Of course, it's their personae that makes the difference to genre, for instance, Bruce Lee's grim tenacity, all the more poignant given his ill-fated death in 1973 which brought enduring apotheosis. It also forestalled any return to Hollywood, plying his trade in second-rate films the way Jackie Chan and Jet Li have done. Jackie Chan and Jet Li both became worldwide action heroes, but their martial arts were diluted in Western projects, a casualty of their success. Jackie Chan advanced his legacy further, with startling out-takes of mis-timed stunts, harrowing falls and fluffed lines. Not only does this accentuate the danger of Chan's more daring acrobatics, proving his refusal to relinquish to stunt doubles; it fulfils another key side of his persona, decent, hardworking and fallible. Jackie Chan is willing to break the superhero illusion to show the backbreaking work of choreography, sets and stunts. Like a magician revealing a trick, Chan exposes his endearing personality and willingness to risk his life for the cause.

Bruce Lee's significance in emerging genre/nation that he brings authentic, teachable martial arts skills to cinema. Alongside real performance, Lee represents a pedagogical impulse. His own martial arts hybrid, *jeet kun do*, had a personal conviction worthy of philosophical devotion, as well as animal magnetism with mystical appeal. This authenticity is a correction to sometimes inauthentic action sequences in Chinese cinema. If early attempts appeared phony, it was often poor technical choices that failed martial artists, with wrong camera placement, misapplied editing, and other shortcomings. In the 1950s, the nineteenth-century figure Wong Fei-hong was committed to the screen in scores of films, revitalising the Cantonese-language film industry. Star Kwan Tak-hing was a practising martial artist, but the techniques used by local directors often blunted his impact onscreen. King Hu's *Come Drink With Me* (Hong Kong/Shaws, 1966) and *Dragon Gate Inn* (Taiwan/Union, 1967) heralded a real fusion of authentic period detail, meticulous action choreography and the operatic orchestration of shots in colour and widescreen. Concurrently, Shaws director Zhang Che moved martial arts toward an aggressive, macho genre of confrontation and homo-social swagger, employing house stars David Chiang and Ti Lung. In the hands of Zhang, martial arts film was a catchall, casually combining fists, feet and swordfights with more exotic weapons, like flying guillotines. Also on offer were optical tricks, post-synchronised sound effects and spectacular scenes of torture and bloodletting. These films of the 1960s and 70s, like *One-Armed Swordsman*, *Boxer from Shantung*, *Blood Brothers*, *Vengeance*, and scores more, flowed directly into the romantic gangster fantasies of John Woo in the 1980s. Whereas John Woo's films were idiosyncratic, Zhang's studio pictures for Shaws were highly conventional and serialised, making up in sheer volume what they lacked in conviction or authenticity.

The industrial key to East Asian martial arts films is that they are spectacle-driven. They may have absorbing, meticulously crafted narratives, but at bottom they are not story-dependent. Their versatility and visual excitement make them highly valued in the global marketplace, despite and sometimes because of their Chinese roots. Their spectacular display, without needing millions for special effects, suits martial arts pictures for low-budget and developing film industries – not just in East Asia, but wherever young audiences seek intense kinetic stimulation. Martial arts, therefore, became the template for Chinese film in global popular culture, breaking out from B-movies into multiplexes, television and animation. Eventually, they may not even seem particularly Chinese any more.

Meanwhile, in Japan martial arts have seen a resurgence; but they don't match the global popularity of Chinese screen martial arts. Japanese martial arts films belong primarily to *jidai geki* period drama, pictures set in the seventeenth to nineteenth centuries, which depict samurai, the sword-wielding warrior class. In sheer numbers, period films were once preponderant in Japanese cinema. Derived from classic chivalry tales and morality plays, they portray exquisite ethical dilemmas and refined sensibilities, as well as spectacular swordplay. Accordingly, Japanese martial arts are about particular figures in the historical or literary record, quite segregated from other genres; only in certain circumstances do samurai, daimyo, ninja and other Japanese martial artists appear. There are exceptions, where merchants, gamblers and lovers are protagonists, or loyal warriors and masterless ronin appear in fantasy films, or tales of time-travel. In general, though, Japanese martial arts genres are specific, occupying a rich but hermetic world. Nonetheless, *jidai geki* and samurai pictures have assisted the revival of Japanese genre pictures, signalling the genre's resilience and versatility. They appealed to younger viewers, evolving to meet the preferences of contemporary audiences – one key change is a 'gamer' sensibility that samurai and ninja films now display. For example, 2005's *Shinobi* (dir. Shimoyama Ten), a hit ninja picture that earned US$15 million and combines martial arts with love story; in 2003 there was *Azumi*, another manga-like female swordplay fantasy. Both these films look and play like videogames, punctuated with romantic interludes. Others include *Owl's Castle*, *Samurai Resurrection* and the occult-themed *Yin-Yang Master* (*Onmyoji*, dir. Takita Yojiro, 2001, part two released 2003). Re-packaging or rejuvenating Japanese cinema for younger generations requires integration with other kinds of platform, like comics, games, internet and mobile phones. The process hastens re-invention of popular cinema itself within the Japanese context.

Old-fashioned 'humanist' samurai pictures were successfully released also: *Twilight Samurai* (2002) and *The Hidden Blade* (2004). These character studies were directed by Yamada Yoji, of Shochiku's Tora-san series. A third film, *Love and Honor*, out-grossed the latest James Bond, *Casino Royale*, in its opening weekend (Gray, 2006c). This had the honour of starring SMAP superstar Kimura Takuya, whose first feature film was Wong Kar-wai's futuristic *2046* (see Chapter 6). *The Samurai I Loved* was directed by Kurotsuchi Mitsu (2005), and all these films were based on the period fiction of Fujisawa Shuhei. *Twilight Samurai* was nominated for an Academy Award, and these quiet costume pictures have the elegiac, pacifist mood of Fujisawa's stories set in the last days of the Tokugawa shogunate. Whether laden with nostalgia, or tricked-up digitally,

Japanese martial arts have flowed in distinct tributaries, one for fantasy-spectacle, and another for traditional costume drama with serious historical themes.

Kung Fu Hustle

Stephen Chow's comedies are flamboyant genre send-ups. His new films provide spectacular physical action with broad humour, and push Chinese martial arts into new digital forms. They use martial arts as a springboard to broader entertainment appeal, capitalising on Chinese-language cinemas' perennial employment of martial arts – their adaptability in vernacular situations in many genres and media. Chow assimilates martial arts conventions with CGI effects (computer-generated imagery), pop culture nostalgia and Western detritus. Martial arts are stretched outward, showing the mega-generic aspects of the form. *Kung Fu Hustle* advances this by touching on other, seemingly incongruous genres, like melodrama, musicals and animated cartoons. These generic experiments started in *Shaolin Soccer* (2002, see Chapter 2) and developed in the 2004 hit *Kung Fu Hustle*. Compared to *Shaolin Soccer*, *Kung Fu Hustle* is more saturated in the traditions and treasures of martial arts. It draws source material from martial arts fiction, martial arts schools and styles, referencing Bruce Lee and Cantonese magic-spirit pictures, a popular subgenre of the 1960s.

Kung Fu Hustle (2004), martial arts sendup

The story begins with a bickering landlord couple who love to terrorise their poor tenants. The couple alludes to the pair Yang Guo and Xiao Longnü, created by writer Louis Cha in his 1959 *The Return of the Condor Heroes* (aka *The Great Eagle and Its Companion*). This novel has been adapted for television and film screens many times and is a household-name martial arts romance. Besides drawing on vernacular fiction, *Kung Fu Hustle* introduces several leading forms and schools of martial arts. The film's action sequences have some ingenious performances. The foul-tempered couple consists of two retired martial artists. The husband is a Tai Chi master while the bitchy wife uses a rare 'lion roaring' kung fu. These two forms also match their personalities – Tai Chi is a subtle, but very effective defensive technique (cf. *Pushing Hands*, Ang Lee's first film in 1992) and the husband is presented as a spineless, hen-pecked man. His obnoxious wife, on the contrary, roars like a lioness to show her ferocious power. Meanwhile, among the poor tenants there are hidden three very skilful, righteous warriors. Again, the film uses these three characters as emblems of more specialised martial forms. Disguised as a noodle man, one specialises in bamboo-cane combat. He wields his noodle cane like a chef, rapidly scattering enemies as if making flour into dough. A 'sissy' tailor is a master of flying iron rings. A coolie with strong legs takes offenders down with his powerful, deadly kicks. Comic business is done with the martial arts' vernacular. Even the blind musicians excel in magical martial arts. Their instruments are lethal weapons that use timbre and vibration to kill. Each of these specific, incredible martial arts can be traced either to previous pictures, fiction or real martial arts.

The final battle between Chow and the Fire-cloud Beast resurrects the ghost of Bruce Lee and pays tribute to Cantonese classics. After a seemingly fatal encounter with the Beast, Chow descends from the sky, posed like a Buddha. This refers to *The Young Swordsman Lung Kim Fei* (dir. Ling Yun, 1964), with its outlandish use of fantasy, animated robots, flying rings and the Million Buddha Palm. Chow as Bruce Lee as a reincarnated Buddha, serenely waving away hundreds of attackers like so many flies, is an image of pop cultural condensation.

To authenticate martial arts in all its variety, Chow casts real-life experts. Fire-cloud Beast is played by former stuntman and action choreographer Leung Siu-lung. Other characters in the film are martial arts instructors, opera performers, dance instructors and even a real Shaolin monk. This gives the cast a fresh look, even though all are (or used to be) show-business veterans.

Chow's elaboration of martial arts goes on. *Kung Fu Hustle* presents martial arts as an ingredient in a soufflé of movie references. The dancing axe gang is a blend of Hollywood musical (à la *Top Hat*) and gangster burlesque. Genre, finance and technology are smoothly folded into a savoury concoction. There are layers of cross-cultural and historical reference, with material from

Hong Kong's treasury of film and theatre. The premise borrows from a Cantonese classic, *The House of 72 Tenants*, about a poor ghetto terrorised by landlords. Tenants band together to defy their tormentors, including the authorities (police, fire department) corrupted by greed. This was first performed as a standup comedy review, then a stage play mounted in Shanghai. The property made the transition to film at least twice, first in 1950 (dir. Zheng Xiaoqiu, Cooperative Huaji Theatre), then remade in Guangzhou as a co-production in 1963 (dir. Wang Weiyi for Zhujiang-Hongtu studios). At that time, the mainland film bureau ruled the film could be made but only in Cantonese, not Mandarin or Shanghainese, thus paving the way to distribution of mainland movies overseas. Within a few years, the film was condemned in China during the Cultural Revolution. In Hong Kong, Hongtu handled the film's release where it was a solid hit, partly because setting and language had been shifted from Shanghai to Guangzhou, and performed in Cantonese (Chi, 2006).

In Hong Kong *The House of 72 Tenants* made yet another transition. It became a box-office smash in its 1973 colour version (dir. Chor Yuen) and brought a renaissance of Cantonese comedy in the following two decades. It returned HK$5.6 million for Shaw Brothers, outstripping Bruce Lee's *Enter the Dragon* at HK$5.3m. The director, who became a force in martial arts pictures, remembered this well, since Run Run Shaw was so happy that he drank too much (Kwok and Ng, 2006: 43). Though it was conceived as a way to introduce TVB television stars to movie audiences, there remains a socialist message about the excesses of capitalist greed, which Stephen Chow then twists into sympathy for his underdog heroics and martial arts.

The use of wirework, familiar to fans of martial arts films, becomes a type of intertextual wirework or substrate in Chow's film. Like subtle nods and allusions used by Hollywood writers, Chow's scriptwriting is of a high order, deftly borrowing generic conventions, character arcs and narrative twists. On the basis of this well-structured material, financing came from Columbia Pictures-Asia, the same corporate sponsor of the *Crouching Tiger* benchmark. Rumours circulate about Chow going to Columbia executives with a one-page outline, expecting to open an account for production. This improvisational approach used to be standard operating procedure in the Hong Kong film industry. Instead, at Columbia Chow was told to return with a complete script – only then would there be instructions about releasing funds (Holson, 2006).

The action's technical wizardry gratifies viewers who might not catch the nostalgia cues. As a tight 'fusion of story and technology', gags and fight scenes are backed by digital effects, which function to 'enhance the overall presentation', not overwhelming performance or narrative. A comic sequence has Chow bitten on the lips by a pair of snakes. A CGI 'wire frame' was made up, into which photographs of face and serpents were composited. These were matched then inserted into the edited sequence. Spectacular gags are not the only use of computer-generated visuals. Changes in scale or simple colour corrections are digitally manipulated, freeing film-makers from building models or waiting for the sun. The digital effects on *Kung Fu Hustle* were done by Centro Digital; it took over eight months to produce 550 shots. The company also did effects work for the *Kill Bill* films, drastically reducing the cost of Tarantino's martial arts pastiche. Not only cost, but the fact Centro and other digital post-production houses are based in Hong Kong – and, increasingly, mainland China – means the work is accomplished by people who know what martial arts should look like. This underlying synthetic 'wirework' between digital imaging and Chinese action choreography means greater value and integration into world cinema production (So, 2005).

Still, *Kung Fu Hustle* resists outright homogenisation. The film's humour is edgy and often violent. Chow's film is fully funded by Columbia-Asia and larded with nods to both Hong Kong and Hollywood; it is nonetheless black comedy and rather sadistic. The opening scene includes spitting on a stricken policeman and blasting a gangster's moll point blank, after a kindly reassurance, 'I never shoot women.' Like characters in Tex Avery or Warner Bros. cartoons, there is much pain and humiliation. Chow's sidekick plunges a knife deep into his leg, then his back, then his shoulder. If it's funny once, then repeat. Fire-cloud Beast smashes Chow's face so hard he drives him deep into the ground, like a pile driver. Of course, the blows keep coming. A group of bullies urinates on a boy's head after he tests his kung fu to save a schoolgirl. In the US, such nastiness stays in R-rated comedies. The toilet humour is mainstream Hong Kong, which, like its martial arts, comes fast and loose, with shocks, knocks and doubtful taste. Despite changing audience tastes in Hong Kong, its box office of US$7.8 million (HK$61 million) made it the year's biggest film accumulated in a continuous run of forty-seven days. To add to the local success was its record in China – grossing US$20 million. In the end, *Kung Fu Hustle* set a global record of US$101 million, next to *Crouching Tiger, Hidden Dragon* and *Hero*. Big budget, impressive digital effects and the brash energy of Stephen Chow, backed by the marketing of a Hollywood studio – all combined to make *Kung Fu Hustle* the top performer not only in Chinese-speaking territories but on a global scale.

CONCLUSION

In one film, we see the incredible fertility and flexibility of Chinese martial arts. *Kung Fu Hustle* may be a little too prolix, sacrificing ethical seriousness and athletic discipline for comic pursuits. But its astonishing capacity, embracing shards of Westerns, musicals, animation, and famous passages from martial arts fiction, displays martial arts' inclusiveness as a mega-generic category. If one allows for Japanese martial arts, including not only *jidai geki*, with their swordsmen and ninja, but judo and kendo, as well as action formula like the violent hoodlum cycles of Sonny Chiba, it's possible to advance some expansive propositions about East Asian genres.

Martial arts in all forms represent paths for industrial design that do not rely on massive capital outlay. Instead, the genre relies on ingenious physical, spatial displays of agility and speed. These are inexpensive, and astonishing. While some appropriations of martial arts are bound up with extravagant digital effects, martial arts spectacle is best when digital-free – thus lowering barriers to entry – just as it is independent of intricate narrative construction. As a physical feat of athletic skill based on real-time human combat, martial arts is a mega-genre with multiple applications. There are any number of films, television series and videogames where this potential is visible in the West, but it has special prospects in Southeast and South Asian industries, where East Asian genres may provide guidance in strengthening popular film and cultural production. But it's not just martial arts, but other genres from East Asia that are travelling far.

If martial arts are globally extensive, then East Asian horror is intensive. We have seen how J-horror has been employed by DreamWorks and other Hol-

Nostalgic, humanist martial arts: *Love and Honor* (Japan)

lywood companies for creative stimulation, citing 'one world market' rationales for options on remakes of East Asian pictures, in pursuit of huge profit margins. In principle, one world market is multilateral, and allows consumer access to a variety of national cinemas through proliferating distribution channels. As Hollywood majors are an oligopoly on global flows, they are preponderant in the release of would-be blockbusters – for now. The mechanism, though, can feed back to the source. The fact that Hollywood finds East Asian source-genres attractive, with hits like *Ringu*, *Ju-On* or *Dark Water* as well as *Infernal Affairs, Il Mare* and *My Wife Is a Gangster*, lets consumers seek these out in their original forms. They might do this through festivals (Chapter 6) or through increasingly specialised cable channels and online access to films, rather than internet movie databases and newsgroups. Another consequence of East Asian genre diffusion is a further attention to former national valences. Shochiku's *Twilight Samurai* and *Love and Honor*, melodramatic elegies for the doomed samurai world, are exemplary. As the global market for theatrical films contracts, it also becomes more diversified, creating new tastes and niches closer to local cultural material. If Western audiences now access and enjoy East Asian genre pictures, if only through remakes, soon East Asian consumers will rediscover the archive of their own national cinemas, catalysed by regional consolidation and competition.

NOTES

1. Qualification: *Rashomon* was seen as an oddity in Japan, certainly not an orthodox *jidai geki*. That it won the grand prize at Venice only confirmed for executives at Daiei and audiences in Japan that Kurosawa's style seemed very 'Western'.
   In Europe and America, Kurosawa's films, despite their driving action, seemed very Japanese. Other *jidai geki* honoured in the West were not just samurai pictures; they include literary adaptation *The Tale of Genji* (Yoshimura Kozaburo, 1951, nominated for Grand Prix, Cannes in 1952), romantic epic *Gate of Hell* (Kinugasa Teinosuke, 1953, Grand Prix, Cannes in 1954) as well as *Seven Samurai* (Kurosawa, 1954). In 1954 *Seven Samurai* shared the Venice Silver Lion with Mizoguchi's *Sansho the Bailiff*, a period film/melodrama with a strong humanist message. Because of *Rashomon*, potboiler genres like *jidai geki* became associated with modernist, though still exotic overtones.
2. Western discoveries of great Japanese directors in the 1960s corresponded to the auteur theory, which was itself a response to European affirmation of distinct signatures in the mostly anonymous studio system of Hollywood.
3. Further reading on Japanese genres should include: McRoy, Jay (ed.) (2005), *Japanese Horror Cinema*, Edinburgh: Edinburgh University Press; Schilling, Mark

(1999), *Contemporary Japanese Film*, New York: Weatherhill; Richie, Donald (1989), 'Japanese Film', Ed. Duus, P., *The Cambridge History of Japan 6: The Twentieth Century*, Cambridge: Cambridge University Press. See also Silver, Alain (2005), *The Samurai Film*, Woodstock/New York: Overlook Press; Davis, Darrell William (1996), *Picturing Japaneseness: Monumental Style, National Identity, Japanese Film*, New York: Columbia University Press. For more specialised studies see Yoshimoto, Mitsuhiro (2000), *Kurosawa: Film Studies and Japanese Cinema*, Durham, NC: Duke University Press; Prince, Stephen (1991), *The Warrior's Camera: The Cinema of Akira Kurosawa*, Princeton, NJ: Princeton University Press; Bordwell, David (1988), *Ozu and the Poetics of Cinema*, Princeton, NJ: Princeton University Press and Nöel Burch's historical survey, from a semiotics-of-culture perspective, in his (1979) *To the Distant Observer: Form and Meaning in the Japanese Cinema*, Berkeley, CA: University of California Press.

4. On their way to the graveyard, Karen and Doug pass three schoolgirls on the street – a reference to Izumi and her friends Chiharu and Miyuki from the original film. This subplot was dropped from the American version. IMDB trivia item.

6

Festivals, Events and Players

A major development in the twenty-first century has been the rise of film festivals as showcases, marketplaces and cultural events. Like elsewhere in the world, Asian film festivals of all kinds are proliferating. They are prime cultural and commercial events – sites for the activities of cultural bureaucrats, governments and international corporations. Today film festivals in Asia compete with each other, not just in programming but also for prime slots in the calendar. Festival directors must ensure their schedules do not clash with the major events of Cannes, Venice, Berlin, Park City and the American Film Market. Given this, we may argue that film festivals have moved beyond their traditional role as gatekeepers of the art of cinema and ventured onto a new international field of transactions in film co-production, investment, promotion and exhibition. Successful festivals tirelessly revamp themselves to maintain a unique regional, and possibly global, leadership; on the other hand, festival branding also relies on a strong domestic cinema and the support of the nation-state. With festivals becoming more internationalised, state support becomes indispensable. It is within a synthesis and tension between the global, regional and national/local that we will chart the recent development of East Asian film festivals.

In 2006 there were around 700 film festivals worldwide (see Table 6.1). These numbers show that film festivals have greatly diversified although they are still associated with art cinema. The numbers also indicate that festivals now tend to be organised by format, such as genres (e.g. science fiction/fantasy), festivals for children, seniors, shorts, silents, animation and digital; topical categories, like gay/lesbian, nostalgia, environmental; or frankly organising purposes, raising social awareness, activism and causes for democracy, women's groups, ethnic pride and so on. In some cases these categories – audiences, format, social agendas – overlap. Such East Asian festivals as Yamagata International Documentary Film Festival (est. 1989), the now-defunct Yubari International Fantastic Film Festival (1990–2005), 'Focus on Asia' Fukuoka International Film Festival (est. 1991) and Taiwan's Women Make Waves Film/Video Festival (est. 1994) have established regional reputations.

General (world cinema)	203
Shorts, independent, experimental, underground	135
Documentary	48
Animation, digital, new media, special effects	33
Television, videos	17
Corporate, industrial, commercial productions	3
Gay, lesbian, bisexual, transgender	21
Women and feminist film	10
Children, youth, family	30
Foreign-language or cultural films	137
Theme-oriented (e.g. human rights, archaeology, arts, environmental)	26
Genre	39
New directors	11
Student, young film-makers	12
Others (e.g. dance, internet, restored films)	22
Unspecified (festivals without specific topics)	34
Total	**699**

Non-competitive	143
Competitive	486
Others	70

Source: *Screen International 2006 Festival Guide*, 2006.

Table 6.1 Breakdown for 2006 Worldwide Film Festivals and Events

In general festivals have become alternative distribution circuits, taking over the functions of 'art-house' exhibition, once a burgeoning network of theatres screening foreign, independent and non-commercial films. In those days of art-house and repertory cinemas ca. 1960–85, commercial movies and art cinema were segregated. Today multiplexes offer a wider range of foreign and festival favourites. While the demise of art houses is due mainly to the proliferation of home video, including cable offerings, festivals do appeal to similar objectives as art-houses: offering international, offbeat and unusual material overlooked by major theatre chains. Furthermore, a festival's priority is maximum publicity, emphasising the event's newsworthiness via celebrity, controversy or competition. Festival organisation consists of a flurry of press, logistical and economic orchestration, as well as the more traditional curatorial tasks of film selection, booking, catalogues, publicity, screening, translation and ticketing. The 63rd Venice Film Festival (2006) boasted an unprecedented achievement: all twenty-one films in competition were world premieres. 'Many producers and sales agents know that only Venice can offer a film something beyond just a launching-pad. Venice allows a film to have special visibility', said Marco Muller, the festival's artistic director (Rodier, 2006). In effect 'festival cinema' has now become completely mainstreamed. It is common to see festival films continuing in a commercial run following a premiere at the festival, with hardly a break.

Contemporary film festivals also work like conventions; they are networking opportunities for like-minded people and groups. Festivals are cultural bazaars, spotlighting films and directors, offering a chance for sales, publicising future programmes and promoting social agendas. East Asian film festivals also func-tion as windows onto national and regional film cultures. They are a good way to produce copy about film trends, and educate the international cohort of film professionals about a given region.

Another salient aspect is the gilding of host cities themselves, as Shanghai, Hong Kong, Tokyo and Pusan, a large Korean port and shipyard city, all jockey for position as must-visit destinations on the festival circuit. These cities compete fiercely not just for film premieres, but also for juries, interesting panels, media markets, networking events, press gambits and international stars. Moreover, cities now want to appear as attractive shooting locations, service providers or showcases of new talent. The latest trend sees festivals offer information on incen-tives like tax breaks or co-production packaging, often with government support.

The growing complexities of film festivals have impacted their financial basis. Their phenomenal expense necessitates the involvement (and interference) of local and state governments, as well as transnational corporate sponsors. This always entails shifting constraints and compromises. In these shifting pri-orities, one can make out the dialectics of global, regional and domestic spheres. While film festivals bring media spotlight to their cities, politicians are capricious in their support. Hong Kong International Film Festival (HKIFF) was shunted between different government bureaus after 1997; it was then fully privatised in 2004, after struggling to maintain corporate sponsors. Cathay Pacific Airways supported it, then abruptly dropped its sponsorship. At this time HKIFF was 'handed over' to the Trade Development Council, a government office that promptly harnessed its commercial potential as a market or trade fair. This was an abrupt turn from HKIFF's traditional reputation as the prime cinephiles' fes-tival for Asian cinema. Meanwhile, Pusan and Bangkok enjoyed rising levels of municipal- and state-funding every year, allowing more press junkets (for Pusan 5,000 fully funded places for journalists, as opposed to just ninety for Hong Kong), more international stars and more lavish parties. Post-coup Bangkok, however, has had its budget slashed.

East Asia's first was the Asia-Pacific Film Festival, established in 1946. It is held annually in a country designated by the board of the Federation of Motion Picture Producers in Asia-Pacific. Once the major film event for area countries,

Wong Kar-wai, auteur *par excellence*

this festival included Australia, Hong Kong, Indonesia, Japan, Malaysia, New Zealand, the Philippines, Singapore, South Korea, Taiwan, Thailand, Vietnam and Iran. The Asia-Pacific Festival was a venue for Asian films to compete with each other and also a site for deals and networking. The fifty-year-old festival has since lost influence but film festivals in the East Asian region have become increasingly important. The importance comes as a melting pot, mixing business with craftsmanship and pleasure, combining studio presentations, art films and independents. More important yet, festivals now provide regular pathways to professional recognition and commercial viability, for anyone from struggling newcomer to bankable film-maker. Celebrity, too, plays an important public relations role, boosting visibility and aspirations. Asia's leading festival darling, Wong Kar-wai, is foremost in his ability to feed (on) festival cachet. Directors, stars, producers and suits all do turns as enticements, and offer marketing hooks for investment, distribution packages and publicity. This chapter covers three festivals in detail.

A TALE OF THREE FESTIVALS

Window on New China: The Shanghai International Film Festival

The Shanghai International Film Festival (SIFF) is China's first and foremost international festival. It was the brainchild of several veteran directors and actors, initiated in 1990. In 1992, a formal application drafted by the Shanghai Municipal Government and Ministry of Radio, Film and Television was sent to the State Council of the People's Republic, and was approved. A year later, the first edition of SIFF was launched. It was held every other year until 2001. The 2003 festival was cancelled because of the SARS outbreak, and in 2004, SIFF became an annual event.

Like other major cultural events in China, SIFF takes place under watchful eyes of national and local governments. Daily operations are run by the Special Events Office through the Shanghai Media and Entertainment Group. Special Events must secure its own financing, since the Shanghai Municipal Government provides no funds. The festival's annual budget is in the region of US$1.1 million and there are two major sources of revenue: sponsorship in cash and materials, as well as box-office receipts (Tan, 2001). SIFF has four sections: competitions including 'Jin Jue' Golden Cup award, and a new prize for young Asian film-makers with an award of RMB 30,000; the International Panorama; the Forum, with panels on directors, topics such as piracy and animation, and 'Master Classes' with prominent figures; and, finally, the International Film Market. SIFF takes place concurrently with the Shanghai television festival and offers a platform for PRC cinema, particularly mainstream, government-produced, 'main melody' films (see Chapter 2). Examples include domestic hits *Tale of the Sacred Mountain* (dir. Feng Xiaoning, 1997), *Purple Sunset* (dir. Feng Xiaoning, 2001), *Deng Xiaoping* (dir. Li Xiepu, 2004) and *On Taihang Mountain* (dir. Zhou Dechang and Li Chongyang, 2005). With its official ties, this festival avoids challenging fare such as Jia Zhangke's debut *Xiao Wu* (1997) or the notorious sexuality of Lou Ye's *Summer Palace* (2006).

For some local journalists and critics, SIFF remains provincial, not 'international' enough, lacking quality screenings and high-profile stars (Zeng, 2005). At Shanghai we encountered some fairly big names such as John Lone and Hong Kong director Stanley Kwan. At a crowded roundtable, there was Ang Lee, in town for pre-production on his new period film *Lust, Caution*; Feng Xiaogang (see Chapter 2), director of *The Banquet* and *A World Without Thieves*; and Hollywood producers Chris Lee and Peter Loehr. But some journalists wrote that reading the catalogue, with its unfamiliar directors and movies, was like visiting an alien world. Moreover, there have been complaints about organisational problems, especially ticket scalpers (Zeng, 2005). Dealings with festival staff were pleasant, but rarely concluded with satisfying results. Passes, tickets or information on sessions were not easily obtainable. The roundtable was dominated by reporters and cameramen covering the guests, and visitors were elbowed aside. Unlike other festivals, little time was made available to the audience for questions.

With China one of the hottest markets in the world, SIFF has intensified engagements with the Chinese film industry. In 2005, it brought together global media executives from companies such as Sony, Columbia and Miramax, directors of prestigious film festivals – Cannes, Sundance, Pusan and Hawaii – as well as key domestic players such as James Wang Zhonglei from Huayi Brothers and Ren Zhonglun, CEO of Shanghai Film Group in the forum. In 2006 it invited Anthony Minghella for intensive Master Classes with producers. Three seminars and roundtables were held to discuss specific issues in financing, marketing, intellectual property and the distribution of Chinese cinemas within global institutions (see Epilogue).

The Hong Kong Film Festival: Overtaken, Not Overcome

The Hong Kong International Film Festival (HKIFF) once enjoyed direct government support and was, throughout the 1980s and 1990s, the most respected film festival in East Asia. But lately HKIFF lost these two advantages. The Taiwan Golden Horse Awards (est. 1962) and affiliated Golden Horse International Film Festival is older, but not as respected as the HKIFF for programming, publications and screenings. HKIFF was founded in 1977 by the Urban Council of Hong Kong, under Governor Maclehose. For over twenty years, HKIFF was funded and run by the colonial Urban Council and, from 1997, the Leisure and Cultural Services Department. From 2000 to 2004, the Hong Kong Arts Development Council, a government arts fund, took over. In 2004, HKIFF was changed to the Hong Kong International Film Festival Society (HKIFFS), an independent, non-profit corporation directed by Peter Tsi, a former banker and financier. The Society is now the sole organiser of the festival. It has contended with a tough transition from public to private standing. Its budget rose from HK$110, 000 in 1977 to HK$6.70 million (US$869,000) in 1996. However, after the formation of HKIFFS, the festival's subsidy was cut because it already had commercial sponsors. The 2005 budget was about HK$9 million (an increase of 2.3 million over ten years), making it relatively small among Asia's top film festivals – Tokyo, Bangkok and Pusan (*bc Magazine*, 2005). Tight budgets forced the curtailment of screenings and the number of films. Aware of the shortfall, Andy Lau, veteran entertainer and show-business spokesman, called publicly on local directors to support the opening of the 2006 festival.

HKIFF is still one of the most important film festivals in Asia because of its critical taste and strong commitment to Asian cinema. Before the rise of Pusan, it was regarded as the best place to watch Asian films. Historically, it pushed the Hong Kong New Wave in the late 1970s, and brought *Yellow Earth*, *Red Sorghum* and the Fifth Generation film-makers to widespread notice when they were still banned in China. In 2006, Hou Hsiao-hsien recalled that meeting PRC 'comrades' in the mid-1980s was his most treasured memory of the HKIFF. Recent years saw new attempts to promote Asian cinema and try to catch up with Pusan. New competitions, including the FIPRESCI Award (Fédération Internationale de la Presse Cinématographique, or International critics' selection) and Asian DV Competition were introduced. HKIFF traditionally scorned competitions, leaving that to the more commercial Hong Kong Film Awards (est. 1982) staged mainly for television broadcast. Except for screening Hong Kong films, HKIFF's engagements in local production are weak.

Unlike other key international film festivals in Asia, the HKIFF lacked its own film market. The SAR government therefore established the Hong Kong-Asia Film Financing Forum (HAF) and the Hong Kong International Film and TV Market (FILMART) as platforms for financing and sales. Orchestrated by the Trade Development Council, HKIFF was integrated into a grand umbrella event, the Hong Kong Entertainment Expo. This included HAF, FILMART and five other activities centring on media and entertainment, including the Hong Kong Film Awards. In 2007, the Hong Kong Music Fair joined the Expo, making the Expo even more comprehensive. The SAR government's effort to spotlight and rejuvenate the entertainment industry is welcomed, but it is a large-scale business proposition, a distant relation to the freewheeling creative sources of Hong Kong cinema (Eder, 2001).

The consolidation of events shows the SAR government's awareness of the stakes in promoting co-productions and transnational investment in the region. Trade press reporter Liz Shackleton writes:

> In a move that appeared to be a reaction to growing competition with the launch of the Asian Film Market in South Korea this October ... the Trade Development Council also announced the findings of a survey in which 70% of respondents described FILMART/HAF as the most significant film event in Asia. Conducted on the first two days of the market, the survey polled 81 exhibitors and 259 visitors. (Shackleton, 2006b)

As the Hong Kong film industry struggles to keep its annual production number above fifty (down from an average of 200 in the 1990s), the SAR government has examined other ways to sustain the city's historical reputation as East Asia's centre of the film trade. Where film production is no longer Hong Kong's competitive edge, large-scale trade fairs and expositions try to rescue Hong Kong as the heart of Asian cinema.

The Pusan International Film Festival: The Way It's Done

In only ten years, the Pusan International Film Festival (PIFF) has become the leading festival in Asia. Its first event was in 1996, seeking ways to boost its own national cinema (see Chapter 1). Approaching 1997, Pusan gambled on the vulnerability of Hong Kong and HKIFF, and won. Clearly outdoing HKIFF, PIFF is now hailed (and touts itself) as

> One of the most vibrant and influential film festivals in the world. PIFF is also the most important place in Asia to conduct film business and 2006 will see the launch of the first Asian Film Market in conjunction with the festival ... now in its 9th year, PPP [is] Asia's leading meeting place and BIFCOM, for film commissions and production services, now in its 6th year. (Pusan International Film Festival Website)

PIFF aimed to avoid the excesses of the Tokyo Film Festival (est. 1985), which began life as a retail/real estate executive's dream, ending as a test market for Hollywood blockbusters (Segers, 2003). Pusan's programmes fall into two categories: (1) a competition open to young Asian directors; (2) eight non-competition sections showcasing Korean cinema and films from around the globe. In addition, its associated market and promotional activities are large, lively and easy to enter.

PIFF is strongly committed to Korean cinema, both contemporary and classic. Borrowing HKIFF's 'Hong Kong Panorama', a programme introduced in 1990, 'Korean Panorama' presents the latest quality Korean films. But it also has cash prizes to reward Korean short films and documentaries. There is also a NET-PAC award (Network for the Promotion of Asian Cinema, est. 1994) chosen by Asian critics for the year's best Korean film.

PIFF's regional prominence comes from its promotion of Asian cinema overall. The festival's only international competition, 'New Currents', is devoted to emerging film movements from Asian countries. Here one finds some of the most exciting talent in Asia – China's Jia Zhangke, Taiwan's Lee Kang-sheng (Taiwan director Tsai Ming-liang's protégé), and Koreans Lee Yun-ki, Park Ki-yong, and Song I1-gon. Like the HKIFF, a FIPRESCI Award[1] is given annually to a new Asian film based on artistic creativity. Film talents from Japan, Hong Kong, Iran and even Bhutan were rewarded by this scheme. Pusan has endorsed gifted directors like Fruit Chan, Hur Jin-ho, Hong Sang-soo and Kurosawa Kiyoshi, leading to its reputation as a place to encounter the brightest lights from every Asian territory (Teo, 2002).

PIFF's importance to new Asian cinema is underlined by its confab, the Pusan Promotion Plan (PPP), a 'pivotal meeting place for Asian Films' (Kim, 2004a: 10).

It has become PIFF's trademark, smoothly combining public funds and private know-how, the fruit of remarkable trust and confidence in each other's expertise. Thus Pusan's PPP exemplifies another contemporary policy buzzword, public–private partnership. Since 1998, Pusan's PPP selects around twenty-five projects and arranges hundreds of one-to-one meetings between film-makers and their potential investors, and co-producers. PPP also initiated a sales market in 2003: it 'provides a free office, a free ID pass, project sourcing, film festival participation … and worldwide location scouting. We also invite buyers. All this happens in three days' (Jeong, 2003: 12). PPP itself offers cash awards totalling one hundred thousand in US dollars, which goes far to reaching its objectives. PPP has become the world's largest project market specialising in Asian cinema.

Successful PPP projects include *Beijing Bicycle* (dir. Wang Xiaoshuai, 2001), *Address Unknown* (dir. Kim Ki-duk, 2001), *Oasis* (dir. Lee Chang-dong, 2002), *Story Undone* (dir. Hassan Yektapanah, 2004), and *Woman Is the Future of Man* (dir. Hong Sang-soo, 2004). In 2001, PPP created another project called 'New Directors in Focus' (NDIF), which is only open to new Korean film-makers. It selects five projects from directors who have not yet made a feature and gives the winners cash awards of over US$20,000 (KRW 20 million). In 2005, NDIF arranged for LJ Film, Korea's leading art-house production company, to produce many of Kim Ki-duk's films (see below), to sponsor the programme, guaranteeing the production of the awarded project.

Comparative Remarks

Shanghai Film Festival is keen to put China, a growth market for commercial film, on the international map. It is still patently government supervised, so its programming is unlikely to include offbeat, experimental or politically sensitive films. Shanghai wants to cultivate its promise as a potential marketplace, where Chinese businessmen can hold meetings with investors under the benign supervision of municipal authorities.

Hong Kong, on the other hand, enjoyed a reputation for critically acclaimed programming. During the 1970s and 1980s, HKIFF was the only place to catch glimpses of mainland cinema, and its programming philosophy embraced dissident and independent film-makers, and extended festivals' role as champions of free speech. At a time of sensitive political transition, it was an institution with the temerity to defy censors. After Hong Kong's handover to China in 1997, this stance required substantial modification, along with the festival's financial footing. There was great uncertainty during this time, moving from government funding to private sponsorship, with continuing government co-ordination under the supervision of the Trade Development Council (TDC). It is a mark of how far the festival has come that TDC, a government body, now directs HKIFF's place in the city's cultural calendar, while tensions and occasional recriminations with its private board often spill into public view.

PIFF, on the other hand, is an effective public–private partnership, with a great international reputation for quality programming and excellent networking opportunities. When we attended, the festival was still split between its seaside and downtown locations, presenting logistical problems. It was difficult to attend all the screenings we wanted. Still, Pusan's foremost reputation is largely deserved, due to its co-ordination between the government and industry representatives, and the skill with which Pusan has leveraged itself into the national and international spotlight. Seeing the great success of Hong Kong FIL-MART, PIFF immediately announced its launch of Asian Film Market in 2006, the first of its kind in the world:

> Asian Film Market brings two vital film business [PPP and BIFCOM] events into one roof [sic] and adds other services to create a total film market serving all aspects of film business: sales offices, market screenings, buyer services, production and co-production services, and financing tools and events. There will be space for 150 Sales Offices and 200 Market Screenings. The Market will hold special events and panels including 'Curtain Call,' a summit of Asia's leading talent and talent agencies which will be the focus of the Co-Production Program this year.
> (PIFF website)

Clearly Pusan wants to be a one-stop shopping destination for anyone seeking business in the East Asian screen trade. This grand addition shows PIFF's untiring aspiration for leadership in Asian film festivals, be it programming, publicity or events. Even the Tokyo Film Festival started an event called Asia-Pacific Entertainment Market in 2006 to promote global trade in entertainment and/or co-production with a focus on Asia and the Pacific. And in Taiwan, five major events were consolidated into the Taiwan International Film and Television Expo including two festivals, two awards ceremonies and a television–film–digital contents exhibition (Cremin, 2006).

Pusan's regional pre-eminence does not go unchallenged. Along with Shanghai's ambition to increase its stakes in the trade, and the Hong Kong SAR government's astute conversion of pop culture to business, PIFF now faces another challenge from a thriving city to the south – Bangkok.

In 2003, the first Bangkok International Film Festival (BKKIFF) was launched by the Royal Thai Government and powerful Tourism Authority of Thailand (TAT). TAT's motivation was to enhance Bangkok's image as a cosmopolitan city and boost tourism. From the beginning BKKIFF received substantial government funding and in 2006 TAT advanced a budget of US$4.5 million for the festival (Feinstein, 2006).

A big attraction at BKKIFF is its ASEAN competition, selecting fifteen films from ten Southeast Asian countries. These are judged by members of FIPRESCI, the International Federation of Film Critics. The festival also places a special emphasis on cinematography: its Cinematographer's Day invites famous cameramen like Christopher Doyle, Eric Gautier and Dante Spinotti.

The festival emerged at a time when the Thai film industry was recovering from a long period of stagnation. In the late 1990s, its domestic film industry was in decline due to the Asian economic crisis and Hollywood's opportunistic moves into the region's cinemas. By 1997 the Thai film industry was averaging ten films per year. But a push to reinvigorate Thai cinema resulted in new waves of talent and production, with directors like Pen-ek Ratanaruang, Jira Maliku and Prince Chatrichalerm with his epic *Suriyothai* (2001). Transvestite comedy *Iron Ladies* (dir. Youngyooth Thongkonthun, 2001) and its sequel enjoyed international acclaim and good domestic box office. Production rose to over thirty films in 2002. The festival positioned itself the following year as a way to bring Thai cinema to the world, and screened international films in Bangkok. Annually, it showcases twenty or more new Thai films, formerly in a separate section called 'Thai Panorama', but now entered in different programmes shows in an attempt to enhance Thai films' competitive edge and critical value. Like the others, BKKIFF hosts a film market, centring on ASEAN production. The Bangkok Film Market invites critics, festival programmers, acquisition and development executives, financiers, producers, writers and talent agents, resulting in US$100 million worth of deals struck in 2005.

BKKIFF was criticised for not showing greater support to local production. This was mainly because it contracted a Beverly Hills consulting firm, Film Festival Management, Inc., to run the festival for the past four years. All festival executives and most programmers were appointed from North America. Moreover, none of the foreign films were given Thai subtitles, alienating the local ticket buyers. Given this, local film associations and societies felt marginalised. The Federation of National Film Association of Thailand called on its members to boycott the 2006 festival because they were excluded from film selection and access to the market (Rosenberg, 2006). Clearly the Bangkok festival is vulnerable to charges of selling out to the international market, given its placement of Western staff in such influential posts. In late 2006, budget cuts of 30 per cent forced the BKKIFF to sever its contract with the American consultants. Organisers insisted this had nothing to do with frictions in the past, and was simply a financial constraint. The tourist authority and organisers were also recruiting a Thai director to head the festival (Wong, 2006b). In their need to balance domestic and international priorities, the major Asian film festivals and markets must carefully consider their objectives, funding and need to recoup the huge expense of mounting festivals.

FESTIVAL PLAYERS
Wong Kar-wai: The First Chinese Jury President
Wong Kar-wai single-handedly held up the 2004 Cannes Film Festival. Like a glamorous latecomer to a party, the most anticipated Hong Kong film not only delayed the Cannes festival but also altered the scheduling of other films, creating havoc to accommodate its arrival. This was because Wong was fiddling with the final cut of his opus, *2046*. While reel one was being projected, the end of the film was still being couriered to the Lumiere Grand Theatre.[2] This created a furore since Wong, awarded Best Director at the festival in 1997, not only squeezed maximum anticipation out of his latest sensation; the stunt also forced other films' rearrangement, ruining the meticulous lineup of high-profile premieres. Despite all the chaos, Wong was still invited back to Cannes, as president of the jury for the competition in 2006. Wong was the first Chinese president of the festival jury, and the official poster featured a silhouette of Maggie Cheung descending a stairway in a scene from *In the Mood for Love* (2000).

The 'final cut' of *2046* screened at Cannes was not final at all. After the film received lukewarm and even hostile reviews, Wong returned to the editing room with collaborator William Cheung and prepared at least two more editions before releasing *2046* in Shanghai in September 2004. The appearance at Cannes reveals a fanatical perfectionist, or someone who wishes to be so regarded, but it also shows a film-maker in control of his image, en route to enhanced newsworthiness of festivals themselves. Many journalists noted with relish that Wong's Cannes performance was completely unprecedented.

Wong's Cannes sensation *2046* (2004)

In Hong Kong dollars

Title	Hong Kong	Worldwide
As Tears Go By (1988)	11,532,283	12,357*
Days of Being Wild (1990)	9,751,942	4,500,307
Chungking Express (1994)	7,678,549	4,668,956
Ashes of Time (1994)	9,023,583	N/A
Fallen Angels (1995)	7,476,505	2,498,606
Happy Together (1997)	8,600,141	3,085,012
In the Mood for Love (2000)	8,663,227	99,998,679
2046 (2004)	6,147,095	149,911,536
Eros (2005) (co-directed)	792,535	11,947,214

*Taiwan Box Office only.

Sources:
Data compiled from Box Office Mojo website, *Cinema in the Republic of China Yearbook* (1989, 1991, 1995, 1996, 1998), *City Entertainment* ('Annual Box Office Supplements'; 1988, 1990, 1994, 1995, 1997, 2000, 2004 and 2005) and *TPBO WRETCH* (2004).

Table 6.2 Box Office of Wong Kar-wai's Films (1988–2005)

Such outrageous ego displayed at the pinnacle of all film festivals lends controversy to a 'must see' film/event. In the long run *2046* was perhaps not up to the director's best work, but Wong skilfully presented it in Cannes as a notorious media incident.

It had been a decade since Wong received his first international award, for *Chungking Express* (1994) at the Stockholm International Film Festival. Since then, Wong has crafted the most enviable reputation in all of Chinese-language cinema, due mainly to his elegant concoctions of stars, voiceover narration and temporal puzzles. But Wong has never been a major player in Chinese-language film box office. Table 6.2 shows the box-office receipts of all his films shown in his home base of Hong Kong.

It would appear that as Wong becomes more internationally successful, his local popularity declines. This needs to be assessed with reference to the changing economy of local cinema since the 1990s. With US$1.3 million (HK$10 million) as a rough guide for modest box-office success, Wong's films have not been runaway hits. But their international visibility and box office have steadily risen since Quentin Tarantino championed Wong's *Chungking Express*, bringing an American release contract with Miramax. On the other hand, seeing the dramatic rise in costs of Wong's successive productions since *Happy Together* (1997), Wong's films are more profitable internationally than in Hong Kong. Take *In the Mood for Love*: the film's international box office is over ten times the local gross. The Hong Kong box office (HK$6.1 million) for *2046* is a disappointment, considering the Cannes hype and the steady flow of press releases since its production plans were announced in 1998. But with co-production and distribution in China, the film's international box office is the best yet for Wong – over twenty times its Hong Kong receipts.

So far, Wong's most commercially successful film in Hong Kong was his debut, *As Tears Go By* (1988), starring Maggie Cheung, Andy Lau and Jacky Cheung. However, this film is usually regarded as the worst, given its plain generic conventions and residual, John Woo buddy-film style. Not until his second film, *Days of Being Wild* (1990), was his talent noted by local critics. *Days* won Wong Best Director at the Hong Kong Film Awards in 1991 and many critics maintain *Days of Being Wild* is Wong's best film of all.

From the start, Wong Kar-wai utilised the myth of auteurism, casting himself as latter-day Jean-Luc Godard or Michelangelo Antonioni, an international spokesman for film art, not merely a talented film-maker. Wong carefully guards his public image, a director hiding behind dark shades, like Godard. It was reported that he would not receive journalists without putting on his sunglasses and cancelled an appointment with *The New York Times* because he had misplaced them. The name of his production company, Jet Tone (est. 1993), indicates this 1960s allusion and perhaps nostalgia, transliterating to English the Cantonese pronunciation of Mao Tse-tung's first name.

By the mid-1990s, Wong had yet to be discovered internationally, though HKIFF programmer Li Cheuk-to was working to promote him to sister festivals such as Toronto, among others (Li, 2004). Wong's breakthrough came with *Chungking Express* at Stockholm where Quentin Tarantino claimed to have fallen in love with the film (Ngai, 1997). With Tarantino's endorsement, Wong's international reputation climbed steadily up. He quickly finished *Fallen Angels* (1995), a follow-up to *Chungking Express* about unrequited love and romanticised gangsterism. The narrative and style of *Fallen Angels* stays in the form of the 'festival gangster' picture (Davis, 2001), like Kitano's *Fireworks* and John Woo's *The Killers*. But it failed to lift Wong's auteur status to the next level.

In 1997 Wong established Block 2, a subsidiary of Jet Tone, to handle international co-productions for foreign art-houses and video/cable markets. Fortissimo, Wong's European sales agent since *Chungking Express*, handled all international sales for Block 2 productions. *Happy Together*, Wong's Cannes winner, was the first Block 2 production with an international finance package from Japan and South Korea. *Happy Together* won Wong best director award at Cannes and became his second breakthrough film. Unlike *Fallen Angels*, a variation on the gangster formula, *Happy* is a carefully planned relationship picture and set the pattern for Wong's bigger and more elaborate productions in subsequent years. *Happy Together* took a calculating approach by directing attention to the 1997 handover via a gay theme, something rarely explored by Asian directors and remaining an anomaly – the only queer film Wong has so far ventured.

Despite its crowning success at Cannes for best director, *Happy Together* was criticised for injecting a heterosexual mentality into a homosexual narrative (Chan, 2004). This 'drawback', however, was precisely Wong's drawing card for acceptance on the global festival grapevine, as well as niche (gay) markets. Though it's sold as a 'gay film', it worked well as a political allegory and a compelling exercise in transcultural film-making. *Happy Together* is thus another clear step toward publicity, market attractions and eventual mainstream establishment. The public relations angle in Wong's activities was further cemented in his next two works, and is clearer and more pronounced in every step he takes.

Wong's projects show different stages, moving from his early experiments with genres to more exotic melodramas capturing the admiration of foreign audiences, to a brand-name auteurism with its attendant celebrity trappings. This climaxed in Wong's behaviour at the 2004 Cannes festival. *Eros* (2005), an omnibus film with featurettes by Wong, Stephen Soderbergh and Michelangelo Antonioni, confirms Wong's international stature, especially as the other two entries were comparatively weak. At the time of writing, there are reports of Wong signing up Nicole Kidman for a remake of the Hollywood classic *Lady from Shanghai*. Wong's projects are so long in the making (up to four years) that press reports and industry rumour are essential parts of their construction process and modifications. If Hollywood perfected the craft of prerelease marketing, then Wong has shown great expertise in leveraging auteur mystique to the highest levels of anticipation, speculation and investment.

From the beginning of his career Wong had remarkable access to the biggest stars in Hong Kong – Andy Lau Tak-wah, Maggie Cheung Man-yuk, Tony Leung Chiu-wai, Leslie Cheung, Faye Wong, Kaneshiro Takeshi, Brigitte Lin Ching-hsia, Katrina Lau, Leon Lai. This list, as of 2004, continues to grow with the addition of Gong Li, Zhang Ziyi, Taiwanese heart-throb Zhang Zhen and J-dorama/pop idol Kimura Takuya. Despite his use of dreamlike artistic imagery, even in gangster and martial arts films, Wong's insistence on stars often boosted their (sometimes fading) reputations. Wong's own visibility as an 'avant-pop' film-maker helped differentiate his work from pulp-genre fare dominating mainstream production in Hong Kong through the late 1990s (Bordwell, 2000: 261–81). Wong's stars were enriched and rejuvenated, and this allowed him further command over stars in subsequent projects. Pronounced differentiation (via stars, genres, art film technique) made Wong's packages stand out, and allowed for ascent to greater international exposure through festivals. This reached a pinnacle in 2000, with seven international awards for *In the Mood for Love*. Wong's facility with stars, exalting their charisma and mystery, with transplantation to his own persona as a name-brand director, emphasised the emphatically 'Oriental' qualities of stars, styles and tradition as precious commodities. Like his stars, Wong fiercely protects his own privacy, and stays on script in the details released about current and forthcoming projects. In many respects Wong is the shrewdest auteur-showman in all of contemporary cinema, consistently leveraging an international artistic reputation into a repeatable formula, and sustaining an East Asian cultural industry. WKW Inc. is now attractive to Hollywood stars, and Hollywood majors, released through his own company Block 2, making and distributing English language-pictures through Fox Searchlight.

Festival Film-makers in Wong's Wake: Jia Zhangke and Kim Ki-duk

Wong Kar-wai's international success began in 1994, in Sweden. In under a decade, Wong became one of the top directors in world cinema. Wong's creative choices and business strategy show that traditional, nation-based theatrical and video markets are no longer the main factors in an intricate, international screen industry where festivals play key roles. Directors need not reach the home market to be able to produce films but, rather, directly access the finance–distribution–marketing packages available at festivals and film markets. For East Asian film-makers, Wong is no doubt the top model; young newcomers repeatedly copied Wong Kar-wai's style and narrative, but so far, few have been able to reproduce his success. Perhaps this signals that it is the business and professional package, not just the gorgeous stars and soundtracks, that confirms Wong's distinction.

Other young film-makers who have chosen to create their own working styles have had better results. As mentioned, reputable festivals have been trying to best each other and it appears that even non-competitive fests (Toronto, Hong Kong, Pusan, Vancouver, Hawaii, etc.) fiercely compete for new works, hungrily seeking prestige through the next big talent, and jockeying as gatekeepers for the most cutting-edge Asian works.

Jia Zhangke, Chinese independent

In 1995, a young Chinese film student from Beijing Film Academy named Jia Zhangke presented a short at the Hong Kong International Film Festival. There, he met producers Chow Keung, Li Kit-ming and cinematographer Yu Lik-wai. Together these people established Hu Tong Communication to make low-budget features that could be screened at festivals (Berry, 2003b). Within two years, Jia's *Xiao Wu* (1997) would win awards at Berlin, Vancouver and Pusan, prompting one American critic to call him 'the world's greatest film-maker under 40' (Lim, 2004). At thirty-two, Jia's third feature *Unknown Pleasures* (2002) was screened in the main competition at Cannes. At the time Jia started in Hong Kong, an unknown Korean, Kim Ki-duk, showed his first feature, *Crocodile* (1996) at Pusan (Korean Panorama) and, within a few years, he would be crowned best director twice in a single year – at Berlin and Venice in 2004.

The career trajectory of Jia and Kim confirms the importance of festivals as avenues into the network of international cinema, avoiding years of haggling with distributors and exhibition circuits at home. This alternative path is especially attractive to young talent from China, Taiwan and Japan and, to some extent, South Korea and Hong Kong.

Screen institutions in China remain under state control, and in recent years, although ideological censorship appears more relaxed, a cartel of distribution and exhibition has quietly formed to ensure the market is limited to the state and state-affiliated private enterprises. Worse, the scourge of piracy prevents films from making a profit on theatrical release. While East Asian piracy is an endless buffet of consumer choices, it works as a powerful disincentive to all but the most connected Chinese film-makers, discouraging independents from any engagement with Chinese audiences in theatres. This is a sad deterioration from the 1980s, when the major obstacles to the Fifth Generation directors were political censorship, a situation partly improved through the efforts of festivals and foreign critics.

In Taiwan, with close to two decades of dormant production, and distribution monopolised by Hollywood majors, there is little opportunity for new blood in feature production. The most vibrant film scene in Taiwan in recent years is non-fiction, documentary, animation and shorts (Davis, 2007). Film-makers in Taiwan have to seek offshore capital to invest in their features, or they have to bid for meagre government subsidy funds, called the *fudaojing*, with a maximum award of US$300,000. Even when their films are completed, they often do not receive any support from local distributors and go straight to the cable networks. On the other hand, Hong Kong has the strongest returns from within the territory; investment and rentals from Southeast Asian markets – Taiwan, Singapore, Thailand, Malaysia, Philippines – also boost revenues to some extent. But with current annual production dropping to the danger zone of under fifty films (see Table 1.2), Hong Kong novices must look for new ways of getting their films made and seen. In the opposite direction, South Korea's film industry enjoyed a remarkable recovery and boom in the late 1990s so domestic films in Korea continue to be very strong, compared to foreign imports. A strong commercial cinema however may impose constraints on alternative film practices. Film-makers whose priorities are not big-budget genre pictures, turn their attention to festival avenues.

Given these conditions, festivals open a smoother pathway to visibility and a chance to show small works on big screens. In addition there is media coverage, another advantage hard to get at home, especially for newcomers without powerful backers or partners. More important, festivals are places where new projects can seek financing and finished products can be marketed. So bypassing the traditional film trade at home, and entering festival markets, new types of films are advantaged and young directors are more likely to be 'discovered', often through extravagant acclaim at international events that feeds back to domestic recognition.

This international pathway that skirts national institutions worked well for Jia Zhangke and Kim Ki-duk. Both came from humble backgrounds and had no affiliations with powerful producers or gatekeepers. Jia has adroitly used festivals and Western critics to build an international reputation and visibility, which in turn helped cast him as an avant-garde artist in the region. As indicated by

Still Life (Jia Zhangke, 2006)

Film	Budget (in RMB)	Financing	Production	Sales and Distribution
Xiao Wu (1997)	30,000	Hu Tong Communication ; Qiang Shexian (a Chinese advertising agency)	Hu Tong Communication	N/A
Platform (2000)	N/A	Pusan Production Project, Office Kitano	Hu Tong Communication; T-Mark Inc. (Japan), Bandai Entertainment Inc. (Japan); Artcam International (France)	International sales: Celluloid Dreams Distributors: Ad Vitam (France); Seville Pictures (Canada); New Yorker Films (USA)
Unknown Pleasures (2002)	5 million	T-Mark Inc.; Lumen Films (France); E-Pictures and (Korea) Hu Tong Communication	T-Mark Inc.; Lumen Films (France); E-Pictures and (Korea) Hu Tong Communication	International sales: Celluloid Dreams Distributors: Ad Vitam, Bitters End and Office Kitano (Japan), New Yorker Films; Seville Pictures
The World (2004)	12 million	Office Kitano; Lumen Film; Xstream Pictures; Shanghai Film Group; Xinghui Production Hong Kong	Office Kitano; Lumen Film; Xstream Pictures; Shanghai Film Group; Xinghui Production Hong Kong	International sales: Celluloid Dreams Distributors: Ad Vitam; Zeitgeist Films (USA) Shanghai Film Group (China)
Still Life (2006)	30 million	Xstream Pictures, Shanghai Film Group	Xstream Pictures, Shanghai Film Group	International sales: Xstream Distributors:Shanghai Film Group (China)

Source: *The Internet Movie Database*

Table 6.3 Jia Zhangke: Film Budget, Financing, Production, Sales and Distribution (1997–2006)

Table 6.3, almost all of Jia's works have backing from Japan's powerful inde-
pendent – Kitano Takeshi (see Chapter 3). Ichiyama Shozo, Office Kitano's film
producer through T-Mark, served as executive producer for all Jia's films since
Platform (2000). According to the source co-edited by Lin Xudong, a patron of
China's young avant-gardes and Jia's production consultant for *Xiao Wu* and
Platform, the collaboration began when *Xiao Wu* caught Kitano's attention.
Shozo Ichiyama was then asked by Kitano to co-produce *Platform* with Hu Tong
Communication. The success of *Platform* built trust between the two companies
and it has been a sound partnership ever since (Ku, 2003).

In recent HKIFF screenings, Jia's works, including both student films and
more mature ones, were immensely popular with advance tickets selling out
quickly. Jia's auteur status is rising and his festival track record allows him to
secure financing from abroad. As shown in Table 6.3, Jia's production costs have
jumped twofold since his second feature, *Platform*. More recently, his international reputation as China's most talented working film-maker has found
resonance at home. In China too Jia is now seen as the most successful young
film-maker, despite having his first three films banned in China for failing to get
permission to produce. But bootleg discs of his films, in either Japanese or
French editions, were always widely available in China. Obviously Chinese audiences are curious about Jia and China is a market not to be ignored. Jia has lately
expressed his desire to get out from the underground and go mainstream, like
many other Chinese directors. Like Zhang Yimou and Chen Kaige, he too wants
to make films that are officially sanctioned and supported by the major distributing lines. So Jia asked the Shanghai Film Group back the domestic
distribution for *The World*, which grossed a modest box office of RMB 2 million (Ho, 2005). In 2006 Jia's *Still Life* won the Best Director award at Cannes.
This film, too, was backed by Shanghai Film Group and was scheduled for
release in China during the New Year holidays. But Jia's road to the mainstream
will remain rough unless he considers making genre pictures – preferably martial arts with major stars and splashy special effects (see Chapter 5).

Kim Ki-duk

Kim's reputation was built on his festival awards, not domestic popularity.
Compared to Jia, who at least enjoyed the pedigree of Beijing Film Academy,
Kim was nobody when he first began. A former Marine and a bohemian art stu-
dent in Paris, Kim was a self-taught film-maker. By constantly submitting his
works to screenplay contests and winning awards, including first prize at the
KOFIC Screenplay Competition (see Chapter 1), he got his foot in the door.

Among his films, only *The Isle* (2000) was backed by big corporations Myung
Film and CJ Entertainment; most were produced by small, obscure companies

Kim Ki-duk, prize-winning
director

(see Table 6.4). In 2000 when *The Isle* was selected as a competition film at the Venice Film Festival, Kim began to attract attention from international critics and festival programmers. Kim Ki-duk had a retrospective at the Czech Republic's Karlovy Vary Film Festival (2002). In the same year, Kim's *The Coast Guard* was chosen as PIFF's opening film. These two events illustrated his rise as a reputable international art director. Further, Kim demonstrated an ability to make *popular* art film with his 2002 *Spring, Summer, Fall, Winter ... and Spring*. Sony Classics picked up the film for US distribution. It grossed US$2.3 million, the highest-grossing return for a Korean film in the US (Russell, 2005). Its international box office exceeded US$9 million (Box Office Mojo, 2004). This film plays on a Zen conceit by depicting nature's cycle as four passages to enlightenment – birth, sex, death and rebirth. Shot on location in a Buddhist temple sitting in the middle of a lake, the film offers sumptuous scenery, laconic dialogue, youthful love, violence and stylised martial arts. With Kim's art training in Paris, the film's cinematography and Zen-like touch captivated art-house audiences in Europe and North America. The film shows that Kim is attuned to the tastes of the main demographic for art cinema. From then on, Kim Ki-duk

Film	Financing	Production	Distribution
Crocodile (1996)	N/A	Joyoung Films	N/A
Wild Animals (1997)	N/A	Dream cinema	N/A
Birdcage Inn (1998)	Partial funding from Korea Broadcasting Advertising Corp. (KOBACO)	Boogui Cinema	KOFIC
The Isle (2000)	N/A	Myung Film	CJ Entertainment
Real Fiction (2000)	N/A	Shin Sung-Su Production & Saerom Entertainment	N/A
Address Unknown (2001)	KOBACO	LJ Film, Kim Ki-duk Film	Local distribution and international sales: Tube Entertainment
Bad Guy (2001)	N/A	LJ Film	Local distribution: CJ Entertainment International sales: Tube Entertainment
The Coast Guard (2002)	N/A	LJ Film	Local distribution: Korea Pictures International sales: Cineclick Asia
Spring, Summer, Fall, Winter ... and Spring (2003)	N/A	LJ Film & Pandora Film Production (Germany)	Local distribution: Korea Pictures International sales: Cineclick Asia; US distributor: Sony Classics, European distributor: Bavaria Film International
Samaritan Girl (2004)	N/A	Kim Ki-duk Film	Local distribution: Show East International sales: Cineclick Asia
3-Iron (2004)	Happinet	Kim Ki-duk Film	Local distribution: Chungeorahm International sales: Cineclick Asia; US distributor: Sony Classics
The Bow (2005)	Happinet and Kim Ki-duk Film	Kim Ki-duk Film	International sales: Cineclick Asia
Time (2006)	Happinet	Kim Ki-duk Film	Local distribution: Sponge International sales: Cineclick Asia; European distributor: Arcam
Breath (2007)	Sponge and Cineclick Asia	Kim Ki-duk Film	International sales: Cineclick Asia Local distribution: Sponge

Sources:
Information compiled from Cannes Film Festival website ('Hwal'), *Han Cinema*, Karlovy Vary International Film Festival website ('Wild Animals') and *Korean Cinema* (2001–5) and *Koreanfilm.org*.

Table 6.4 Kim Ki-duk's Film Production, Financing, Sales and Distribution (1996–2007)

and his own company have taken charge of production (see Table 6.4), working with Cineclick Asia, a major representative for international sales of Korean art cinema. It has handled international sales for Kim's more recent works, including *Spring, Summer, Fall, Winter ... and Spring, The Coast Guard, Samaritan Girl* (2004), *3-Iron* (2004), *The Bow* (2005), *Time* (2006) and *Breath* (2007). Strangely, this independence paid off handsomely, when Kim would become the world's most honoured director in the year 2004 – awarded Best Director at Berlin with *Samaritan Girl* and best director for *3-Iron* at Venice.

Despite this high international profile, Kim Ki-duk remained at the margins of the South Korean industry. While *Spring, Summer* was the 'most successful Korean film ever in the US market', it made less than US$300,000 at home (Russell, 2005). Kim's working pattern and style is fast paced, efficient and tight (Park, 2006), resembling that of low budget V-cinema (straight-to-video) directors in Japan. Most of his later work's funding came from abroad, mainly from Japan. For Kim local sources of funding play auxiliary roles (Han, 2005). An important investor is Japan-based Happinet Pictures (Paquet, 2006a). This connects with the fact that Kim's work is not profitable in Korea, with the exception of *Bad Guy* (2001), which grossed US$3.5million (*Korean Cinema*, 2002), thanks to the male lead Jo Jae-hyun (Paquet, n. d. b) and its masochistic theme of sexual exploitation. On the other hand, his *Address Unknown* (2001) grossed only US$ 30,000 and was yanked from theatres a week after release – the typical response to Kim's films in Korea (*Korean Cinema*, 2001).

Some of Kim's earlier works were released by big companies: giant media conglomerate CJ Entertainment picked up *The Isle* and *Bad Guy*, and Tube Entertainment distributed the ill-fated *Address Unknown*. However, as Korea's screens have become more centralised and 'the increased dominance of entertainment companies is reducing the number of screens for specialized productions', art directors like Kim struggle to get their films widely distributed (Leong, 2005). This might explain the gap in revenues between the home market and abroad. Opportunity costs forestall any strong commitment to marginal films like Kim's, in spite of international festival acclaim. And being distributed by big firms does not translate into marketing clout or strong box office.

Compared to more prominent directors such as Park Chan-wook (*JSA, Old Boy* and *Sympathy for Lady Vengeance*), Kim Chi-yun (*The Foul King, A Tale of Two Sisters*) and Hur Jin-ho (*Christmas in August, April Snow*), Kim Ki-duk is not known in Korea. Worse, while enjoying recognition in the West, Kim was greeted with divided responses at home. According to Darcy Paquet, critical notices are mixed – some liked his films, but others condemned them for their misogyny and brutal treatment of the innocent (Paquet, n. d. b). Tension with local critics prevented any interviews with the Korean press in 2002. Twice crowned the world's best director in 2004, Kim was reported to look for a warmer, more positive reception at home (Soh, 2004). But Kim's next picture *The Bow* was only screened in one theatre in Korea and recorded only 1,400 total admissions (Park, 2006). *Time*, Kim's latest, had difficulty getting any release at home, and testifies to continuing tension between festival-lauded art directors and the commercial cinema of South Korea. For this film-maker, as for Tsai Ming-liang, Hou Hsiao-hsien, Jia Zhangke, and many others, there is limited crossover between the two spheres, and much likelihood of misunderstanding.

CONCLUSION

Certainly Jia and Kim are not the first to benefit from overseas awards and international acclaim from writers at *The Village Voice*, *Film Comment* (New York), *Sight and Sound* (London) and *Positif* (Paris). Their successes belong in a continuing line of ardent reception of Asian film-makers in the West. A variety of East Asian new cinemas (Taiwan New Cinema, Korean New Wave, Hong Kong New Wave and China's Fifth Generation) sought Western appraisal and created new springboards for Asian film-makers to finance and screen new work, and accumulate cultural capital. It is international festivals where this can take place. The epitome of this is Taiwan director Hou Hsiao-hsien's *City of Sadness* winning Best Picture at Venice in 1989, he also won Best Director at Cannes for *The Puppetmaster* in 1991; China's Zhang Yimou received a Golden Lion with *The Story of Qiuju* at the 1992 Venice Film Festival; a year later, Chen Kaige's *Farewell My Concubine* shared the Palm D'Or at Cannes with another 'Asian' director, Abbas Kiarostami, from Iran; Taiwan director Tsai Ming-liang won the top prize at Venice in 1994 for his *Vive L'amour*. Still in Venice, Japan's Kitano Takeshi's *Fireworks (Hana-Bi)* received the Venice Golden Lion in 1997. In the 1990s, these directors were struggling with severe conditions (political or commercial censorship, personal trauma) but festivals encouraged them to persevere, and compete with the world's top film professionals. The result was a steady stream of fine work coming out of East Asia.

Another payoff is that foreign festival success facilitated directors' journeys home with heads held high. These international awards changed the mindset of industry insiders and government bureaucrats; they began courting these film-makers for their cultural and political significance, not just their commercial worth. Festivals therefore helped bestow cultural capital that could be converted and used at home.

These people set the artistic benchmark, to inspire newcomers and to maintain a parallel – not hostile – structure to the commercial cinema. Hou Hsiao-hsien is now the doyen in Taiwan, a sought-after public intellectual, even though his films try in vain to reach local young audiences (Yeh and Davis, 2005: 176). Chen Kaige and Zhang Yimou have become the top players in the world's most populous market. Once controversial at home, these senior East Asian directors have all become world artists, creating not just films, but Olympic ceremonies, opera performances and museum installations. Their visibility in the world comes in multiple roles – cultural ambassadors as well as film–artists. Festivals are the means, not the end, to prompt both commercial and cultural achievement.

NOTES

1. Comprised of the national organisations of professional film critics and film journalists from around the world for 'the promotion and development of film culture and for the safeguarding of professional interests'. It was founded in June 1930 in Paris. At present it has members in more than fifty countries worldwide.
2. The authors thank Li Cheuk-to and Wong Ain-ling for providing this information.

Epilogue: Problems and Prospects for East Asian Screens

Instead of a conclusion, we will follow some of the narratives begun in earlier chapters. Here we will provide updates on some of the key issues. These include South Korea's protection of its own screens; the need for greater overall protection and extension of intellectual property in East Asian screen industries; the increasing co-operation between Hollywood and East Asia through co-production, Asian subdivisions and remakes; and finally the outlook for a new Chinese film industry bent on marketisation and (like Hollywood) oligopoly. These issues are presented anecdotally, since they are ongoing and will continue to play out over the coming years.

Certain broad themes can nonetheless be distilled from these specific issues, such as the question of cultural exemption, often invoked in trade negotiations over screen entertainment. This will be central to the discussion on Korea's screen quota, below. Another is the status of intellectual property (IP) itself and whether efforts to police it – as well as IP violation – can sometimes get out of hand. There are stories of traditional agricultural-craft practices suddenly falling under IP provisions wielded by multinational pharmaceuticals, for instance. Such cases are anomalies now but they show just how great the potential of IP applications and 'protections' are in the twenty-first century. Economists recognise IP as a problem for free trade, extending monopoly rights to IP owners for the sake of promoting new ideas, a trade-off 'between the evil of discouraging competition and the virtue of encouraging innovation' (Gittins, 2004). It's conceivable that ordinary discourse, including stories, names and events, will be readily packaged, managed and tendered within the informational surfeit of electronic communication circuits. In China, this is already happening with politically sensitive topics. Keywords like democracy, Falun Gong or Tiananmen crackdown attract attention in local ISPs (internet service providers), and there are over 10,000 security officers patrolling the worldwide web for potential troublemakers (Hachigian, 2001). Since these systems, including security and surveillance, are installed and maintained by Intel, Microsoft and Google, extrapolation into commercial (not just political) trafficking is assured. Such a trademarked, copyrighted, intertextual, cross-referenced all-rights-reserved world extends the logic of IP into the most intricate (and intimate) of human transactions.

One way of apprehending this is the notion of 'total marketisation', and how governments respond to capitalism's rampant globalisation. What role do governments and authorities play in the screen industry game? Most opinion assumes an either-or, binary relation between marketisation and state regulation as in the case of China:

> crossborder market pressure, when present, makes it even more difficult for the state to withstand the pressure of marketisation … a regionalizing force as in the case of Phoenix Satellite TV or a globalizing force as in the case of China's ascension to the WTO. [Which] leads us to this conclusion: there is no denial the state-market tension is fundamental to the understanding of media development in China. (Chan, 2003)

That may be, but it is also true that marketisation can be a tool of state repression rather than a force of liberalisation. As Wang Hui writes, 'market expansion took the form of coercive intervention by the state, and because of this, the notion of a binary market/state opposition was shattered' (Wang, 2003: 116–17). He goes on to say that in China, 'The creation of today's market society was not the result of a sequence of spontaneous events, but rather of state interference and violence' (Wang, 2003: 6).

As governments are not immune to the forces of globalisation, they no longer play just the role of regulator/referee, monitoring corporate behaviour and the progress of marketisation in the field. In fact, government authorities now behave more like players in the market, which often result in contradictions and ambiguities. This is visible in mainland China, Taiwan and South Korea, which was recently caught in a bind between screen protection and open trade in other areas.

Total marketisation takes other forms as well. We might also note how cultural products can be blueprints for a production line of ancillary commodities (sequels, spin-offs, soundtracks, taglines, merchandise, theme-park rides, remake rights, etc.). These are multipliers in an exponential table of intellectual property values, outlining a complex linkage of commercial contracts (Donald, Keane and Yin, 2002: 11). The screen industry calls this copyright enterprise 'the long tail', but our study has shown how screen institutions themselves – finance packaging, adjustable templates, multiple formats and festivals – are also subject to total marketisation through competitive replication.

East Asian producers are fully capable of meeting and exceeding the entertainment benchmarks of Hollywood and Western films (Chapter 1). While noting that East Asian production and policy benchmarks are comparable with the West, we remain sceptical of directly comparing and contesting the two. East Asian or Hollywood: which will prevail? Scenarios of conquest going either direction are simplistic and not very helpful, though it is necessary to describe specific mutual influences. These influences will be limited because East Asian screen industries cannot reproduce Hollywood's hegemony at will, just as Hollywood pictures cannot simply devour domestic and local entertainment. What's more likely to emerge are heavily interdependent industries and audiences worldwide, leading to unforeseen agglomerations of regional consumption. Also, East Asian screen industries have a treasury of intellectual capital at their fingertips, including audiences, infrastructure and all the cultural archives – the stories, stars, languages and collective experience – that constitute East Asia (Chapters 2 and 5). At century's end many investors and producers successfully capitalised on these local resources, leveraged into sustainable industrial templates that might end up transcending Asia altogether. Consider how manufacturers provide hundreds of variations on basic models (cars, mobile phones, search engines, etc.) to accommodate specific markets anywhere in the world, all tailored with different configurations, buttons and functions. East Asian design and product development has an enviable track record, particularly in embedding them in Western markets. Regional producers have already appeared, intent on making multi-inflected films that will expand and sustain various East Asian markets. Total marketisation also suggests co-ordination with cognate industries such as television, games design, digital and telephony applications so that film industries are integrated, and not competing with, other entertainment activities (Chapter 3). The Japanese television industry exemplifies a pursuit of multiple platform production, and its animation industry has become a major global export. There's a delicate balance in the world marketisation of anime, wherein *Astro Boy* needed major retailoring for Western tastes in the 1970s; but in the 1990s *Pokemon* capitalises on its Japanese origins. We also covered the regional consolidation and co-ordination of pan-Asian cinema, which actively takes steps to enlarge the pool of audience members primed for East Asian pictures (Chapter 4). It's noteworthy that while Japan represents the power of small screens, it is the least active in pan-Asian co-production, mainly because of the size of its home market (Shackleton, 2006c). With respect to content, total marketisation governs the updating of Chinese martial arts, with a quickening slate of state-of-the-art blockbuster co-productions made in China, increasingly destined for global distribution (Chapter 5). Story ideas from East Asia, especially horror franchises, migrate to remake sites elsewhere, in Hollywood and also with the Asia-ready horror cycles of Applause Pictures. But it is instructive that other properties besides horror, such as Media Asia's *Infernal Affairs* and Korean melodrama *Il Mare*, rounded out exports of East Asian films to prominent US remakes. Remakes are only that, but it is hard not to conclude that East Asian formats and stories have found a measure of global success. Finally, we showed how festivals and associated confabs of East Asia are proliferating, aggressively competing to attract expertise, stars and investment from the region and the world (Chapter 6). Here too there's an explosion of market possibilities, as film-makers, events and festivals themselves rush to capitalise on novelty and market access to every form of linked audiovisual commerce. In this and in every sphere of activity, it seems competition, innovation and intensive marketisation rules the orientation of East Asian screens.

The remainder of this chapter returns to accounts of marketisation in specific contexts, describing the dialectics of intellectual protection and new market trajectories. Perhaps 'intellectual property' harbours impulses that are self-contending, an expectation that storytelling, spectacle and stars are universally desirable, against a need for recouping investment with secure transactions that buyers can efficiently access – and thieves cannot easily flout. But first, an update on South Korea's screen quota conundrum.

SCREEN QUOTA UNDER SIEGE

As shown in Chapter 1, South Korea's culture industry is sustained by government fiat, with legislative backing. The South Korean film-cultural policy has different aspects: appeals to pride in Korean craftsmanship backed by promotional campaigns, and business incentives provided by tax packages, subsidies and investment schemes. The screen quota has elements of both – as economic barrier erected and maintained by the state – though its origins lie in an industrial consolidation and control by a right-wing dictatorship (Lee, 2006: 187). Impulses to control wrestle with desires to compete on level playing fields, though the objects and rules of the game themselves are also fiercely debated. This dilemma of control and unfettered commerce remains alive in South Korean screen policy. It indicates possibilities and contradictions of national competitiveness within what will become a genuinely world market for film and media. As that market grows, it responds primarily to conglomerates and multinational activities promoting global entertainment on the widest possible scale. These worldwide conglomerates, Korean, Japanese, European or American, have a disproportionate impact on markets that governments must regulate and protect.

In 2003 these contradictions were exposed as relations between global market and national policy were acutely strained. Unlike the US, South Korea upholds distinctions between market, nation and culture.[1] Korean cultural policy supports in principle the exemption of culture in international trade negotiations, instead of unbridled 'free trade'. American negotiators demanded they scrap the screen quota of 146 days reserved for Korean films. Since April 2002, the French made offers of co-production treaties in the form of agreements to quota-exempt joint projects. This first-ever Franco-Asian co-production treaty was carefully timed to support Korean resistance to American tactics (Paquet, 2003b). In effect the French were offering relief and compensation for South Korean resolve in the face of American pressure to end the quota. There was also pressure, however, from Korea's Ministry of Foreign Affairs, which had concerns about the country's most-favoured-nation status. So instead of a formal treaty between countries, a co-operation agreement between the Korean Film Council and Centre National de Cinematographie was signed in late 2002. Not until October 2006 did South Korea sign its first official co-production treaty with France (Noh, 2006f). By this time, Korea's screen quota had been halved.

Lee Chang-dong, a respected novelist and award-winning director (*Peppermint Candy*; *Green Fish*; *Oasis*; *Secret Sunshine*) was named Minister of Culture and Tourism in March 2003. Lee's cultural policy, driven by high profit yields, was also nationalistic, promoting Korea's regional leadership in film production. But one year later, Lee found himself in the quandary of what to do with the 40 per cent quota that protected domestic films. The 146-day reserve was not acceptable to distributors of foreign films and to other branches of government. Finance ministers argued that since Korean films held a domestic majority, the quota had served its purpose, and should go. Theatres should be free to show as many imports as they liked. As a prominent film director and cultural bureaucrat, Lee was on a collision course with further free-trade pacts such as BIT (bilateral investment treaty) and the most-favoured-nation status. Lee's unyielding position shows how national cinema may be used as a wedge or 'stumbling block' to the passage of major international trade agreements. A single industry might delay approval of multiple agreements and trade pacts, employing a rhetoric of patriotism and cultural pride: 'A nation whose mass media is controlled by foreigners cannot be called a nation, ... Without the quota system, Korean films could be thrown into a spiral of decreasing investment and production, leading to an irreversible quagmire,' stated an industry coalition in June 2003 (Paquet, 2003a). To protect the quota, the film industry turned an economic policy into a question of national pride. In 2004 Lee's ministry folded, and reversing its support agreed to a 50 per cent reduction of the 146 days to seventy-three days. Lee Chang-dong, reviled and pilloried by Chungmuro, was sacked from his government post (Paquet, 2004b).

The reduced quota came into effect on 1 July 2006. Some 10,000 protesters – most were film-makers – rallied in Seoul to rage at the government's betrayal of the industry (Noh, 2006b). Despite strong letters and appeals issued by the Korean Screen Quota Action Alliance warning of the loss of cultural diversity and the dwindling vitality of Korean films,[2] the box-office receipts of summer blockbuster *The Host* (dir. Bong Joon-ho, 2006) said otherwise. *The Host*, a

The Host (2006): allegory
monster film

monster film with political subtexts, could itself stand for Korean anxieties in
the way it narrates the panic and ensuing resolve aroused by a ghastly foreign
mutant. This picture broke all previous records, bringing US$64.6 million in the
first seven weeks of domestic release (*ScreenDaily.com*, 2006). The film also had
a wide release on 250 screens in Japan in early September 2006 (Noh, 2006c).
Its commercial success even sparked a public brawl from festival maverick Kim
Ki-duk, who questioned Korean audiences' taste and the increasing centralisa-
tion of movie distribution (Noh, 2006d). As for Lee Chang-dong, he received
the French Legion of Honour for his heroic efforts to promote cultural diversity through protectionism.

Judging from the events taking place on Korean screens in 2006, the future
looks uncertain. But it is assured that earlier collusion between national screen
policy and the rules of the capitalist game has gradually unravelled. Colonisa-
tion of the market by commercial genre pictures and continuing difficulty the
artists like Kim face in accessing screens tell a story of painful 'diversification'
in the Korean screen industry. In South Korea over 60 per cent of internet users
download films and many report that they curtailed their visits to cinemas and
DVD purchases. It is hard to tell if this escalating blockbuster race will provide
for alternative directions in Korean screen culture. At the same time, festivals
are proliferating, becoming a burgeoning industry of their own in trade fairs and
popular exhibition. It is harder to distinguish between festivals and multiplex
screenings as both platforms are equally important places for marketing, promotion and sales.

IPR, PIRACY AND GLOBAL MEDIA INTEGRATION

Beyond such national struggles, intellectual property rights (IPR) is the defining
obstacle to the region's full integration into the global media system. The IPR
issue surpasses the trade in entertainment to threaten overall reliance on authen-
tication formalities in pharmaceuticals, aviation, trademark design and basic

research and development. IP violations endanger China's hopes of full parity in negotiating an accommodation with international norms of trade, contracts and arbitration.[3] Like debates over human rights and environmental crises, IPR raises a host of related issues and possible solutions. In the view of the Motion Picture Association (MPA), intellectual property violations are opportunistic, feeding on market distortions like protectionism, crony capitalism and other restrictions on trade. (Established in 1994, MPA is the international branch of the Motion Picture Association of America, the formidable trade association dominated by the Hollywood studios.) But if opportunism and piracy are a problem, another is whether IP protection itself is appropriate, excessive or unfair. There may be cultural and intellectual resources that do not fall under the 'property' rubric at all, whether private or public. An emerging legal field called 'rights management' seems to sidestep the proprietary assumptions of 'intellectual property', but it is really a refurbishing of existing norms.

In general, discourses on IPR involve presumptions of universal compliance with legal protection of entertainment and information. This is a basic requirement for access to global markets, as supervised by bodies such as the World Trade Organization. When protections are ignored, punitive measures go into effect and steps are taken to ensure long-term compliance and fair play in the market. Thus, the industrial side of IPR is the basis of macroeconomic structures serviced to keep up with market developments. If macroeconomic incentives and penalties are one side of IPR, another is the sociological dimension that involves ethical values and judgments. These in turn divide into the rights of artistic creation on the one hand, and the responsibilities of consumers on the other. In our discussion, we treat these related aspects in turn.

For years, panels on piracy, intellectual property and investment prospects have been regular events at Asian film festivals and markets. At the 2006 Shanghai International Film Festival, a panel presented views on contemporary IPR in East Asia. With representatives from industry associations, film-makers, law firms and government officials, the discussion hit some surprising notes, even while sounding many familiar refrains.

Mike Ellis, the MPA representative, began with a claim that the international market was worth more than 50 per cent of MPA's revenues and that 'criminal gangs' exploited loopholes, snags and other impediments to an open, level marketplace. By the end of 2006 piracy would cost MPA members around US$6.1 billion, while non-members were losing $2.6 billion a year – and over half of that in the PRC film industry. He argued that IPR was a global not just American problem, to be tackled co-operatively. The cleanup would benefit not only American firms, but would staunch the haemorrhaging of Chinese revenues as well. Post-9/11 the MPA and other industry lobbyists have maintained the link between IP violations and funding for terrorist associations. Instead of the narco-terrorism of Iran-Contra in the twentieth century, now we allegedly face IP terrorism.

Hong Kong's 'zero tolerance' policy was praised, where in 2006 an individual caught circulating illegal films online was prosecuted for the first time. Still, these efforts need to be seen in perspective: in 2005, 95 per cent of American DVDs in China were pirated, and in 2006, the figure came down to 93 per cent. On a micro level, the MPA uses software that tracks minute-by-minute downloading of clients' wares.[4] The MPA sees this as techno-crime, though East Asian trafficking in feature films also stimulates new business initiatives. State-of-the-art copyright-tracking tools include BayTSP, a search engine to capture copyrighted material, Sony's Blu-Ray DVD standard and Dolby subsidiary Cinea, which supplies 'clean', protected players to studios wishing to circulate screeners during awards periods. (Awards screeners on DVD are a major source of unauthorised copies.) This means not only various preventative and punitive responses to illegal distribution, but also a chance for MPA clients to rethink, and possibly attempt wholesale re-defining and reorganisation of world cinema – especially in distribution and marketing.

In Shanghai, the MPA stressed the macroeconomic consequences of IP violations; a single commercial film costs around US$100 million to make and market, Ellis pointed out. With such costs, there *must* be recovery on investment to continue to have any film industry at all. MPA is therefore committed to building an industrial framework in which motion pictures can be sold without fear of imitations that dilute or distort the market.

Others saw the problem differently, but agreed with the MPA's structural emphasis. This position casts IPR violation as a pervasive moral rot or pollution, like an environmental pestilence. This sociological perspective demands action at the level of consumer behaviour. A representative of FIAPF, the French trade association, produced a locally bought DVD of *The Music Box*, a Chinese film that was supposed to debut at the festival that evening! This seemed to bear out the MPA's insistence that IPR was not just the West's problem. FIAPF's response was to go after demand and stigmatise it. Public service announcements from Europe and Mexico were presented with punch lines like 'Be Original' (Spain), 'Five Years' Prison' (Germany) and a Mexican Happy Birthday scenario. Papa gives his daughter a gift, only to find it won't work because it's a knockoff. 'Pirated movies look bad – and make you look bad. What are you teaching your kids?' admonishes the narrator.

In these public campaigns, IP was personalised, turning it into an issue of a moral judgment and of ethical conduct in the home. Using illegal content typifies a mentality that tolerates theft, plagiarism and short-cuts, leading soon to destruction of youngsters' moral fibre. This appeal differs from the MPA's, akin to a 'say no to drugs' crusade that alternates between cajoling and threatening users, in those 'halo or horns' moments when faced with a harmful product. It targets the demand for cheap but illegal entertainment through emotional association and negative reinforcement. In this way the IPR stakeholders are expanded to include the public at large, addressed in the privacy of their most treasured and intimate family relations.

At the panel, Hong Kong director Jacob Cheung (*A Battle of Wits*) offered a mix of ethical and economic arguments, citing the low-budget *Made in Hong Kong* (dir. Fruit Chan, 1997), an acclaimed film that could not recoup its cost because the market was ruined by illegal dupes. To Cheung, non-mainstream, independent and 'creative' movies were hardest hit because it made investors risk-averse. Traffickers in illegal copies reaped the greatest rewards, said Cheung, and made it all but impossible to get innovative, challenging works off the ground. According to Cheung, piracy had driven creative people out of the industry. In the 1980s there were around 200 independent producers in Hong Kong, whose output ranked third in the world per capita. In 2006 there were fewer than 100, with half of Hong Kong's film people fleeing into television, to Southeast Asia and to other industries with less criminal activity. More crudely, Feng Xiaogang criticised Chinese consumers' 'low moral standards' and regards rampant piracy as reflecting the inferiority of Chinese culture (Pang, 2004: 30).

Where does this leave the state, whose officials are charged with managing intellectual property in turbulent conditions? Li Guomin, deputy president of the China Film Copyright Protection Association, addressed this. He framed China's IPR decisions in terms of its inexperience. It was only in 1980 that China joined the World Intellectual Property Organization, followed by the acceptance of many international conventions, treaties, agreements and accords governing copyright, patents and trademark. China's first trademark law was passed in 1983. It thus had over twenty years experience in IPR, compared to 200 years in the US and 300 in Europe. 'If some person demands that PRC should go through the same road in 20 years which the USA cost 200 years and Europe cost 300 years [sic] I think it is unbelievable' (Li, 2006).

Since the 'PRC has implemented planned economy for a long time and people don't have the conception of IPR', Li seemed to accept some awkwardness in the compatibility of IP, a novel idea, with the reality of a planned economy. It appeared Li reluctantly took China's responsibility to be a good IP umpire but preferred the role of coach. In the matter of co-productions, China always insists on being a player. Delicately, Mr Li addressed the macroeconomic distortions the MPA blames for IP violations in China. Li allowed that planned economies are inhospitable to creative discoveries that are protected in capitalist countries. Under socialist regimes, all property belongs to the state.

But this seems an excuse, not a rational defence. If East Asia wants better credibility in the global media economy, it needs to look beyond conventional decisions about movie production to affirm IPR's importance. IP stakeholders are not just Hollywood majors and their army of lawyers and compliance officers, or even Asian or European film-makers. The affected community includes investors, inventors, artists and retailers everywhere. To the trade, this extends to professions as well: educators, policemen, students and parents with children – anyone concerned with the civilised exchange of reliable goods and services. FIAPF's Valerie Lepine-Karnick said, 'it's about learning how to behave with cultural goods'.

SCREEN CONVERGENCE, TOTAL MARKETISATION?

Do East Asians know how to behave with cultural goods? The MPA's Ellis offered a conclusion admiring China's decisive planning, its authoritative, executive-led policy as a benefit to IPR: 'in my experience, when they want to do something in China, they can *really* do something'. Here Ellis praised effective IPR protection of China's own *dapian* (big pictures), many of which were made under CEPA provisions. In this statement there's an implicit plea: to extend the same protection of China's own pictures to imports or, put differently, to make IPR indiscriminate. This is what is needed in an umpire or referee. China's reputation as 'the Wild West' of capitalist development also makes it the best lab to test technical and educational breakthroughs in IPR. The combination of population, technological savvy and powers of 'persuasion' gives China and East Asia huge advantages in pursuit of innovations in IPR – so long as it has a sufficient stake in the hunt. East Asian screen industries already play a disproportionate role in global cinema, but this is negligible compared to the awesome potential to harness the region's markets to drive IPR into a new era. This could mean a brave new world of punitive enforcement (online prosecution, cyber-spooks, etc.) but many more creative solutions can be devised, addressing the realities of consumer preference, open-source systems and expanding information access.

Given the claims by MPA and other trade bodies, we can end this study on a speculative note. Convergence usually means the industrial-technological integration of moving images across broadcast, computer and telecommunications channels (Sinclair and Turner, 2004: viii). But here we indicate a simple yet extraordinary convergence, the emerging reciprocal structures between greater China and the West. For both sides, co-productions, branch offices or transnational enterprise will need to cross more than one boundary: a cultural gap between China and the world, and a legal-economic one between public and private ventures. This crossover brings diffusion of once clearly marked spheres of control, ownership and reward. It means commercial operations are literally co-operating with government bodies, which are not just regulators but also participants and aggressive players in the marketplace. Microsoft and Google are just two recent examples of corporate compromise to suit Chinese conditions, adapting standards and practice to the requirements of Party ideology. Likewise, Warner China-HG is a recently formed joint venture between state-owned China Film Corp, Warner Bros. and Heng Dian Group. It is the only production-cum-distribution company with a large foreign component, and yet, for purposes of state regulation, is still considered Chinese. This represents potential for collusion and fraud (since these foreign companies have to adjust their practices to accommodate state demands) but also a chance for creative discoveries in profitable innovation.

Another way to view this convergence is as an exchange of places between China and the West. America's obsession with security, stability, financial accountability and sound regulation in the post-Enron era faces China's exuberant turn toward marketisation, internationalisation and raging consumerism. It almost seems the two systems are trading features, and incrementally becoming more like one another. Trading features, by means of feature (film) trading, is a process that involves economic, policy and cultural assimilation without a clearly predictable destination.

Like South Korea, China has fewer releases but higher box-office gains as the industry consolidates, with rising proficiency in marketing and promotional

Curse of the Golden Flower: Shakespearean epic or gaudy exploitation?

blandishment. As we saw in Chapter 4 with audience mockery of blockbusters like *The Promise*, state-supported film-makers appear to be taking a high-handed road. Feng Xiaogang was loved for his witty social satires (Chapter 2) but his 2006 film is a Shakespearean tragedy that opened simultaneously in China, Hong Kong, Malaysia, Singapore and Taipei. In Guangzhou, *The Banquet*'s unnatural dialogue brought much laughter, which offended the Beijing-based director. Feng immediately commissioned an online poll whose results showed, not surprisingly, unqualified appreciation. Other audiences ridiculed Zhang Yimou's *Curse of the Golden Flower* (2006) whose use of Gong Li's cleavage brought negative remarks. 'Must Chinese films resort to this?' was an all-too-common response from ordinary moviegoers who went of their way to post criticism. But just as the films' production, publicity and reception are all reported and monitored by state-backed conglomerates, blockbuster mentality is itself state-owned enterprise. Though it might appear as populist rejection of forced marketisation and *dapian* triumphalism, China's tight control is a foregone conclusion. This is why Li Guomin's protests that IP is a foreign notion ring hollow.

So before applauding the cheek of viewers who would really prefer modest comic pleasures to state-sponsored epics, we must remember that even this apparent tension is sustained by the Party-controlled media. Control is exercised and then relaxed by Chinese bureaucrats, but also by corporate strategies and agencies imported from outside. Once inside China, the new entity awkwardly adjusts and accommodates, whether its origins are in Hong Kong, Taiwan, Japan or Hollywood. Companies like Media Asia, Emperor Media Group, Jackie Chan Productions, Kadokawa Inc., CJ Entertainment, Warner China-HG and Columbia-Asia are all active in China. They pursue financing, production slates and media infrastructure, the better to secure regular revenue streams. It is significant, though, that distribution remains firmly in Chinese hands. Encouraging foreign participation in its screen industries, China in this way transfers private expertise into public enterprise. Public projects are taking on unexpected features, becoming more lean, efficient and responsive. Access to a practically limitless market is possible ('one billion consumers') but only through absorption into a 'China-ready' economy. Ultimately, marketisation should be a means to an end, offering abundance in ideas as well as goods. Certainly it means prosperity, sustainability and progress in efforts to entertain more people, more effectively. But if marketisation is heavily imposed, by governments or by consumerist dogma, can East Asia's screens continue to offer appealing, liberal entertainments?

NOTES

1. The contradiction is visible precisely in Hollywood's global hegemony: 'For all its rhetoric of pure competition … the US government has devoted massive resources to generate and sustain its "private sector" film industry in the interests of ideology and money' (Miller *et al.*, 2001: 25).

2. In March 2006, the Korean Screen Quota Action Alliance, an association of film-makers and professionals opposed to the US–Korea Free Trade Agreement, sent out an open letter called 'Korean Film Industry Asks the US and the Rest of the World's Cooperation' to call for support for cultural diversity. Citing an agreement passed in the 2005 UNESCO Convention on Cultural Diversity that protects cultural products, the letter argued that cultural products, unlike other global products, should be exempted from free-trade agreements. The Alliance 'held a series of protests and events at the Cannes Film Festival in May, which successfully led to the Cannes board announcing a joint statement of support for the screen quota'. The same campaign was also held at the 63rd Venice Film Festival later that year (Noh, 2006d).

3. Typical headlines related to IPR: 'Suspected kingpin of fake drugs ring netted' and 'Internet sales of fake Viagra "out of control"', *South China Morning Post*, 23 September 2006: C1.

4. "The MPA's MediaSentry search engine – which only looks for titles produced by MPA member companies – detected 2,770 cases of peer-to-peer piracy in Hong Kong in 2004 compared to just 107 the previous year. The MPA also detected that within a 10-second period in December, 153 people were downloading Sony's Chinese-language *Kung-fu Hustle*. More than half of these were in China' (Shackleton, 2005a).

References

Barlett, C. A., and Ghoshal, S. (1998), *Managing Across Borders: The Transnational Solution*, Boston/MA: Harvard Business School Press.

bc Magazine (2005), 'The Most Wonderful Time of the Year', No. 179, 3 March, <hk.bcmagazine.net/cgi-bin/output.cgi?issue=179&&id=28> (accessed 10 June 2006).

Beals, Gregory (2001), 'The Birth of Asiawood', *Asiaweek*, 21 May, pp. 57–60.

Beech, Hannah (2001), 'Keeping It Reel – Don't Look for Magic Swords in a Feng Xiaogang Movie. He Prefers Contemporary Comedies', *Time Asia*, 158, no. 3, 23 July, <www.time.com/time/asia/arts/magazine/0,9754,167619,00.html> (accessed 15 May 2006).

Berry, Chris (2003a), 'What's Big About the Big Film? "De-Westernizing" the Blockbuster in Korea and China', *Movie Blockbusters*, Ed. Stringer, Julian, London and New York: Routledge, pp. 217–29.

Berry, Michael (2003b), 'Cultural Fallout: An Interview with Jia Zhangke', *Film Comment*, 39, no. 2: 61–4.

Bordwell, David (2000), 'Avant-pop Cinema', *Planet Hong Kong: Popular Cinema and the Art of Entertainment*, Cambridge, MA: Harvard University Press, pp. 261–81.

Box Office Mojo (n. d. a), 'Movies', <www.boxofficemojo.com/movies/> (accessed 13 December 2006).

Box Office Mojo (n. d. b), 'South Korea Box Office', <www.boxofficemojo.com/intl/korea/> (accessed 8 September 2006).

Box Office Mojo (n. d. c), 'Taiwan Box Office', <www.boxofficemojo.com/intl/taiwan/> (accessed 8 September 2006).

Box Office Mojo (n. d. d), 'Thailand Box Office', <www.boxofficemojo.com/intl/korea/> (accessed 8 September 2006).

Brodlie, Matt (2003), 'Miramax Pictures', FILMART Successful Marketing Seminar, Hong Kong International Film & TV Market, 23 September.

Cannes Film Festival (2005), '*Hwal* (*The Bow*)', <www.festival-cannes.fr/films/fiche_film.php?langue=6002&id_film=4283110> (accessed 1 August 2006).

Chan, Joseph Man (2003), 'Administrative Boundaries and Media Marketization: A Comparative Analysis of the Newspaper, TV and Internet', *Chinese Media,*

Global Contexts, Ed. Chin-Chuan Lee, London and New York: RoutledgeCurzon, pp. 159–76.

Chan, Ka-ming (2004), '*Happy Together*: Embrace Oneself and Tango Alone', *The Cinema World of Wong Kar-wai*, Eds. Pun, Lawrence and Lee, Bono, Hong Kong: Joint Publishing (Hong Kong) Company Limited, pp. 156–65. (Chinese)

Chan, Peter (2005), 'Pan-Asian Cinema', Asian Cultural Cooperation Forum, Hong Kong Academy of Performing Arts, 11 November.

Chen, Huanzong (2005), 'From the Initial: *Initial D*'s Commercial Operations', *China Film Market*, December, pp. 22–4. (Chinese)

Chen, Qingwei (2000), *The Structure and Marketing Analysis of Hong Kong Film Industry*, Hong Kong: City Entertainment. (Chinese)

Chi, Robert (2006), 'The House of 72 Transformations', *Cultural Studies: Exploring Cross-disciplinary Perspectives*, Department of Cultural and Religious Studies, Chinese University of Hong Kong, 8–9 May. Conference talk.

China Film Yearbook (1991), Beijing: China Film.

China Film Yearbook (1992), Beijing: China Film.

China Film Yearbook (1993), Beijing: China Film.

China Film Yearbook (1994), Beijing: China Film.

China Film Yearbook (1995), Beijing: China Film.

China Film Yearbook (1996), Beijing: China Film Yearbook Society.

China Film Yearbook (1997), Beijing: China Film Yearbook Society.

China Film Yearbook (1998), Beijing: China Film Yearbook Society.

China Film Yearbook (1999), Beijing: China Film Yearbook Society.

China Film Yearbook (2000), Beijing: China Film Yearbook Society.

China Film Yearbook (2001), Beijing: China Film Yearbook Society.

China Film Yearbook (2002), Beijing: China Film Yearbook Society.

China Film Yearbook (2003), Beijing: China Film Yearbook Society.

China Film Yearbook (2004), Beijing: China Film Yearbook Society.

China Film Yearbook (2005), Beijing: China Film Yearbook Society.

Ching, Leo (2000), 'Globalizing the Regional, Regionalizing the Global: Mass Culture and Asianism in the Age of Late Capital', *Public Culture*, 12, no. 1, pp. 233–57.

Chung, Thomas (2002), 'Personal Observations on Asian Movie Marketing', Symposium on Hollywood, Asian Media and the Global Market. University of Notre Dame, 28 February–2 March.

Cinema in the Republic of China 1989 Yearbook (1989), Taipei: ROC Film Development Foundation.

Cinema in the Republic of China 1991 Yearbook (1991), Taipei: Taipei Film Archive.

Cinema in the Republic of China 1995 Yearbook (1995), Taipei: Taipei Film Archive.

Cinema in the Republic of China 1996 Yearbook (1996), Taipei: Taipei Film Archive.

Cinema in the Republic of China 1997 Yearbook (1997), Taipei: Taipei Film Archive.
Cinema in the Republic of China 1998 Yearbook (1998), Taipei: Taipei Film Archive.
Cinema in the Republic of China 1999 Yearbook (1999), Taipei: Taipei Film Archive.
Cinema in the Republic of China 2000 Yearbook (2000), Taipei: Taipei Film Archive.
Cinema in the Republic of China 2001 Yearbook (2001), Taipei: Taipei Film Archive.
Cinema in the Republic of China 2002 Yearbook (2002), Taipei: Taipei Film Archive.
Cinema in the Republic of China 2003 Yearbook (2003), Taipei: Taipei Film Archive.
City Entertainment (1988), 'Annual Box Office Supplements', Hong Kong:
    City Entertainment.
City Entertainment (1990), 'Annual Box Office Supplements', Hong Kong:
    City Entertainment.
City Entertainment (1994), 'Annual Box Office Supplements', Hong Kong:
    City Entertainment.
City Entertainment (1995), 'Annual Box Office Supplements', Hong Kong:
    City Entertainment.
City Entertainment (1996), 'Annual Box Office Supplements', Hong Kong:
    City Entertainment.
City Entertainment (1997), 'Annual Box Office Supplements', Hong Kong:
    City Entertainment.
City Entertainment (1998), 'Annual Box Office Supplements', Hong Kong:
    City Entertainment.
City Entertainment (1999), 'Annual Box Office Supplements', Hong Kong:
    City Entertainment.
City Entertainment (2000), 'Annual Box Office Supplements', Hong Kong:
    City Entertainment.
City Entertainment (2001), 'Annual Box Office Supplements', Hong Kong:
    City Entertainment.
City Entertainment (2002), 'Annual Box Office Supplements', Hong Kong:
    City Entertainment.
City Entertainment (2003), 'Annual Box Office Supplements', Hong Kong:
    City Entertainment.
City Entertainment (2004), 'Annual Box Office Supplements', Hong Kong:
    City Entertainment.
City Entertainment (2005), 'Annual Box Office Supplements', Hong Kong:
    City Entertainment.
City Entertainment (2006), 'Annual Box Office Supplements', Hong Kong:
    City Entertainment.
Cremin, Stephen (2006), 'Taiwan Gears up for Five-Pronged Film & TV Expo',
    ScreenDaily.com, 12 October, <www.screendaily.com/story.asp?storyid=28097>
    (accessed 1 November 2006).

Curtin, Michael (2003), 'The Future of Chinese Cinema: Some Lessons from Hong Kong and Taiwan', *Chinese Media, Global Contexts*, Eds. Chin-Chuan Lee, London and New York: RoutledgeCurzon, pp. 237–56.

Curtin, Michael (2007), *Playing to the World's Biggest Audience*, Berkeley: University of California Press.

Davis, Darrell William (2001), 'Reigniting Japanese Tradition with *Hana-Bi*', *Cinema Journal*, 40, no. 4, pp. 55–80.

Davis, Darrell William (2007), 'Cinema Taiwan, a Civilizing Mission?', *Cinema Taiwan: Politics, Popularity and State of the Arts*, Eds. Davis, Darrell William and Chen, Ru-shou Robert, London and New York: Routledge, pp. 1–13.

Davis, Darrell William and Yeh, Emilie Yueh-yu (2003), 'Inoue at Shaws: The Wellspring of Youth', *The Shaw Screen: A Preliminary Study*, Ed. Wong, Ain-ling, Hong Kong: Hong Kong Film Archive, pp. 255–71.

Davis, Darrell William and Yeh, Emilie Yueh-yu (2004), 'VCD as Programmatic Technology: Japanese Television Drama in Hong Kong', *Feeling Asian Modernities: Transnational Consumption of Japanese TV Dramas*, Ed. Iwabuchi, Koichi, Hong Kong: Hong Kong University Press, pp. 227–47.

Donald, Stephanie Hemelryk, Keane, Michael and Yin Hong (2002), *Media in China: Consumption, Content and Crisis*, London: RoutledgeCurzon.

Dorfman, Ariel and Mattelart, Armand (1975), *How to Read Donald Duck: Imperialist Ideology in the Disney Comic*, New York: International General.

Eder, Klaus (2001), 'Interview with Freddie Wong', *Filmfestival.com*, <www.filmfestivals.com/cgibin/cannes/read.pl?site=us&type=article&text_id =18700> (accessed 10 May 2006).

Elley, Derek (2001), 'Shaolin Soccer', *Daily Variety*, 28 September, p. 14.

Feinstein, Howard (2006), 'An Uneasy East-West Fusion: The Bangkok International Film Festival', *indiewire.com*, 2 March, <www.indiewire.com/ots/2006/03/ an_uneasy_east-.html> (accessed 10 May 2006).

Film Art (Dianying yizhu) (1999), no. 3. Beijing: China Film Archive. (Chinese)

Film Art (Dianying yizhu) (2000), no. 3. Beijing: China Film Archive. (Chinese)

Film Art (Dianying yizhu) (2001), no. 3. Beijing: China Film Archive. (Chinese)

Film Art (Dianying yizhu) (2002), no. 3. Beijing: China Film Archive. (Chinese)

FILMART 2004 Brochure (2004), Hong Kong International Film & TV Market, Hong Kong: Hong Kong Trade Development Council.

Frater, Patrick (2003a), 'Remaking the Remake', *Screen International*, 30 May, p. 9.

Frater, Patrick (2003b), 'Chasing the Dragon', *Screen International*, 19 September, p. 29.

Frater, Patrick (2004), 'Driving Hong Kong's Film Industry', *Screen International*, 26 March, pp. 20–3.

Frater, Patrick and Kay, J (2003), 'What Makes a Good Remake?', *Screen International*, 6 June, p. 9.

Friedman, Jonathan (1990), 'Being in the World: Globalization and Localization', *Theory, Culture and Society*, 7, pp. 311–28.

Fujisankei Communications Group (2005), 'Fuji TV Outline', <www.fujitv.co.jp/en/overview/outline/group.html> (accessed 24 August 2006).

Fung, Anthony (2003), 'Marketing Popular Culture in China: Andy Lau as a Pan-Chinese Icon', *Chinese Media, Global Contexts*, Ed. Chin-Chuan Lee. London and New York: RoutledgeCurzon, pp. 257–69.

Gamble, Adam and Takesato Watanabe (2004), *A Public Betrayed: An Inside Look at Japanese Media Atrocities and Their Warnings to the West*, Washington, DC: Regnery Publishing Inc.

George, Sandy (2005), 'Fortissimo Partners Still Happy Together', *Screen International*, 29 April, p. 8.

Gittins, Ross (2004), 'Costs Aplenty in "Free" Trade IP Deals with US', *The Sydney Morning Herald*, 24–5 July, p. 46.

Gray, Jason (2006a), 'Japanese Box Office Poised to Beat 2005 Numbers', *ScreenDaily.com*, 10 August, <www.screendaily.com/story.asp?storyid=27215&st=2005+box+office&s=3> (accessed 11 August 2006).

Gray, Jason (2006b), 'Japanese Films Moving Toward 50% Market Share', *ScreenDaily.com*, 24 November, <www.screendaily.com/story.asp?storyid=28725&st> (accessed 25 November 2006).

Gray, Jason (2006c), '*Love and Honor* Beats Bond at Japanese Box Office', *ScreenDaily.com*, 6 December, <www.screendaily.com/story.asp?storyid=28852&st> (accessed 10 December 2006).

Grove, Martin A. (2004), '"Grudge" Reflects Hollywood Taste for Asian Horror', *The Hollywood Reporter*, 30 January, <www.hollywoodreporter.com/hr/search/article_display.jsp?vnu_content_id=2081691> (accessed 8 December 2006).

Hachigian, Nina (2001), 'China's Cyber-Strategy', *Foreign Affairs*, 80, no. 2, March–April, <www.foreignaffairs.org/20010301faessay4267/nina-hachigian/china-s-cyber-strategy.html> (accessed 15 July 2006).

Han Cinema (n. d.), <www.hancinema.net> (accessed 13 September 2006).

Han Cinema (2007), 'Korean Films Take 60% Share', 3 January, <www.hancinema.net/news_50.php > (accessed 15 January 2007).

Han, Eun-jung (2005), 'Director Prefers to Get Funding from Abroad', *The Korea Times*, 9 March, <search.hankooki.com/times/times_view.php?term=kim+ki-duk+kim+ki+duk++&path=hankooki3/times/lpage/culture/200503/kt2005030918080811710.htm&media=kt> (accessed 10 June 2006).

Hannerz, Ulf (1996), *Transnational Connections,* London and New York: Routledge.

Havis, Richard James (2004), 'Cell Phone', *Hollywood Reporter*, 385, nos. 2, 3, pp. 64.

Hayes, Dade (2001), *Daily Variety*, 26 March, p. 1.

Ho, Yanning (2005), 'Jia Zhangke Corrected the Box Office Figure of *The World*', *Yanzhao City Daily*, 15 June, <ent.sina.com.cn/x/2005-06-15/0304752072.html> (accessed 10 May 2006). (Chinese)

Holson, Laura M (2006), 'Hollywood Seeks Action Overseas', *International Herald Tribune*, 3 April, pp. 11, 12.

Hong Kong Film Archive (n. d.), Hong Kong Film Archive Website, <www.lcsd.gov.hk/CE/CulturalService/HKFA/hip/index.html> (accessed 13 September 2006).

Hong Kong Trade Development Council (n. d.), 'Weekly Box Office', *hkfilmart.com*, <www.hkfilmart.com/weeklyboxoffice.asp?lang=cn> (accessed 15 December 2006).

Hopewell, John (2004), 'Gaga, Avex Partner on "Initial" Pickup in Japan', *Variety.com*, 19 May, <www.variety.com/article/VR111790524?categoryid=1706&cs=1> (accessed 8 August 2006).

Internet Movie Database (n.d.), <imdb.com> (accessed 13 September 2006).

Jäckel, Anne (2003), *European Film Industries*, London: BFI Publishing.

Jeong, Taesun (2003), 'Down by the Seaside', *Moving Pictures*, p. 12.

Kadokawa Holdings, Inc. (2005), 'Annual Report', <www.kadokawa-hd.co.jp/annual/2005/02_network/02_network.html> (accessed 5 August 2006).

Kaifu, Michi (2006), 'Ryoichi Kimizuka Talks about *Suspect* and *Bayside Shakedown* Series', *HollywoodNewsWire.net*, 2 November 2005, <www.hogacentral.com/Special_RJ_SMS.html> (accessed 14 August 2006).

Kan, Wendy (2002), 'Applause Pics Bring Asian Talent Together', *Variety*, 22 April.

Karlovy Vary International Film Festival (n. d.), 'Wild Animals', <www.kviff.com/?m=25&id=20021255> (accessed 1 August 2006).

Kateigaho International Edition (n. d.), 'Horror on the Horizon', <int.kateigaho.com/win05/horror-previews.html> (accessed 13 September 2006).

Kawamoto, Mamiko (2005), 'Japan's Ace Plays a Winning Hand', *Screen International*, 15 July, pp. 13, 14.

Kay, Jeremy (2005), 'Intermedia, Kadokawa Extend Co-pro Pact', *ScreenDaily.com*, 12 September, <www.screendaily.com/ScreenDailyArticle.aspx?intStoryID=24328> (accessed 1 October 2005).

Kehr, Dave (2002), 'Anime, Japanese Cinema's Second Golden Age', *The New York Times*, 20 January, p. 1.

Kim, Keu-young *et al.* (2004a), *PPP Projects: 7th Pusan Promotion Plan*, Pusan: Pusan International Film Festival Organization Committee.

Kim, Kyung Hyun (2004b), *The Remasculinization of Korean Cinema*, Durham, NC and London: Duke University Press.

Klady, Len (2006), 'Japan's Box-office Takings Down 8%', *ScreenDaily.com*, 10 January, <www.screendaily.com/story.asp?storyid=24701> (accessed 15 August 2006).

Klein, Christina (2004), '*Crouching Tiger, Hidden Dragon*: A Diasporic Reading', *Cinema Journal*, 43, no. 4, pp. 18–42.

Korean Cinema (Hanguo ying hua) (2001), '*Address Unknown*', 3 June, <www.krmdb.com/office/krbo-2001061.b5.shtml> (accessed 1 August 2006). (Chinese)

Korean Cinema (Hanguo ying hua) (2002), '*Bad Guy*', 17 February, <www.krmdb.com/office/krbo-2002023.b5.shtml> (accessed 1 August 2006). (Chinese)

Korean Cinema (Hanguo ying hua) (n. d.), 'Korean Films Weekly Box Office' (Hanguo dianying meizhou piaofang), <www.krmdb.com/office/index.b5.shtml> (accessed 8 September, 2006). (Chinese)

Korean Film Council (2002), *Korean Film Newsletter*, no. 7, Autumn, <www.koreanfilm.or.kr/news/newsletter.asp> (accessed 1 September 2004).

Korean Film Council (2004), *Korean Film Newsletter*, no. 12, September, <www.koreanfilm.or.kr/news/newsletter.asp> (accessed 1 September 2004).

Korean Film Council (2006), 'Statistical Review of Korean Film Industry 2005', *Korean Film News*, <www.koreanfilm.or.kr/statistics/pop_statistics.asp?tabName=a> (accessed 28 April 2006).

Korean Film Council (n. d. a), 'Korean and Foreign Films Produced, Imported and Released by Year', *Statistics*, <www.koreanfilm.or.kr/statistics/pop_statistics.asp?tabName=a> (accessed 28 April 2006).

Korean Film Council (n. d. b), 'Nationwide Box Office Sales by Year', *Statistics*, <www.koreanfilm.or.kr/statistics/pop_statistics.asp?tabName=f> (accessed 20 August 2004).

Kraicer, Shelley (2001), 'Interview: Johnnie To and Wai Ka-fai', <www.sensesofcinema.com/contents/01/18/to_and_ka-fai.html> (accessed 9 May 2004).

Ku, Zheng (2003), 'Platform in Four Seasons', *The Cinema of Jia Zhangke*, Ed. Lin, Xudong *et al.*, Beijing: Manwen Press, pp. 231–7. (Chinese)

Kwok, Ching-ling and Grace Ng (eds) (2006), *Director Chor Yuen*, Hong Kong: Hong Kong Film Archive.

Lau, Shirley and Chan, Felix (2001), 'Shaolin Monks Give Kick to Blockbuster Summer', *South China Morning Post*, 18 January, p. H03.

Lee, Chin-Chuan (1979), *Media Imperialism Reconsidered: the Homogenizing of Television Culture*, Beverly Hills, CA: Sage.

Lee, Dong-Hoo (2004), 'Cultural Contact with Japanese TV Dramas: Modes of Reception and Narrative Transparency', *Feeling Asian Modernities: Transnational Consumption of Japanese TV Dramas*, Ed. Iwabuchi, Koichi, Hong Kong: Hong Kong University Press, pp. 251–74.

Lee, Hwangjin (2006), 'South Korea: Film on the Global Stage', *Contemporary Asian Cinema*, Ed. Ciecko, Anne Tereska, Oxford: Berg Publishing, pp. 182–92.

Lee, Hyangjin (2000), *Contemporary Korean Cinema: Identity, Culture, Politics*, Manchester: Manchester University Press.

Lee, Keun-sang (ed.) (2001), *Korean Cinema 2001*, Seoul: Korean Film Council, <www.koreanfilm.or.kr/img/kofic/KoreanCinema2001.pdf> (downloaded 28 April).

Lee, Keun-sang (ed.) (2002), *Korean Cinema 2002*, Seoul: Korean Film Council, <www.koreanfilm.or.kr/img/kofic/KoreanCinema2002.pdf> (downloaded 28 April).

Lee, Keun-sang (ed.) (2003), *Korean Cinema 2003*, Seoul: Korean Film Council, <www.koreanfilm.or.kr/img/kofic/KoreanCinema2003.pdf> (downloaded 28 April).

Lee, Keun-sang (ed.) (2004), *Korean Cinema 2004*, Seoul: Korean Film Council, <www.koreanfilm.or.kr/img/kofic/KoreanCinema2004.pdf> (downloaded 28 April).

Lent, John A. (1990), *The Asian Film Industry*, Austin: University of Texas Press.

Leong, Anthony C. Y. (2002), *Korean Cinema: The New Hong Kong*, Victoria, BC: Trafford Publishing.

Leong, Anthony (2005), 'Bubble Trouble? Local Film Biz Keeps Expanding, but Some Fear a Burst', *Variety.com*, 14 May, <www.variety.com/article/VR1117922833?categoryid=1912&cs=1> (accessed 10 May 2006).

Li, Cheuk-to (2004), 'Overseas Receptions of Wong Kar-wai's Films', *The Cinema World of Wong Kar-wai*, Eds Pun, Lawrence and Lee, Bono, Hong Kong: Joint Publishing (Hong Kong) Company Limited, p. 242. (Chinese)

Li, Guomin (2006), 'International Cooperation Against Piracy', The 9th International Shanghai International Film Festival. (Unpublished handout)

Li, Jack C. C. (2003), 'A 'Connectivity' View on Media Firms' Management Strategies in Media Globalization', *Mass Communication Research*, 75, pp. 1–36. (Chinese)

Liang, Liang (2002), '*Double Vision* Creating Taiwan Box Office Miracle: Interview with Chen Kuo-fu', *City Entertainment*, no. 616, pp. 48–9.

Lim, Dennis *et al.* (2004), 'Autumn Sonata: Young Guns Mingle with Old Masters at NYFF', *The Village Voice*, 28 September, <www.villagevoice.com/film/0439,nyff,57138,20.html> (accessed 10 May 2006).

Liu, Joey (2006), 'Redeeming Features', *South China Morning Post*, 22 January, p. 4.

Media Asia (2003), 'Profile', <www.mediaasia.com/eng/aboutus.php> (accessed 4 May 2006).

Mes, Tom and Sharp, Jasper (2005), *The Midnight Eye Guide to New Japanese Film*, Berkeley, CA: Stone Bridge Press.

Midnight Eye (n. d.), <www.midnighteye.com> (accessed 13 September 2006).

Milkyway Image (HK) Ltd. (n. d.), Milkyway Image Website,
   <www.milkywayimage.com> (accessed 28 April 2006).
Miller, Toby, Govil, Nitin, McMurria, John and Maxwell, Richard (2001),
   Global Hollywood, London: BFI Publishing.
Minns, Adam (2004), 'Foreign Language Films Take on Popcorn Crowd',
   Screen International, 15 October, p. 9.
Mok, Kin-wai (2002), 'Hong Kong Film Industry and Film Policy', *Media Digest*,
   December, p. 6. (Chinese)
Mosco, Vincent (2004), *The Digital Sublime: Myth, Power, and Cyberspace*,
   Cambridge, MA: MIT Press.
Motion Picture Producers Association of Japan, Inc. (n. d.),
   <www.eiren/org/statistics_e/index.html> (accessed 8 August 2006).
Muzushi, Kunio (2002), 'Interview with Nakata Hideo', *Koukoku Hihyo* (Advertising
   Review), no. 261, pp. 125–33. (Japanese)
Ngai, Jimmy (1997), 'A Dialogue with Wong Kar-wai: Cutting Between Time and Two
   Cities', in Jean-Marc Lalanne *et al.*, *Wong Kar-wai*, Paris: Editions Dis Voir, p. 83.
Noh, Jean (2006a), 'Korea's YedangOnline Acquires ShowEast', *ScreenDaily.com*,
   16 May, <www.screendaily.com/story.asp?storyid=26208> (accessed 16 May 2006).
Noh, Jean (2006b), 'Korean Filmmakers Protest as New Quota Becomes Reality',
   ScreenDaily.com, 3 July, <www.screendaily.com/story.asp?storyid=26865>
   (accessed 3 July 2006).
Noh, Jean (2006c), '*The Host* Breaks Korean Box-office Records', *ScreenDaily.com*,
   31 July, <www.screendaily.com/story.asp?storyid=27148>
   (accessed 31 July 2006).
Noh, Jean (2006d), 'Kim Ki-duk Stirs Controversy in Korean Film World',
   ScreenDaily.com, 23 August, <www.screendaily.com/story.asp?storyid=27362>
   (accessed 23 August 2006).
Noh, Jean, (2006e) 'Korean Screen Action Alliance to Hold Venice Campaign',
   ScreenDaily.com, 31 August,<www.screendaily.com/story.asp?storyid=27446>
   (accessed 15 September 2006).
Noh, Jean (2006f), 'South Korea Signs Co-production Agreement with France',
   ScreenDaily.com, 30 October, <www.screendaily.com/story.asp?storyid=28331&st
   =South+Korea&s=3> (accessed 1 November 2006).
Oei, Lily (2006), 'The Big Unknown', *Screen International*, 14 February, p. 9.
Okakura, Kakuzo (2005), *The Ideals of the East with Special Reference to the Art of
   Japan*, Eliborn Classics Replica Edition, Boston, MA: Adamant Media Corporation.
   Originally publlished in 1903.
Onishi, Norimitsu (2006), 'Seoul Train', *South China Morning Post*, 7 January, p. C7.
Otto, Jeff (2004), 'IGN Interviews Sam Raimi', *IGN Filmforce*,
   <movies.ign.com/articles/558/558371p2.html> (accessed 8 December 2006).

Pacific Friend (2002), 'Return of the Japanese Film', 29, no. 11, March, p. 21.

Pang, Laikwan (2004), 'Mediating the Ethics of Technology: Hollywood and Movie Piracy', *Culture, Theory & Critique*, 45, no. 1, pp. 19–32.

Paquet, Darcy (2003a), 'Korean Film-makers Rage Against Quota Threat', *ScreenDaily.com*, 13 June, <www.screendaily.com/story.asp?storyid=12847> (accessed 13 June 2004).

Paquet, Darcy (2003b), 'South Korea, France Re-open Co-production Treaty Talks', *ScreenDaily.com*, 19 June, <www.screendaily.com/story.asp?storyid=12900> (accessed 13 June 2004).

Paquet, Darcy (2004a), 'Festivals: Focus on 9th Pusan Film Festival', *Screen International*, 1 October, p. 17.

Paquet, Darcy (2004b), 'South Korean Film-makers Stunned by Quota Reversal', *ScreenDaily.com*, 13 June, <www.screendaily.com/story.asp?storyid=18041> (accessed 13 June 2004).

Paquet, Darcy (2005), 'The Korean Film Industry: 1992 to the Present', *New Korean Cinema*, Eds Shih, Chi-yun and Stringer, Julian, Edinburgh: Edinburgh University Press, pp. 32–50.

Paquet, Darcy (2006a), 'Cineclick Asia Taking Kim's *Time*: Presale Will Open at the European Film Market in Berlin', *Variety.com*, 11 January, <www.variety.com/article/VR1117935929?categoryid=1442&cs=1> (accessed 16 June 2006).

Paquet, Darcy (2006b), 'What's New?: Prediction for 2007', *Koreanfilm.org*, 28 December, <www.koreanfilm.org/new.html> (accessed 3 January 2007).

Paquet, Darcy (n. d. a), 'A Short History of Korean Film', *Koreanfilm.org*, <www.koreanfilm.org/history.html> (accessed 10 August 2004).

Paquet, Darcy (n. d. b), 'Kim Ki-duk', *Koreanfilm.org*, <koreanfilm.org/kimkiduk.html> (accessed 16 June 2006).

Paquet, Darcy (n. d. c), 'Commercial Releases in 2003', *Koreanfilm.org*, <www.koreanfilm.org/films2003.html> (accessed 1 August 2006).

Paquet, Darcy (n. d. d), 'Commercial Releases in 2004', *Koreanfilm.org*, <www.koreanfilm.org/films2004.html> (accessed 1 August 2006).

Paquet, Darcy (n. d. e), 'Site Updates and Darcy's Weblog', *Koreanfilm.org*, <www.koreanfilm.org/new.html> (accessed 1 August 2006).

Park, Daniel D. H. (ed.) (2005), *Korean Cinema 2005*, Seoul: Korean Film Council, pp. 50–1, <www.koreanfilm.or.kr/img/kofic/KoreanCinema2005.pdf> (downloaded 28 April).

Park, Soo-mee (2006), 'Escape Artists: Korean Directors Head Overseas to Find Audiences', *JoongAng Daily*, 16 June, <joongangdaily.joins.com/200606/15/200606152148312239900091009101.html> (accessed 16 June 2006).

Plate, Tom (2006), 'Thoughts Best Left Unsaid', *South China Morning Post*, 23 February, p. A15.

Rayns, Tony (2004), 'Deep Cover', *Sight and Sound*, 14, no. 1, January, pp. 26–9.

Richie, Donald (2001), *A Hundred Years of Japanese Film*, Tokyo and New York: Kodansha International.

Ridout, Cefn (2006), 'Anime Conquers the World', *The Australian*, 16 August, p. 18.

Robertson, Roland (1995), 'Globalization: Time-Space and Homogeneity-Heterogeneity', *Global Modernities*, Eds Featherstone, Mike *et al.*, London: Sage.

Rodier, Melanie (2006), 'Venice Competition Includes 21 World Premieres', *ScreenDaily.com*, 27 July, <www.screendaily.com/story.asp?storyid=27114&st=Venice+competition+includes+21+world+premieres&s=3> (accessed 28 July 2006).

Rosenberg, Scott (2006), 'Boycott Festival Urges Thai Film Association', *movies.monstersandcritics.com*, 25 January, <movies.monstersandcritics.com/news/article_1079271.php/Boycott_festival_urges_Thai_Film_Association> (accessed 10 May 2006).

Russell, Mark (2005), 'Sector Report: Korea', *The Hollywood Reporter*, 24 May, <www.hollywoodreporter.com/thr/international/feature_display.jsp?vnu_content_id=1000930566> (accessed 10 August 2005).

Ryall, Julian (2006), 'The Man in Bleak', *South China Morning Post*, 23 February, p. C7.

Sata, Matsunori and Hirahara, Hideo (eds) (1991), *A History of Japanese Television Drama*, Tokyo: Japan Association of Broadcasting Art.

Schiller, Herbert (1976), *Communication and Cultural Domination*, New York: M. E. Sharp.

Schilling, Mark (1999), *Contemporary Japanese Film*, New York: Weatherhill.

Schilling, Mark (2003), 'Spirited Performance', *Screen International*, 14 February, p. 19.

Schilling, Mark (2004a), 'Horror King: Here to Stay', *Screen International*, 30 July, p. 9.

Schilling, Mark (2004b), 'Trendspotting', *Screen International*, 26 March, p. 34.

Schilling, Mark (2004c), 'The Japanese Bruckheimer', *Screen International*, 30 April, p. 9.

Schilling, Mark (2004d), 'The Future is Bright: Kadokawa's 60th Year', *Screen International*, 15 October, pp. 17–20.

Schilling, Mark (2005a), 'Japan's Rising Fortunes', *Screen International*, 18 February, pp. 4, 5.

Schilling, Mark (2005b), 'Sea, Samurai and Zatoichi', *Screen International*, 18 February, p. 5.

Schilling, Mark (2005c), 'Kadokawa to Enter Chinese Market', *ScreenDaily.com*, 19 October, <www.screendaily.com/story.asp?storyid=23785> (accessed 19 October 2005).

ScreenDaily.com (2006), 'Screen Global Box Office', <www.screendaily.com/boxterrdisp.asp?TerrId=75&NC=True> (accessed 15 September 2006).

Screen International (2004), 'Anime and Fraternité', 24 September, p. 21.

Screen International 2006 Festival Guide (2006), London: Emap Media.

Segers, Frank (2003), 'Pusan Blossoms', *Moving Pictures*, Pusan Festival Official Guide, p. 2.

Shackleton, Liz (2005a), 'Hong Kong Industry Urges Anti-online Piracy Action', *ScreenDaily.com*, 24 January, <www.screendaily.com/story.asp?storyid=20695> (accessed 26 July 2006).

Shackleton, Liz (2005b), 'Europe Chases the Dragon', *Screen International*, 30 September, p. 6.

Shackleton, Liz (2006a), 'Warner Bros. Goes West with Sichuan Partnership', *ScreenDaily.com*, 22 January, <www.screendaily.com/story.asp?storyid=24820&st=Warner+Bros&s=3> (accessed 22 January 2006).

Shackleton, Liz (2006b), 'Filmart Wraps with Record Attendance', *ScreenDaily.com*, 23 March, <www.screendaily.com/story.asp?storyid=25622&st=Filmart+wraps+with+record+attendance&s=3> (accessed 10 June 2006).

Shackleton, Liz (2006c), 'Japan Still on Outer Edge of Pan-Asian Market', *ScreenDaily.com*, 25 October, <www.screendaily.com/story.asp?storyid=28285 25 October> (accessed 1 November 2006).

Shackleton, Liz (2007), 'Hong Kong Box Office Remains Flat in 2006', *ScreenDaily.com*, 14 January, <www.screendaily.com/ScreenDailyArticle.aspx?intStoryID=30214> (accessed 15 January 2007).

Shek, Kei (2002), 'Is *Shaolin Soccer* Funny?' *Apple Daily*, 4 May, E10. (Chinese)

Sinclair, John and Turner, Graeme (eds) (2004), *Contemporary World Television*, London: BFI Publishing.

Singapore Film Commission (n. d.), 'List of Singapore Films: 1991–2005', <www.sfc.org.sg/statistics/List%20of%20Singapore%20Films%20(Updated%202006).pdf> (downloaded 2 June 2006).

So, Sherman (2005), 'Snakes Alive – It's Special Effects', *South China Morning Post*, 18 January, TEC 1.

Soh, Joon (2004), 'Back From Venice, Kim Ki-duk Looks for Understanding', *The Korea Times*, 14 September, <search.hankooki.com/times/times_view.php?term=kim+ki-duk+looks+for+understanding++&path=hankooki3/times/lpage/culture/200409/kt2004091421465411720/htm&media=kt> (accessed 16 June 2006).

Standish, Isolde (1994), 'Korean Cinema and the New Realism', *Colonialism and Nationalism in Asian Cinema*, Ed. Dissanayake, Wimal, Bloomington: Indiana University Press.

Taiwan Cinema Year Book 2004 (2004), Taipei: Chinese Taipei Film Archive.

Taiwan Cinema Year Book 2005 (2005), Taipei: Chinese Taipei Film Archive.

Taiwan Cinema Year Book 2006 (2006), Taipei: Chinese Taipei Film Archive.

Tan, Qin (2001), 'Deficit Over One Million: Shanghai International Film Festival Running in Reds', *Zhongguo jingying bao*, 27 June, <ent.sina.com.cn/48237.html> (accessed 10 May 2006). (Chinese)

TBS Global Site (2005), <www.tbs.co.jp/eng/corporatedata/cd_co.htm> (accessed 22 August 2006).

Teo, Stephen (2002), 'The Pusan International Film Festival – Mature and Independent', *Senses of Cinema*, 18 January, <www.sensesofcinema.com/contents/festivals/01/18/pusan.html> (accessed 7 May 2006).

TPBO WRETCH (n. d. a), '2002 Box Office Billboard' (Taibeishi dianying piaofang paihangbang), <tpbo.wretch.cc> (accessed 8 September 2006). (Chinese)

TPBO WRETCH (n. d. b), '2004 Box Office Billboard' (Taibeishi dianying piaofang paihangbang), <tpbo.wretch.cc> (accessed 10 May 2006). (Chinese)

TPBO WRETCH (n. d. c), '2005 Box Office Billboard' (Taibeishi dianying piaofang paihangbang), <tpbo.wretch.cc> (accessed 15 January 2006). (Chinese)

TPBO WRETCH (n. d. d), '2006 Box Office Billboard' (Taibeishi dianying piaofang paihangbang), <tpbo.wretch.cc> (accessed 15 January 2006). (Chinese)

Tsui, Clarence (2005), 'Pictures Imperfect', *South China Morning Post*, 29 December, p. C7.

Tsukeda, Naoko (2002), Asian Co-production Panel. Seminar on Asian Convergence, the 21st Hong Kong Film Awards, Intercontinental Hotel, 20 April.

Uni Japan (2001, 2002), Tokyo: Association for the Diffusion of Japanese Film Abroad.

Wallerstein, Immanuel (1974–1980), *The Modern World System*, New York: Academic.

Wang, Hui (2003), *China's New Order: Society, Politics and Economy in Transition*, Ed. Theodore Huters, Cambridge, MA and London: Harvard University Press.

Watanabe, Takesato (2003), 'Status of Media in Japan', *Encyclopedia of International Media and Communications,* Ed. Johnston, Donald. H. Vol. 2., San Diego, CA and London: Academic, pp. 641–54.

Weinstein, Harvey (2004), 'Scaling the Chinese Wall', *Variety*, 31 August.

Wong, Silvia (2006a), 'Asian Film Finance Forum (HAF) Selects 25 Film Projects', *ScreenDaily.com*, 3 January, <www.screendaily.com/story.asp?storyid=24635&st=HAF&s=3> (accessed 1 May 2005).

Wong, Silvia (2006b), 'Bangkok Festival Ends Contract with FFM', *ScreenDaily.com*, 30 November, <www.screendaily.com/story.asp?storyid=28786&st=Bangkok&s=3> (accessed 1 December 2006).

Yeh, Emilie Yueh-yu (2006), 'Taiwan: Popular Cinema's Disappearing Act', *Contemporary Asian Cinema: Popular Culture in a Global Frame*, Ed. Ciecko, Anne T., Oxford/New York: Berg Press, pp. 156–68.

Yeh, Emilie Yueh-yu and Davis, Darrell William (2002), 'Japan Hongscreen: Pan-Asian Cinema and Flexible Accumulation', *Historical Journal of Film, Radio and Television*, 22, no. 1, pp. 61–82.

Yeh, Emilie Yueh-yu and Davis, Darrell William (2005), *Taiwan Film Directors: A Treasure Island*, New York: Columbia University Press.

Yeung, Fredrick (2007), 'Mainland Box-Office Sales Hit Record 2.6b Yuan', *South China Morning Post*, 11 January, p. B1.

Ying, Hong and Wang, Xiaofeng (2005a), 'Current Industrial Structure of Chinese Film', The Center for Film and Television Studies, Beijing: Tsinghua University, <www.tsinghua.edu.cn/docsn/cbx/cft/xueshu/xueshu-yingshi-industry.html> (accessed 9 September 2005).(Chinese)

Ying, Hong and Wang, Xiaofeng (2005b), 'The Industry Year of Chinese Film', *Contemporary Cinema* (Dandai dianying), no. 2, pp. 18–26. (Chinese)

Yu Mo-wan (1997), *Eighty Years of Hong Kong Cinema*, Hong Kong: Regional Council. (Chinese)

Yu, Sen-lun (2001), 'Passing the Torch of Taiwan Film', *Taipei Times*, 4 March, p. 17.

Yu, Sen-lun (2006), 'Crazy Stone Becomes China's Biggest Local Film in 2006', *ScreenDaily.com*, 12 July, <www.screendaily.com/story.asp?storyid=26962&st=crazy+stone&s=3> (accessed 14 July 2006).

Zeng, Xinwen (2005), 'Tough Embarrassments for Shanghai International Film Festival', *Jinghua Times*, 20 June, <ent.sina.com.cn/x/2005-06-20/0215756508.html> (accessed 15 May 2006). (Chinese)

Zhang, Jingpei and Lee, Ang (2002), *My Ten-year Dream as a Filmmaker*, Taipei: Times Culture. (Chinese)

Zhang, Zhen (2005), 'Bodies in the Air', *Chinese-language Film: Historiography, Poetics, Politics,* Eds Lu, Sheldon and Yeh, Emilie Yueh-yu, Honolulu: University of Hawaii Press, pp. 52–75.

Zhu, Yuqing (2006), 'Century Celebration: Commentary on Chinese Cinema and Film Market in 2005', *China Film Market*, March, pp. 8, 9. (Chinese).

Index

Page numbers in *italics* denote illustrations.

LIST OF ILLUSTRATIONS

While considerable effort has been made to correctly identify the copyright holders this has not been possible in all cases. We apologise for any apparent negligence and any omissions or corrections brought to our attention will be remedied in any future editions.

Crouching Tiger, Hidden Dragon, © United China Vision Incorporated/© UCV LLC; *Memories of Murder*, © Sidus Corporation; *Shiri*, Kang Je-gyu Film Company; *Taegukgi*, Kang Je-gyu Film Company; *Joint Security Area*, Myung Film Company; *Typhoon*, Zininsa Film; *Friend*, Korea Pictures; *Infernal Affairs*, © Media Asia Films (BVI) Limited; *Shaolin Soccer*, © Star Overseas/© Universe Entertainment; *Election*, © Milkyway Image (HK) Ltd; *Double Vision*, Nan Fang Film Productions; *Howl's Moving Castle*, © Nibariki - GNDDT; *One Missed Call*, Kadokawa-Daiei Eiga; *Perhaps Love*, Ruddy/Morgan Productions/Applause Pictures; *Iron Monkey*, Long Shong Films/Film Workshop; *Kung Fu Hustle*, Columbia Pictures Film Production Asia; *Love and Honor*, Love and Honor Film Partners/Shochiku Co. Ltd; *2046*, Block 2 Pictures/Paradis Films/Orly Films/Classic Srl/Precious Yield Ltd; *Still Life*, Xstream Pictures Limited; *The Host*, Chungeorahm Film; *Curse of the Golden Flower*, © Film Partner International Inc.